From the Rhondda to the Ebro

Warren
&Pell

From the Rhondda to the Ebro

The story of a young life and its
survival in the first half
of the 20th Century

by
Alun Menai Williams

Text © Alun Menai Williams.

First published 2004 by Warren & Pell Publishing,
The Old Bible Christian Chapel,
High Street, Abersychan, Pontypool, Torfaen,
NP4 7AG, United Kingdom.
Tel: 01495 775561.
E-mail: warren.ofbooks@virgin.net
Web: www.warrenandpellpublishing.co.uk

ISBN 0 9548904 0 X (Softback)
ISBN 0 9548904 1 8 (Hardback)

Edited by Alan Warren.
Design and Artwork by Nigel Pell.

All photographs by kind permission from the author's
collection with the exception of Britannic Colliery
© National Mining Museum of Wales, Blaenavon
and National Museums and Galleries of Wales.

Printed and bound in Great Britain by
J & P Davison, 3 James Place,
Treforest, Pontypridd.

Contents

Foreword

Ninety-one year-old Alun Menai Williams is the last surviving Welshman who left Britain to serve in the International Brigade alongside the Spanish people in their struggle against the military rebellion of July 1936.

The story of the disproportionately high number of Welsh volunteers who fought in the British Battalion of the 15th International Brigade is told in Hywel Francis's *Miners Against Fascism: Wales and the Spanish Civil War.* Typically, as will become apparent in this account of an unusually eventful early life, Alun saw action not just with the British, but with three other battalions in two brigades.

Four years ago I set out to make *Voices from a Mountain*, a documentary film about five British volunteers who were killed at the Battle of the Ebro in summer 1938 and whose names are crudely inscribed on a makeshift cement memorial that lay undiscovered on a Catalonian mountainside for more than sixty years. The idea was to recreate their lives – and deaths in Spain – through the testimonies of British veterans who actually knew them.

One of the five men – Harry Dobson – was a Welsh miner and active anti-fascist from the Rhondda Valley. At the time of my research, in winter 2000, I learned there were just three International Brigade veterans in Wales. Edwin Greening was naturally reluctant to talk to a stranger from London. The erudite Lance Rogers was too frail to be interviewed on camera. Alun, however, was keen to participate in the project. I wondered if he had known Harry Dobson.

"Did I know Harry Dobson? I was torpedoed with Harry Dobson."

This was almost too good to be true. And it got even better a few months later, when – weighed down with boxes of cameras and sound equipment – we descended on Alun's spotless home to rearrange the furniture and mystify the neighbours. What followed was not an interview in the conventional sense, but a powerful, articulate and emotional performance from an eighty-eight year-old man in full and energetic possession of his marbles.

In *From the Rhondda to the Ebro* Alun writes of his difficult relationship with his father, the poet Huw Menai Williams, and suggests that in temperament he took after his mother. But on paper and in person it is evident that Alun inherited Huw

Menai's poetic sensibility. In places the book has the rhythms and imagery of a prose poem. Similarly there are moments on camera when Alun breaks unconsciously into verse. Of the betrayal by the western democracies of the elected government of the Spanish Republic, for example, he says:

"The cry was '*no pasarán*'. Chamberlain and Daladier sold the pass. To World War Two and the bloody holocaust."

Our cameraman was himself a veteran - a documentary film veteran, battle-scarred from interviews with feral American Heavy Metal bands. From the outset he was dubious about our ability to weave a coherent narrative from the reminiscences of five disparate octogenarians. But at the end of our session with Alun - after a morning of passion, intelligence, sad reflection and humour - he turned off his camera and simply observed:

"You now have your film."

And he was essentially right. A boy from the Welsh Valleys, Alun was in the East of London for the Battle of Cable Street. He arrived in Spain to serve as *sanitario* - paramedic - with the German anti-fascist volunteers of the Thaelmann Battalion at the Jarama Front in spring 1937. He served with the Americans of the Washington and Lincoln Battalions at Brunete, Belchite and Teruel. He joined the British in time for the Ebro Offensive and was repatriated with the remnants of the battalion in December 1938. He was there, *mas o menos*, for the duration.

In *Voices from a Mountain*, Alun says his mother knew he was safely back in Britain because she saw his photograph in the *Daily Express*. This image of Alun - tall and dark-haired and wearing a distinctive polka-dot muffler - also appears in a sequence of rare black and white footage of the British volunteers arriving at Victoria Station in London. Composed and elegant, Alun holds the British Battalion banner. He stands head and shoulders above most of his comrades, an understandably scruffy crew in their Spanish berets and ill-fitting 'demob' suits or overcoats.

At the end of the editing process, I showed a 'rough cut' of the documentary - which includes the Victoria Station footage - to a female friend, a woman of impeccable socialist and feminist credentials with an appreciation of the history and politics of the 1930s.

In the film there are interviews with four other veterans: George Wheeler and Sol Frankel from London, John Dunlop from Edinburgh and Jack Jones from Liverpool. In addition to Alun's memories of Harry Dobson, we learn about the other men commemorated on the mountainside memorial: Lewis Clive, David Guest, Morris Miller and Wally Tapsell. And we hear from three of the Catalans who found the memorial and subsequently oversaw its restoration.

"Well, what do you think?" I asked nervously.

"I think", she replied, "that Alun Williams was an incredibly good looking young man."

Her remark was by no means flippant, but a demonstration that Alun was and indeed still is a striking individual. He has an effect on people.

From the Rhondda to the Ebro is one of the more engaging International Brigade memoirs to be published in recent years. It succeeds specifically because Spain concludes but does not dominate the story. Of his decision to volunteer, Alun writes:

"I have no facile or ready answer available, and the truth on offer is only partial. The emotions and motives for my decision were complex."

As you will discover, he is modest and self-effacing, guarded and oblique. But in fact the reasons for Alun's genuinely heroic commitment to the cause of democracy in Spain are there – beautifully expressed and developed in the first eight compassionate chapters of the book.

Es la historia, es la leyenda.

David Leach
leachdjr@hotmail.com
Batea
Catalonia
October 2004

For
Maudie Goldie
My lovely wife and best butty
and Robert, our son.

Introduction

I have a story to tell. It is a simple story devoid of the historian's hindsight or the student's selective delving during research.

It is a tale of the happenings to me and many of my contemporaries throughout the turbulent years of the 20th Century.

I tell it as it was, how it was, together with my feelings, thoughts, opinions and interpretations of why it was and which were being men tally registered as the events were actually taking place in moments of real time, and beyond the capture of historians of whatever their hindsight's views of the past reveals.

My interpretations of real time events may not square with the academics' interpretation of hindsight. But it does not diminish my opinions or deny the facts of the effects the actualities of the time had over my life and the lives of my contemporaries.

I want to write and tell my story in the only way I know how. In my own style, without pretensions of literary skills or merit in composition or the etiquette of grammatical correctness.

I will not subsume semantics to derail, be an obstacle or inhibit me in my desire to gather together my scatter of memories and put them in a simple and cogent way, compatible with my literary capabilities. Even if in so doing the English language is adulterated and suffers in the process of the telling.

I have time on my hands to indulge myself in a project my lovely wife wanted me to undertake. To write down my life's experiences in a way that can be read, understood and evaluated, by peoples of a different century, and to let them know the 20th Century has been the most violent in human history, as well as the most humiliating for mankind, to the point of making us question our idea of man and his place in the world as a rational being, in the face of so many disasters and massacres of innocent beings. A Century now fading into history where war was the norm and peace an event.

This revisiting will be time consuming, consequently, passing my remaining years in a pleasant occupation, of awakening memories, of the "long ago" of a very dangerous and sometimes stupid life style.

One's youth is full of anomalies and it is only when looking back, do you see that these unrelated anomalies had a pattern that dictated the actions that fundamentally guided and shaped the future to what it eventually became.

This trawling through the memory bank also has the positive bonus of rekindling memories of a very special lady. To again savour six decades of exemplary companionship, unquestioning loyalties and fidelity.

She was my "best friend", and as she so often said, I was her "Best Butty" and above all, mutual love and respect for each other that never goes away.

This may also act as an antidote to ease the pain of her death.

The sequences of my narrative will sometimes be out of kilter, and the interspersing of philosophic asides and digressions may seem to be out of place, but will nevertheless be in keeping with the overall context and the spirit of the telling.

To exhume dead memories of a personal nature and exposing them to scrutiny in a contemporary setting is a hazardous undertaking.

They arrive eroded by nature, sanctified by time and all mixed up.

I have therefore taken the liberty of constructing a kind of "memory fit" to overcome this inherent weakness in memory recall.

The physical aspects of these memories, locations, incidents, friends, people and "explosions", are easily identified. The conversation, the exact words, the heartaches, the loves, sorrows and fears, the joie de vivre, are all hidden away somewhere.

This ephemeral baggage is difficult to quantify and can be suspect. Hence my attempt at reconciling these two component parts of the memory into a whole, where truth and integrity are neither compromised nor jeopardised. The particular period of my story is self-revealing. I have purposely omitted precise dates other than thirteen years following the end of the nineteenth century - 1913 - the year I first made my acquaintance with this most beautiful of planets.

CHAPTER ONE

The Valley, its people and growing up

My mother decided one cold February morning at the beginning of the twentieth century that it was about time I made my entry on to this planet.

This event took place in a little valley bounded on three sides by mountains, a cul-de-sac, one way in, same way out.

A narrow valley with a small river coursing down the centre.

A few years before I arrived the valley was a beautiful, pristine work of time and nature. Trees adorned the mountainside, trout ran in the clear river, wild flowers in profusion along its banks, and green grass on the virgin soil.

The hands of the gods that created this idyllic scene, was now being replaced by the hands of man, who was now indulging in corporate vandalism on a gigantic scale. Tearing it all apart, bit by bit.

The natural beauty of this green and lovely valley was being systematically obliterated.

Vast holes excavated, trees uprooted, the river dammed and polluted. The mountain scarred with quarries. The valley floor flattened for railways and roads. The edges of the valley broken, levelled and covered with concrete and tarmacadam.

The mountains disfigured with tracks on which ramshackle terraced streets of houses, pubs, chapels and shops were built.

The holes in the ground were festooned with masses of ironwork with big winding wheels atop.

There were engine rooms, winding rooms, pump rooms for water, pump rooms for air, boiler houses. Steam locomotives, all the necessary gear and mechanical aids for extracting coal from the ground a quarter mile deep down.

The reason and cause of all this feverish human activity had been hiding down there for millions of years and was once again going to see the light of day and the heat of the same sun that shone upon the ancient Cambrian Seas, swamps and prehistoric forests that were now being resurrected as coal.

The destruction of this tiny and insignificant corner of the planet up in the hills without a map reference in the middle of nowhere, in the pursuit of Mammon was a calculated atrocity of entrepreneurial overkill.

The inhabitants of the hills of this isolated valley before the discovery of coal beneath were the sheep that grazed upon them with shepherds in attendance. This pastoral scene was shattered with that discovery.

The hills were gutted, the sheep dispersed, the shepherds becoming miners, and part of a great influx of people from the quarries of North Wales, the tin mines of Cornwall, the fields and orchards of Somerset.

The quarry men and the tin miners were inured to hard work that is accompanied by danger.

They came into the valley in hundreds bringing their wives and children along to share the hopes and good life that was rumoured to be available in the South Wales Coalfield.

My parents made the journey from North Wales with Welsh as their mother tongue. In the new setting of a polyglot society, English was the normal language of discourse. Their Welshness enveloped in the process.

To accommodate these hopeful migrants, the coal owners built "overnight" terraced houses that were no more than designer hovels. Jerry built from local quarried stone and timber of the indigenous trees and woodlands.

These "houses" consisted of a flagstone-floored living room, two small bedrooms, and a scullery cum-kitchen with a stone sink, water being obtained from a standpipe at the end of each terrace.

The lavatory was outside at the bottom of a small garden, ostensibly a vegetable plot.

Cooking facilities were a source of great ingenuity and confined to an open coal fire, with brick hobs either side of the fire grate, with an oven underneath one of the hobs.

Street after street of terraced jerrybuilt "houses" were "flung up" keeping pace with the mine constructions and the arrival of new families.

Within a period of six years two pits were sunk, and peak production reached by some six hundred miners and ancillary workers.

The population of the valley had stabilised around three thousand including children.

To teach and accommodate these children, three schools were built at various sites in the valley. Two at the entrance to the valley, one each side of the river and crossed by a small concrete bridge. The third at the top of the valley, the cul-de-sac. This was the little school, the only school I attended for nine years, from five to fourteen. Its total intake of seventy pupils including infants was taught by two females and one male, including the Headmaster.

The boys and girls were mixed during lessons and separated at playtime. The Headmaster was a big man with a walrus moustache to match. He was tyrannical in his maintenance of discipline. His cane came down very heavy on the hand of the owner of any recalcitrant tendency. Most of us boys were his victims at one time or another. We were terrified of him.

When he was involved with the children during out of school activities he was a different person; kind, considerate and concerned for the welfare of his pupils. During class his presence always frightened us, yet at the same time it engendered great respect.

He somehow achieved the impossible task of maintaining discipline and at the same time instilling in us the value of such discipline and its place in life, as we grew older.

His tactics of gentle persuasion with a big stick behind his back worked, his efforts were successful.

In later years we talked about our headmaster with a mixture of awe and affection.

From the commencement of our schooling at infant's class until standard three, he insisted that boys and girls be mixed when in class. There were twin desks, boy and girl at each desk. After standard three we were free to sit anywhere and with whom of our choice.

At first that freedom was rarely exercised, but as we grew older, preferences were being made, girl with girl and boy with boy.

By the age of eleven, the class was almost split even. With the exception of Priscilla insisting on sitting with me, and Megan with Brinley.

Priscilla and I sat together for nine years, from the age of five at infants, until we left together at the age of fourteen.

The change of desk positions was gradual and imperceptible. There never seemed to be a difference or problem.

The friendships formed during these early years were unique and lasting. There were a dozen of us boys and one girl, who became very close, loyal and dependable in our attachment to each other.

This group divided into two or three separate little cliques of extra "special best friends". Brinley, Billy, Bobbie and Dai were my four "best friends". I was also their best friend.

The five of us young boys were to have a great influence on each other during our childhood play years and early adolescence and later on as adults. Oh yes! The one girl, our wonderful Priscilla. She was the "best friend" to all of us.

Brinley's father was a chimney sweep and a reformed "hell raiser" who had come over all "Jesus" and was now a member of the Salvation Army and the big bassoon player in the band.

Billy's father was a minor local government official and was known by all the valley as "Will Transvaal", he having served in the Boer War, as a sergeant.

Bobbie's father was a coal cutting miner slightly eccentric in that he was always chewing tobacco and of dubious accuracy in his spitting. He was also, never without "yorks" on his trousers, whatever the occasion. To the uninitiated "yorks" are a small leather strap fitted around each trouser leg just below the knee.

Dai's father was a haulier underground, whose job is to attach the special harness of the horse (pit pony) to a tub of coal and haul it away from the coalface to an assembly point where they are coupled together to form a "journey" or train. Then pulled along the rails by means of an endless steel rope to the pit bottom. He was also an official of the Miners Federation or the "Fed" as it was more commonly called.

My father was a colliery official of some standing and privilege. He lived in a company owned house, with four bedrooms, two living rooms and a lounge, a kitchen and inside toilet facilities. In his spare time he was a writer, a poet and a person of some note.

He was the author of four books of poems which were well received by the critics of the day. The Daily Sketch on one occasion had the whole front page devoted to him, including photos of his family. He was also well known in Welsh literary circles.

Our mothers! Marvellous women, all childbearing chattels of great efficiency and stoicism of legendary proportions.

My mother and the mothers of my four best friends had thirty children between them. I was the second of eight, five girls, three boys. How many miscarriages or self-induced abortions took place can only be at best an educated guess. The intervals between live births are some kind of measure. My mother's first four were at intervals of twenty months, the last four were spaced at thirty months to three years.

Bobbie's mother had nine children, the first four at intervals of eighteen months with the last five averaging twenty-four months.

When as children we went calling on each other, our mothers would invariable be suckling the latest arrival or washing napkins and baby clothes in between preparing a meal and always in the same pinafore; their main and only item of apparel, so it appeared to be.

My recollection of all those brave mothers is of suckling the new arrival with the previous one howling its lungs out nearby. Dirty napkins, a scrubbed deal table top, cluttered with dirty dishes, with a bottle of Alley Sloper sauce in the middle and a look of resignation on their lined and worried faces.

Every terraced house was the same to "that man from outer space"; the whole valley would appear to be one massive crèche.

The babies were carried by the mothers "Welsh fashion", wrapped tightly in a shawl draped over one shoulder and held in place by the left hand. The other free to do whatever?

Carriages and feeding bottles were luxuries used only by the bosses' wives or city women. My mothers would do without. They preferred to feed their babies, free milk, on the hoof, the natural way.

When a small child, I was always fascinated with the suckling action of the baby at its feed.

When my mother opened her blouse and took out her swollen tit, I would bend over to watch the baby suckling away, and nearly always (I never learnt), she would whip her nipple out of the baby's mouth point it at me and squeeze!

The milk would squirt out all over my face at the same time and she would laugh heartily at my embarrassment.

I can hear that lovely laugh now, after all these years as I write and tell.

The suckling child at its mother's tit is to me, one of the most beautiful sights in nature.

The tenderness, security, warmth and love in full measure all for free and without conditions attached.

This picture of natural altruism should evoke in men the possibilities of peace and serenity that lurks out there somewhere.

The overall existence of these wives and mothers was of never-ending drudgery and of self-sacrifice, but with a determination to make the best of their situation for the children's sake.

Their daily lives were of sameness, no end in sight. No rainbow on the horizon. A sterile philosophy of grin and bear it on the journey to nowhere, a courage of despair prevailed.

This amoral outlook may have been a sub-conscious defence mechanism in the acceptance of the standards of the day – "a women's place is in the home looking after the kids."

The children were their priority over what might be, or could be. It was a self-imposed programming and hacker-proof.

During the school summer holidays, we would vanish from the sight of the grown ups and their interference.

We roamed wild and free, in woods, gullies, streams and pools that lay hidden in the architecture of the mountains that surrounded our valley.

We swam naked in the crystal clear pools. Drank the sweet water from the springs that fed the pools, to wash down the thick bread and jam the mothers had prepared for us. The water was always ice cold, we would be shivering with teeth chattering when we emerged from the pool. We would dry and warm ourselves by running around chasing one another, tumbling about and sham wrestling in the grass.

Dried and warmed by the sun, a short rest with the exercise repeated again and again, all the time stark naked with not a care in this world.

Another of our pursuits was chasing some wild ponies which would be grazing quietly with the sheep. One pony in particular was partial to bread and jam. We would entice it, catch it, slip a rope around its head, and attempt to mount the animal; with patience and many bumps and falls we would succeed.

Over time, many holidays and weekends, the pony became docile and quite willing to play with us. We named him (or was it a her?) Lousy, after that fact. We did not mind the odd louse or tick, we were having great fun and as long as we fed him with bread and jam, "Lousy" was always ready and game for riding.

One summer holiday around ten, eleven years of age, we went through the same routine of exploring the mountain gullies and hollows and swimming naked in the pools.

This particular day we made an exception; we decided to bathe in a big pool called "Pond Mawr", Welsh for Big Pond. It was a much bigger pool than we were in the habit of frequenting. This was where the older teenage boys did their swimming. We would join them; we were good swimmers, self reliant and capable.

This day, a newcomer had infiltrated into our little gang. David Davies, a cousin of Billy. We undressed, placed our clothes in neat bundles and ran shouting and laughing into the icy water. There, larking and splashing, swimming, diving and thoroughly enjoying ourselves at the moment. Out we all came, cold, shivering and teeth chattering as usual, then running around shaking the water off and getting some warmth into our bodies, only to repeat it again later.

We then settled on the grass each by our respective bundle of clothes. All the bundles were occupied except one. It belonged to Billy's cousin, David Davies. Where was he? It dawned on us that he wasn't in the melee of our drying and warming exercise.

We shouted, calling his name, stood up and scanned the surroundings, all in vain. Where could he be? We looked at each other for an answer as to who saw him last. Billy volunteered the information that he and David had been indulging in the sport of who could swim the farthest under water without coming up for air. Slight panic ensued before we questioned Billy. What part of the pool did the diving take place? He had an idea, but wasn't quite sure.

With that knowledge, we ran to the older teenage boys of sixteen to eighteen years and told them what we "thought" had happened to David and where. Without hesitating three or four of the lads jumped into the pond, diving and searching for David. This diving went on in relays by the teenage boys without thought of abandonment. When a shout went up from one of the divers, the others quickly rallied to the spot, dived down, and came up with David. He was immediately brought to the bank.

The older boys were methodical and completely in charge. They placed David on his side, massaging and pumping his back in attempts to expel the water from his lungs. They continued working on David for a good twenty minutes without a break, to no avail.

One of the boys turned to our gang and said, "Your friend is dead". It was a terrible shock. David was the first dead person any of us had ever seen. His body was carried to where he had left his bundle of clothes and laid gently on the grass; his naked body was covered with his shirt. Somehow we felt responsible for this tragic accident. We remained by his side in sombre silence and bewilderment.

To be dead was for grown-ups; they were always dying, we were forever. A young life of the living had inexplicably and suddenly got mixed up with the old and the dying.

David's forever was for real; his young life had ended.

As children, death was an abstract notion that had not yet permeated our innocence. We had seen many dead "things"; birds, rats, worms, beetles, flies, but to our infantile way of thinking, they were simply not alive.

The equation is obvious. Is it alive, or is it not alive? The concept of death and its totality was completely absent: our games of cowboys and Indians, cops and robbers, fighting the Germans, all involved the fun of being dead and cheating by suddenly coming alive again.

This time, David's death was a game that was different. He wasn't going to cheat and come back alive. We knew that David would never live again.

Death in all its stark reality was lying on the grass by our side, we were looking at a dead David, but he couldn't see us. Billy started to cry. Meanwhile, one of the teenage boys went for the police. We were as silent as David and transfixed by the sight of his partly naked body lying on the grass by our side, with his face to the sky, covered by a towel, placed there by one of the older boys.

They arrived about two hours later with a stretcher party. The pool where David met his death was over two miles away over undulating territory with only sheep tracks to aid the walking. The long trek back to our valley was interminable.

The news of the drowning had preceded us. When we finally arrived at the base of the mountain, we were met by half of the valley people, with our five mothers in tears. They knew it was somebody of our little gang, but were not certain whom.

They shed more tears when they saw us travelling behind the stretcher - all safe. The five mothers were greatly relieved when they could see it wasn't their son who was lying on the stretcher. It was somebody else's son. There was no sixth mother; David was an orphan.

The mental grasshopper resident in my memory becomes a problem on occasion. It jumps and stops without warning such as now as I pause in the telling of my story to relate the story of Billy's father and mother, his two older brothers and his adopted brother and sister, David and Dodau.

David and Dodau's father was killed in the last year of the Great War. Their mother died later of the Spanish Flu. I am unsure of their parents' relationship to Mr Davies and his wife, however suffice it for me to say that it was close enough for them to take into their care the two orphaned children and treat them as their own.

Billy's two older brothers, Emlyn and Phillip, joined the Army, both doing service in India. After seven years with the Colours. Emlyn transferred to the Reserve and found employment as a postman.

Emlyn's service in India had by all who knew him affected his personality to such an extent that he was accused of strangling his girlfriend to death with a silk stocking. At his trial he was found guilty but subsequently acquitted on appeal.

Phillip, the older brother, was discharged from the Army as unfit, repatriated from India, given a small pension and left to his own devices

Phillip was a quiet and unassuming gentleman who "wouldn't hurt a fly".

Billy, the youngest of Will Transvaal's sons was in London and on the dole. Phillip went to join him.

The politics of the day was of confusion and appeasement, in tune with the Conservative's dominance of the national government.

The subject of European Fascism was beginning to have an effect on the British political scene. A pivitol role in the rise of fascism in this country was the attitude and support of the press barons and prominent members of the Conservative establishment.

Rothermere and the Daily Mail gave Mosley and his Blackshirt followers, the thumbs up and a big 'hurrah' and I also suspect, bank rolled his organisation.

The country's awareness of the political implications of fascism was becoming polarised with the majority as the undetermined middle. This polarisation became very heated, and sometimes bloody.

Billy, being an ex-miner of a radical background, was inevitably motivated to throw in his lot with the anti-fascist movement and any organisation that supported his point of view.

Phillip for no reason other than solidarity with his brother, followed.

Both were unemployed with time and inclination in abundance, and they decided to put Billy's words into action. It goes without saying that this was Billy's decision; Phillip going along for the ride.

It was decided that they sell the 'Daily Worker', because of its virulent anti-fascist campaign, outside the gates of Hyde Park, and adjacent to Speakers Corner. This action furthered Billy's obsession and detestation of Mosley and his Blackshirt thugs, as well as for the commission on the sales of the paper.

For a while it was a pleasant and novel experience, with goodwill shown by good people and supporters of the antifascist cause. Until one evening as dusk fell, a gang of Blackshirt thugs turned up and smashed Phillip's small stand scattering his papers to the wind, mercilessly beating him up, and vanishing as quickly as they came.

Passers-by went to his aid. Police and ambulance arrived, taking Phillip to a hospital where he lay in a coma for seven days, to be eventually transferred to an institution for the mentally disabled, where he died one year later.

Shortly after this incident Billy, true to his anti-fascist principles, volunteered his services to the International Brigades and the war in Spain.

He was killed at the Battle of Brunete. Will "Transvaal's" four sons were dead, killed or died in curious circumstances. One drowned, one died in jail, another in a mental hospital and the youngest killed in a war in a distant land.

With the death of Billy, Mrs Davies finally collapsed, her grief silent and pervading. Dodau, her daughter by adoption was married with a new baby. She went shopping in the High Street, pushing baby in a pram. A lorry veered off course, mounted the footpath, crashing and killing both mother and child.

A family calamity of gross misfortune was reaching its climax. Mrs Davies died shortly after her daughters' funeral. Desolate and prostrate with grief.

This heart-rending misery ended with Will "Transvaal" dying quietly and alone. Fate having dealt him a dud hand of marked cards at the beginning.

The tragedy that fate bequeathed to Will and his wife, was of an agonising, gut wrenching nature. The cry of "What have I done to deserve this?" calls for a response.

Methinks that riddle will be for always. My atheism exonerates me of the possibilities of an answer. Fatalism makes a voluntary pact with man not to resist it. What must happen can be left to take its appointed course.

The valley had become a thriving close-knit community. Due partly to its geographical location it was isolated. We had become a village, with a map reference and a postal address.

The houses were numbered, the terraced streets were given names, a parish council formed and a police station erected and manned by Sergeant Hamm, Constables Beynon and Edwards.

To us children they were known as Bobby Beynon and Copper Edwards. Bobby Beynon was a menace, Copper Edwards was a softy. He always seemed to be engrossed with Rowena, the Postmaster's daughter, to bother about us.

We had many a slap across the head by Bobby Beynon. No complaint was ever made for this action. It was apparent the parents approved of this method without exception of keeping us naughty children under control.

One time, Billy, Brinley and myself were caught red-handed pinching apples from Joby Henderson's small orchard. We were marched by Bobby Beynon without ceremony to the police station, placed in a little anteroom with the door left open so that we could see into the adjoining cell which also had its door open. We were on our own for what seemed an eternity.

Eventually, Sgt. Hamm appeared bearing three mugs of water and three slices of bread. He handed this "feast" to us individually and without a word being said, he left. By now we were in one big sorry state; we were very young.

Unbeknown to us, our parents had been informed of where we were and of our plight - and were at the station.

Sgt Hamm returned to where we were with a pair of handcuffs dangling in his hand. He looked at us and with the hand that held the handcuffs he pointed his finger at the open cell opposite and said if ever we were caught being naughty again, he would lock us up in there forever.

During the whole of this episode from the time of our apprehension for stealing apples to his finger pointing moment, those were the only words spoken to us either by the Sgt or Bobby Beynon.

On being released from "jail" a reception party of three very irate fathers greeted us as we were handed over by Sgt Hamm with the handcuffs still conspicuously swinging in his hand.

A salutary lesson was given; a salutary lesson was learnt by three very contrite children.

The only harm or consequence of any note that flowed from our incarceration was of annoyance at being sidelined and absent when other members of our gang were scrumping Joby's apples. We would remember bread and water as a very unappetising meal.

This incident must have registered subconsciously with the three of us, with the exception of Billy who was always in trouble later with his antifascist activities. I can safely state that we have steered clear of the police and the law.

I can also say with information from an impeccable source (my mother), that Sgt Hamm and my father, who were good friends, hatched this conspiracy in conjunction with the other two fathers to put the frighteners on us. How could they be so insensitive with three very young boys?

The top end of the valley was reasonably flat with plenty of pastureland for sheep grazing and long grass for other "activities".

This was Joby Henderson's fiefdom, where he tended his sheep and maintained a smallholding. Containing among other things a small orchard of apple and cherry trees, he also kept geese, chickens, and pigs.

"Joby's land" and his orchard of goodies was a prime target for the children and the "big boys".

He allowed us without hindrance to roam his pastures and meadows. But look out if we strayed anywhere near his smallholding.

The piggery was a little way from the farmhouse hidden from its direct view. This allowed us surreptitiously to watch his pigs play and go about their business of snorting and grunting. He would however, let us watch him feed the pigs if we were anywhere near at the time. He was human after all.

Once a year, the boar would come to town. We knew the day and time of its arrival. (Children are experts at confirming rumours).

At this annual event, crowds of us youngsters would gather at the little railway station to watch the boar being pulled by the nose out of the guards van, grunting and squealing, one of his handlers with a rope on the nose ring of the beautiful creature, the other handler with a rope attached to one of his rear legs.

This mobile pantomime would begin on the road in the middle of the valley accompanied by cheering crowds of children urging and encouraging the boar on the trek to his harem. His keepers bawling and shouting at us to keep clear of the beast, as he grunted and snorted, while plodding his way to his assignment.

The boar was intent on fulfilling his mission. His keepers were hard at work holding him from breaking into a gallop as well as berating the boar's young followers. On arrival at the piggery, the boar and his handlers would pass through the gate which Joby would close behind them and at the same time, chase the children off the premises. We had vague ideas of the purpose of the boar's visit, but were never allowed to witness the creature perform his "duties". Our ideas were never fully confirmed.

The prosperity enjoyed by the people of the village was being demonstrated by the various enterprises and activities now taking place.

The Miners' Federation was the guiding hand and promoter of many of the enterprises.

It was agreed that every miner and colliery worker, who was a member of the Union, would contribute an amount of money from his pay to be deducted at the source and used by the Federation for purposes beneficial to its members.

A "Workman's" Hall was built which included among other things a library, reading rooms, recreation rooms, as well as a cinema with upholstered seating accommodation for up to four hundred persons.

The subscription was also to finance a scheme whereby all the members and their families would receive medical attention, without payment as and when required.

This innovation of free medical support when needed was in sharp contrast to the existing state of a somewhat spasmodic and expensive service of the only doctor available.

Under the "scheme" as it was now called, the doctor would be under contract and paid by the miners for his exclusive services when called upon, which by the nature of the hazardous work involved in and performed by his patients would be of frequent occurrence, as well as a lifesaving one.

When the scheme was proposed for our valley, a committee was formed to undertake the task of setting up an organisation, and to find a suitable candidate for the post. The local union officials were diligent in carrying out the responsibilities placed upon them. A list of applicants was finally whittled down to one of unanimous preference. He was a negro – a "black man."

It does not take a great deal of imagination to realise that when this became a rumour our childish fantasies ran riot.

We had never seen a black man, what sort of person could nine and ten years olds conjure up? All we knew was, they were cannibals who lived in the jungle, wore grass skirts, with rings in the noses and spears in their hands.

A black man was coming into the valley. The rumour had been confirmed, the day and time of his arrival became known.

With great excitement amongst the children, a crowd of us turned up, with three union officials on the appointed day and time.

Though the stationmaster kept us children a distance away from the platform, we nevertheless had a good view of the proceedings.

The train stopped, the official welcoming party stepped forward to greet a tall, slim handsome young negro in bowler hat and pin-striped trousers with a suitcase in his hand "and no spear." The "Black Doctor" had arrived in our valley.

We were bitterly disappointed there was no grass skirt or ring in his nose, we were baffled and crestfallen. Our impression and fantasy of a black man was completely destroyed. The Black Doctor was exactly like all the other grown-ups we saw with no difference.

The General Strike "came and went" with chaos in its wake.

The Valley was quiet, the noise from the Collieries had ceased. It was a strange silence, a dead silence. The industrial heart of the valley would never again find the same rhythm. This interruption was eventually to prove terminal.

The short duration of the General Strike had little effect on the miners' resolve. Their struggle continued for many months into the future.

The deprivation and suffering of the miners and their families, was to upset the body politic and shatter the status quo. Scabs, blacklegs and traitor were epithets bandied about and used to describe those who were once friends and butties.

The valley was a verbal battleground of public meetings, street gatherings, demonstrations, police confrontations and neighbour against neighbour,

Concurrent with this mayhem was a fine streak of compassion which showed itself in a multitude of ways. Soup kitchens were organised and staffed by union members for the children of those in most need. Charities donated clothing and footwear, like-minded friends and neighbours helped one another.

A great sense of identity and comradeship developed. Welding together antagonisms and hate for the scabs and coal owners, who were perceived as the cause of their suffering.

We were young boys on the edge of puberty. Scanning our lower anatomy for the first signs of hair, and looking forward to the day, which was not far away, when we would be leaving school.

To us the strike was exciting, a novelty and a time of new and unusual educational experiences. We would creep into public meetings and listen to the dedicated speakers, with special attention to the questioners and hecklers. We volunteered to distribute handbills, relay messages and sweep out committee rooms.

Billy, Brinley and I were also required on two separate occasions to assist in sheep rustling.

We were asked to join this "enterprise" by a few desperate miners in their endeavour to supplement the protein requirement of their hungry families. We were "co-opted" in as trustworthy accomplices, primarily because of Brinley's known prowess with the trumpet.

The requirement of our assistance in the furtherance of the rustlers' intentions was to find a high point, from where we could scan a large area of mountain and its small hollows and valleys, in the vicinity of the operation. We should be on the look out for Joby Henderson, the police or any suspect interloper, while they went about the business of catching the sheep, dispatching it, disembowelling, skinning, burying the unwanted results of the kill and finally carving it into joints for easy carrying. All done with lightening speed and efficiency in the time of one half hour.

While this work was going on, our job as lookouts was for Brinley to blow hard on his trumpet and make a loud tune, to warn the sheep stealers of approaching danger. Brinley's music would resonate throughout the mountain. In more normal times we would often, in our moments of leisure, sit on the mountain and listen to Brinley practice his trumpeting. It would therefore not be unusual to see us on the mountain and hear the trumpet being played.

One of the priorities of a coal strike of some duration, is the welfare of the pits ponies. They must be raised to the surface. The day the ponies were brought up, a group of us would gather at the pithead and watch the animals exit the cage. On reaching daylight the poor things seemed dazed and were very docile.

The man in charge would give each boy a pony with halter and rein and instructions to lead the animals to Joby Henderson's enclosed pasture. The ponies were easy to handle, and we were well trained by our wild pony "Lousy" It was no problem whatsoever when out of sight of the pit head to mount the pony and gallop or canter the rest of the way to Joby's farm where we handed them over to a stable man, an employee of the mining company.

The strike had compensations for us boys. The surfacing of the ponies together with sheep rustling were pleasant distractions from the mayhem, acrimony and misery that we were witnessing daily.

Three months into the strike the pit where my father was employed was closed for good. The reasons for such drastic action was obscure, but the consensus was the Coal owners closed it as an example of what could happen to the other pits if the strike was indefinitely prolonged. My father was unemployed and on the dole, with seven children, and one on the way.

The Company house was sold to an estate agent, thereby obliging father to find money for rent. Up to now the house was rent free, a perk of the job. Besides money for rent there was clothing and food that had to be paid for. His wife and young family depended upon him. My mother was in great distress in her attempts at coming to terms with the new regime endured by her family.

It was a case of scrimping, making do and mend. With the children it was more or less first up best dressed.

Our new circumstances were not any different from the rest of the valley people. With the exception that our standard of living and prestige had further to fall because of my father's position as a colliery official, living in a big house, and of being a literary figure of some note.

My mother was a very proud person, come what may, she would hide our poverty from the world with the pretence that nothing had changed.

My father became very withdrawn, morose and indifferent in his attitude to our predicament.

His writing skill and poetic imagination, temporarily deserted him. He became depressed, melancholy and prone to quarrel with my mother on any pretext. According to him it was her fault that the children were hungry. She was to blame that the rent was in arrears.

My poor mother was at her wit's end in trying to maintain a semblance of family cohesion aswell as putting up with my father's rantings. Her only income at the moment was the dole pittances.

My elder sister, Ethel, had won a scholarship to a grammar school, which was fifteen miles travel by train to another valley. Our village was devoid of any educational establishments other than the elementary schools.

She had won the Scholarship when the family circumstances and finances were of a good standard, and when fares, uniforms and other student accessories were not of a monetary problem. The sudden and dramatic turn around in the family's way of life, and the resulting deterioration in the domestic harmony, prompted my mother to withdraw Ethel from the grammar school. My sister would now be of help and assistance in regards to the welfare of the younger children.

Over the next two to three years my sister would be a surrogate mother, my mother being overtly concerned with the baby and her seemingly paranoid husband.

Both my parents had lost their sense of direction. They were benumbed by the sudden turn of events.

My mother avoided contact with her friends. She cut herself off from reality, became introspective and short tempered with the children.

My father only emerged from his dreams and self induced nightmares to sign on the dole.

They were fully aware of the children's needs regarding food and clothes, but were incapable of wanting to alleviate the situation.

My sister was now in charge of the children. She was fifteen years old and of a willingness to undertake any action that would be of value to the family.

Soup kitchens were organised and manned by union members and their wives for all strikers' children. All my friends would be there with their mugs or bowls for the hand out.

I tried to join them, but was found not eligible for partaking of this bounty. My father was not on strike, further more he had been a Company man who was now unemployed and drawing dole money.

I was upset at the rejection and my inability to be with my pals who were enjoying themselves with food which seemed very appetising. I was also disappointed for my siblings who, whilst not starving were nevertheless as hungry as I was.

Ethel to her credit and persistence tackled the people running the "soup kitchen" in the vicinity. She pestered and wore them down to let us join the other children at the table. They grudgingly conceded.

Huw Menai's children were now being fed by a charity.

My mother's pride would have to bend, my sisters' efforts made her realise that inaction was part of the problem. To fold her arms and look on wasn't the solution. Her favourite hobby was knitting and crocheting. She now turned this hobby into a job of work. She buried herself in knitting and crocheting of which she was a master craftsman. Most of our outer garments, dresses, jumpers, pullovers, jerseys, socks and gloves were either knitted or crocheted. She was clever; she would knit and simultaneously continue a conversation without looking at the needles flashing in and out with speed and accuracy.

This new interest maintained her equilibrium and patience to her advantage in her dealings with my father. There were moments when in dark moods of depression a chink of light would appear, illuminating the corner of his mind where in lay his poetic instincts to emerge in attempts of expiation for his behaviour toward my mother. A little poem inspired by her knitting, conjured up by his vivid imagination during the mental agony he was suffering as he surveyed the disintegration of his family and where might lay the blame.

This poem is from the Simple Vision, the last of his four books of published verse.

Nystagmus
(To Mammy)

Slip one - purl two:
Strong in thy virtue knit along;
And I'll mind not the knavish tricks
That would disturb my song.

Knit one - make two:
Away from my wits I once did roam,
When some wee devils, from out the dark,
Would have me wreck my home.

Slip one - knit three;
For this , too, is art, if homely art
And though a dream once held my head
'Tis thou who holdst my heart.

Make three - slip two:
Slipping the faults that have been mine -
Thou, who provest great in cloudy weather,
Would greater prove in fine

Make two - knit two:
There dwells something fatal about thy skill!
And all this knitting, late of nights,
Must knit us closer still.

During this period of change and upheaval, I spent a great deal of my time of an evening reading books recommended by my father and by the Workmans' Hall librarian. Most of these books were topically relevant to the conditions appertaining to the valley and the lives of its inhabitants, such as Jack London's "Iron Heel" and Robert Tressel's "Ragged Trousered Philanthropist", Zola's "Germinal", Upton Sinclair's "Profits of Religion" and Sexton Blake!

I was young with an appetite for reading and easily impressed. The early reading of radical literature was of a permanence that has never been equalled and which has remained with me throughout my life.

You will have noticed in most of this telling that the "We" is used more often than the "I". The old bolshevik in me can't rest. My early education conditioned by its surroundings and sometimes appalling circumstances, won't be shrugged off.

The Workmans' Library had a good selection of books together with a librarian who was very tolerant of us young lads, and who gave freely of advice and guidance which more often than not was of a radical nature. Hence the radical view of me and all my best friends. It is no wonder therefore that we were always in agreement at the unfairness that greeted us on a daily basis, and that a solution to address this apparent disparity must be in the hands of its victims.

My father had always been a closet radical, in the present adverse conditions he threw all his natural caution to the wind and declared in favour of a socialist solution to the problem. He was at the receiving end of a national economic disaster under the camouflaged description of depression with its connotations of a natural phenomena.

My own burgeoning socialism spawned by what I was daily witnessing and by listening to the bolshevik sentiments expressed by the adults and my own contemporaries as well as by the radical books and literature provided by the workman's library and recommended for my delectation by our worthy librarian.

This was now being reinforced by the sight of my father's impotence in his desire to shield his family from the harshness and misery that confronted him. Watching his children go hungry was no help to his moods of depression.

To help my mother who was suckling her eighth child, I obtained a job in a new small cinema that had been built in the locality. I was the re-wind assistant to the projectionist, a job that entailed the rewind of reels of films, the subject of the show. This business was not as easy as it sounds. The film stocks of the day was a compound of nitro cellulose which would break easily if the rewind was not carefully controlled. The sprocket holes would crack and only reveal themselves when the film was run in the projector at its showing.

The film would break up in the optical gate and because of the intense heat of the carbon arc lights; would catch fire with the necessary intermission for rectification.

This break would always be accompanied by whistles, shouts and cat-calls of an impatient audience.

The repairs could take up to fifteen minutes, for reasons of the obligatory fire precautions.

There was a one "house" showing on weekdays from seven to ten of an evening, and two "houses" on a Saturday evening, from six to nine and from nine to midnight. The timing had to be precise and spot on. It would be unlawful to continue into Sunday. Welsh licensing laws were very strict. Continuous performances had yet to be invented.

I received the sum of five shillings for my efforts and paid after the last show on Saturday. The money small as it was, was a little help for my mother as well as making me feel of some value. My school day was normal, but time after school with my friends was restricted. My cinematic occupation took precedence, a few of my friends also had after-school jobs.

Brinley was helping his father sweep chimneys as well as attending evening classes at the Salvation Army hall in the art of trumpet playing. Billy was working at the local bakery, cleaning and greasing bread tins.

The world of work was impinging on the already tarnished fantasies of our private universe. The last of our illusions was in the process of final demolition, and gradually being replaced by a reality and certainty, that could also be prone to erroneous interpretation.

This shift in our young lives was happening the same time as our biological mechanism was changing gear in obedience to nature's first call of her Sovereign and quintessential principle. The conservation and continuity of life; a process that is impervious to strikes, wars or any other manmade event. As well as the parental advice and exultations of the dangers they perceive as inherent in nature's billion year old dictum. That all living things must reproduce.

Our idling hormones were getting excited and latent instincts being revealed with. arrogance, confidence and twinges of independence, consistent with the onset of puberty. Also noticeable were voices getting deeper, hair growing where before there was none. We became shy of girls, but more conscious of the difference. Macho-male in its infancy, with growing pains.

The coalfield strike ended. The miners returned to work. Chastened but proud of their solidarity in the face of overwhelming odds. The return to the pits was not a victory for the coal owners; it was in reality a victory of compassion over principle.

The hardship endured by the wives and children became a burden. Wearisome and too heavy a price to pay for a principle that set the strike on its course in the first place.

The price already paid by the miners was later compounded by the coal owner's policy of cutbacks. Short-time working and the closure of some pits. These closures were creating a pool of unemployed miners and radicalising the politically apathetic of an easygoing hard working body of men. A Conservative Association was formed and club premises obtained.

The predominant group, the Labour Party, with its sponsors the Miners' Federation were given a room at the Workmans Hall.

This hitherto political apathy of the valley had metamorphasised into party constituents. The once close-knit community was ripping itself apart.

The first Labour administration with its demise   after nine months in office rankled with the politically conscious union members. Their hopes once again lay in the future.

My future and that of my friends would be determined by youthful impulse and progress along a different route to that of the frustrated political and union members.

The Britannic Colliery, one of the deepest pits in the coalfield, had the reputation of mining the highest quality steam-producing coal.

Its total production was earmarked for His Majesty's Britannic Navy. Our valley was on the Admiralty Supply list. The Navy was converting to oil.

It would not be too long before the valley would be on the Admiralty's Hit List for pit closures.

A new seam of coal had been discovered at the pit. The event coinciding with myself and friends terminating our school careers. We were fourteen years old.

The new coal seam was about to go into production. Men and boys were required to do the job. Without much ado, and less thought, my friends and I presented ourselves at the pithead and applied. Within ten minutes of our application, all five of us got the jobs. The only qualification demanded was "Have you left school?" In chorus, "Yes!" "Right", said the deputy, "Start Monday morning six o'clock."

Leaving school never to return was an emotional episode I found difficult to define. A door that had been wide open for nine years was suddenly being closed, shut and locked. A mixed class of thirty boys and girls who had sat together, played together, quarrelled together, learned together for nine years. Children of a close knit incestuous terraced community was no longer a viable unit.

Friendships that had been formed and maintained during the most important years of our lives were now being reassessed. New cliques would replace old ones. Some friends would drift apart, others come closer. It was inevitable; Billy, Brinley, Bobbie, Dai and me would become closer, as would a few others. Thirteen of us in total.

The people who had taught and guided us these past nine years will have left a piece of their personalities in our subconsciousness. We will all hold something in common.

A dispersed class of thirty boys and girls unaware that they have little bits of their teachers and of each other hidden away in their identities. Our guides and mentors together with other factors peculiar to our geographical cul de sac imprisonment will always have a profound and residual effect on our lives.

A consensus of the exceptional individuals who had the most effect on our childhood and boyhood years by their sometimes involvement with us on a one to one basis would be Chas Davies, our Headmaster. We would deliberately go out of our way to salute him. It was part of his disciplinary side he frightened into us.

Bobby Beynon – we always ran like cornered rats whenever he was sighted and believe me we could see him coming from miles in the distance, other than when he would pop out of the ground in front of us. Mr Jeans; he in the blue uniform, peaked cap and yellow stripe on his trouser legs. The "whipper in", whose official title was School Attendance Officer. We would always hide from him, we were not aware of the difference between a legitimate and illegitimate absence from school. If we were not in school he would put our parents in jail, such was the rumour.

Huw Menai Williams and sons, 1948. Alun, Arfon, Glyn.

Five sisters in 1957. Jean, Betsi, Peggy, Olwen and Ethel.

My lovely mother, 1956.

CHAPTER TWO

Down the Pit and in the dark

At fourteen years of age I went from pen and ink at a school desk to pick and shovel down a coalmine. "Six o'clock Monday morning!"

My perfunctory interview with the colliery deputy and given a job in the mine was an item of information that I knew would not be welcomed by my parents and especially my mother.

On my arrival home, without gradual introduction or ceremony I blurted out that I had taken a job at the "Britannic" and was to start on Monday. My mother dropped her knitting and with an angry look and equal angry words, she reprimanded me in no uncertain terms for being so stupid without first asking her permission.

Her vehemence temporarily knocked me off balance. I eventually gained my composure by explaining I went along to the deputy's office with my pals because we were of the idea that our parents could do with the money we would earn. Furthermore, I had left school and what else was there for me in the valley, but coal pits.

Her anger subsided, tears came to her eyes, she nodded her consent and went back to her knitting.

My father on hearing the news left the room without uttering a word. As far as I was aware he appeared not to care or be concerned one way or the other, that his son was going to work in a coal mine. I could not have been more wrong.

After his death, many years later my mother whilst sifting through his papers, discovered a poem he had written at the time of my outburst and which had been in his possession over the years. With a touch of sorrow I now realised that my unpremeditated job seeking action had deeply affected him.

He expressed his feelings in solitude and in the penning of this poem, the contents of which he would keep secret unto himself alone.

His sense of martyrdom shown in the last verse was typical of the self-centred mental turmoil he was enduring at the time, and which he vented on my mother.

I reveal his secret poem with pride, as his testament to all my best friends and their parents whose precarious existence necessitated their children undertaking work of a hazardous nature to be a supplementary bread-winner.

To my Son Alun.

Take courage son! 'Tis hard I know
To sweat and labour deep below.
Down in the pit when still so young
With your sums' tables on your tongue.

No "higher grade" for you my boy;
You were not born for play, for joy,
But thus to shoulder best you can
The many worries of a man.

Your strength for growth in work to shed
To help us get our daily bread,
Which, when I eat it, bitter thoughts
Does find it sticking in the throat.

But courage son! Heed what I say,
A question will be asked some day,
Why were you, too, forced to become
A party to my martyrdom?

Huw Menai

I was awakened by my mother at five o'clock Monday morning to start a new chapter in my life. I dressed in the oldest and most decrepit clothes that fitted me. My breakfast of porridge was attended by my siblings, teasing and poking fun at my "fancy dress" and laughing at me. My mother had prepared bread and cheese sandwiches for my dinner break, which she had packed in a tin box, and together with a tin bottle of water was handed to me on my way out.

She was crying as she kissed me on the cheek. Without a word being exchanged I left the house. My father was in bed.

On the way down the terraced street towards the pit, I was greeted by Priscilla, my desk companion and shadow of the past nine years. She had purposely got out of her bed early to see me on my way.

I acknowledged her salutations as I hurried on. I was now a big boy and could not be bothered with silly school girl friends. I had more important things on my mind, such as coal mining.

At the end of the terrace, I joined Billy and Brinley, we looked at each other and burst into hearty laughter with our appearance.

Bobbie and Dai were already at the pithead, from where we were taken to the deputy's office.

Here our names and addresses were taken and we were given a small brass disc with a number stamped thereon. We were then told to make for the lamp room and hand in the brass disc in exchange for a lamp with the same number as the disc embossed on its side.

There is a strict safety procedure with the issue of lamps. The place where the lamp is kept and recharged when not in use is marked with the same number as the lamp. A lamp is drawn in exchange for the little disc. This disc is then hung on a hook in the position previously occupied by the lamp. At the end of the shift, the recharging benches are checked and should a disc be where a lamp should be, enquiries are immediately instigated.

The light given by the lamp was of a dim quality, but long lasting. The contraption weighed about three pounds, had a hook for a handle and could either be carried or hung on the trouser belt - which was more often the practice, thus leaving both hands free. After being issued with a lamp we were mustered outside the lamp room to be introduced to the man to whom we were apprenticed (a misnomer for cheap labour). He was to be my "butty" and I was to be his.

My "butty" was a man of middle age, gruff and not too pleased at having to break in a new boy. A miner at the time was paid by the ton of coal, cut and sent to the surface.

It was a backbreaking slog of pick and shovel in cramped and dangerous surroundings. Machinery had not yet been installed.

A coal miner does not dig for coal he "cuts" it. Tin miners and gold miners 'dig'. Coal mining is a skill, unlike any other, complete with hard labour.

It was to be expected that a man with a new boy would not produce the same tonnage; as such his pay packet would be lighter. Hence the cool reception by the older miners of the new.

Preliminaries over, we were escorted by our "butties" to the pithead, where we were searched for contraband, tobacco, cigarettes and matches. This is a normal and random exercise but because we were new it was obvious that a special and thorough search was being made to impress.

We then entered the cage, holding twenty to thirty men and boys. Together with all the new lads, who were placed by the adults in the middle of the cage for security and confidence building precautions.

They were all very patient and understanding of our apprehensions. The gate closed, a loud bell rang, and the cage started to descend slowly at first, quickly gathering speed, ears clicked, stomach raised and subsided in quick succession.

The sudden darkness and the glimmer of the lamps were eerie. The silence of the men during the descent was strange. Arriving at the pit bottom with a slight bump and stepping out of the cage was tantamount to discovering a New World of which the imagination was unaware.

In contrast to the darkness of the descent, the pit bottom was a blaze of light from hundreds of electric lamps. The iron girders bricked into the cavernous roof looked

© National Mining Museum of Wales, Blaenavon and National Museums and Galleries of Wales.

Britannic Colliery, Gilfach Goch, in the early years of the Twentieth Century. The one pulley shaft was the "upcast" or "return", which vented the foul used air after it had circulated the workings of the colliery.

immense. There were small gauge railways and sidings in all directions. Full and empty coal tubs on the lines. Stacks of timber of all kinds on the sides of the railways, engine rooms, pump rooms hewn into the sides of the tunnel. First aid posts, foreman's office, all there as well as stables for the ponies. The stables were well lit, clean, whitewashed and well appointed and would bear comparison with horse accommodation on the surface.

The ponies when not worked were groomed, pampered and cared for by the farrier and his assistants.

The atmosphere (the weather) at the pit bottom was cool with a slight breeze. This being the downcast shaft where the air it sucked in and starts its circulation around the geography of the pits, many tunnels, by-ways and coal faces. To eventually be exhausted in the upcast shaft warm and foul after its long journey by a very large extractor fan.

My initial awe-inspiring impression of this underground world was quickly modified by the sight of a series of dark tunnels some yards away from the pit bottom pointing in different directions and on which rails were laid and leading to different coal seams. These tunnels were not very big. They were however wide enough to allow coal tubs to travel on the rails to and from the coal face and high enough for man and horse to walk without bending head or ears.

The roofs of these tunnels were supported every ten feet apart by stout timber logs. As coal was cut and surfaced the tunnels move forward. The particular one my butty, companions and I were walking was one mile from the pit bottom to the coalface.

We walked crocodile fashion, following the swaying lamplight of the person in front. Conversation was limited and then only when necessary. The coalface was reached where my butty instructed me to follow to a site at the coalface where his tools were stacked; he then proceeded to explain my duties and methods of helping him in the job of cutting coal and sending it to the surface.

My particular part of the operation was to manipulate a "coal box" a big glorified shovel without a handle but with three raised sides, with which I had to scoop up the coal cut by my butty and push, shove and drag it to the empty coal tubs some fifteen to twenty feet away from the coal face and into which its contents would be emptied.

One third of my daily life for the next three years would be committed to the difficult and painful task of working where a billion years ago the sun shone upon seas and forests and where trilobites and strange insects lived and thrived.

The sun did not shine on me an industrial troglodyte (a distant cousin of those ancient trilobites) and who now inhabits that same world where a half mile of earth and rocks is an impenetrable barrier to the light and warmth of its long, long ago. It was now dark down here.

Not the dark of a moonless night or of an unlit room. It was inky "black and invisible". It shrouded me, you can feel it, you can taste it, you know its there.

Total absence of light is fearful! If the lamp failed whilst working at the coalface, however perfect the eyes, blindness is immediate. Twenty-twenty vision is zeroed.

I would have to trust the efficiency of my acid generated light and live with the fear. The height of the coal seam cut by my butty was three feet nine inches. It was therefore necessary to push or drag the loaded coal box on all fours or on my knees with only the last few feet in the upright position. Enabling me to lift the heavy coal box and tip its contents into the tub on the rails, at the end of the tunnel, which was high enough for man and pony to work and walk.

At the end of my first shift as a "miner", my back was one big ache. My knees were very sore, and fingertips almost raw. I knew if I was to survive this gruelling work of coal mining, I, like my friends, would have to adapt. The older miners told us we would get used to it in time. The evolutionary gene of adaptability is programmed for change. It is insidious and persistent in its progress towards the inevitable. It diverts from this pattern only under duress of a sudden environmental or habitat change. Or of a catastrophe, an event now engulfing five young boys as they migrate from a quiet and safe class room to a life of work and danger, in the dark; a quarter mile underground.

A time would come for me when new conditions would determine again, the course of my adaptability. At the moment I was neither disposed nor ready to argue with or question nature's ultimatum of adapt or die! I kept my job at the cinema. The five shillings I could now keep all for myself. My colliery wages of fourteen shillings a week I gave to my mother.

The cinema had modernised and equipped for the showing of talking pictures. The all-talking, all-singing, all-dancing films had arrived. Broadway had become available to the valley and its inhabitants. Until then this event, the silent film was our only avenue to a world outside our village, it was a silent world. The coming of sound with its brash accents, the glamour of Broadway, the new musical sounds was such a revelation that we young ones sent our fledgling aspirations soaring. Our awareness of a life different to what was accepted by us as normal had become visible and articulated even if it was out of reach.

A subtle change was in the offing; dress and attitude would be influenced. The button-through shirt with collar attached became a novelty that we desired. The Fedora signalled the demise of the bowler. Patent leather shoes the end of naily boots.

The slick American slang and witticisms were quickly adopted O.K. Chewing gum and popcorn replaced mintos and tiger nuts. The talking pictures came as a cultural shock to the chapel-going elders of this isolated valley. To us it was wizardry. Beautiful long-legged girls, scantily dressed, high kicking to the sound of jazz.

Shadows maybe, and inaccessible, they were nevertheless included on our wish list, and fantasised over during conversations of what we would do, if only we had the chance.

The stars of silence with exaggerated gestures were eclipsed by the bright, articulate and sophisticated. My heroes, Buck Jones, Tom Mix and Pearl White were killed by the electronic sound of their voices. It did not match their silent personas.

The new pin ups, the talking handsome lovers, the leggy girls, the suave Romeo's, would be the topic of the day and subject of much chit chat, speculation and hilarity by the "Young Turks" as they sweated at the coal face.

I enjoyed my stint as "assistant projectionist". My love of the cinema has never waned and will always be a place for me where its fantasy is an elixir of magical potency that alleviates and wishes away the pain of life's relentless struggle.

My mother was concerned about me and the two jobs I was doing. The lack of leisure time of an evening was also a concern of mine.

My friends were free to cavort around, to talk to and wink at the girls. To boast and tell lies about their phantom amours and easy conquests. I wanted to join in with more lies.

I was fifteen years old when I left my cinematic occupation. I became once again a fully participating member of my old small clique, which was a member of a bigger clique. Thirteen in all and with the exception of "one" all young colliers working down the Brittanic pit.

The financial position at home was still in a perilous condition. My mother had emerged from her semi vegative state and was beginning to assume and take an interest in her motherly responsibilities. My father was not of this world; he was in his tormented mind an absentee. There was however, occasions when he would "clock in" and write a poem. The odd guinea's payment by a publisher was welcomed by my mother as an addition to her limited budget.

His aggression towards my mother showed no signs of abatement. His meaningless outbursts were of such frequency that her defence was to completely ignore them and to mentally "exclude" him. He did not exist when ranting.

The children also took very little notice of these verbal fireworks. They were never accompanied by physical violence of any kind or threat of any description. The noise was of little consequence and nothing to fear.

It was his habit after one of his aggressive turns to retire to his room and spend the rest of his time pouring over the chessboard, solving problems set by various publications and periodicals.

He was a great chess player and it was the one passion that remained with him right through out his life.

He taught all his children to play chess, though for my part I cannot recall ever being taught.

He always had his chessmen at the ready. We would watch the moves. He would explain in great detail the intricacies of the game. He would watch us and give encouragement as we played amongst ourselves. He would play the game with us, it somehow seemed natural. I learned the game of chess like my brothers and sisters without consciously realising it. The game of chess was later on in life to be of great value.

In the library section of the Workman's Hall, a small room was set aside for study and quiet game of chess and draughts. There was also a small Chess Club which the librarian encouraged me to join.

I was a fairly good player and could hold my own. It was however with some trepidation that I became a member. My best friends were somewhat annoyed by my going it alone. They could not play chess at the moment. With lots of persuasion and arguments I finally got them to agree to sit in with me and watch the game being played, and if they liked what they saw they might like to learn the game and join in.

At the end of only one session they were indeed so inclined by what they had seen, within a matter of a few months they were challenging the experts, and like myself they became so enamoured of the game, that one day a week was henceforth prescribed as our chess day.

In the evening after work we would retire to the chess room at the library and indulge in chess rivalry and meditation.

Leisure facilities in the valley for young people were to all intents and purposes non-existent. The contours of the land precluded any attempts at serious ball games. Indoor facilities were also limited to either the Church Hall the Chapel Vestry or the Salvation Army Citadel,

The workman hall did however offer a billiards room and facilities for small functions. The Saturday night "hop" was a well-attended affair.

The valley's lack of physical aspects for leisure was of a minor inconvenience to friends and myself; we created entertainment of our own and of a unique kind. My particular clique of twelve young colliers formed a select club. With the help of the Librarian we obtained permission and for free the use of a small room in the Workman's Hall, where every Sunday for one hour we would hold meetings to discuss our business. At our first meeting Mr. Morgan, the Librarian sat in with us, guiding and advising us on the methodology of organising and conducting ourselves.

We appointed a chairman, a secretary and treasurer. The Librarian (patient man) taught us how to set our agenda, as well as the elements of Parliamentary procedures, as the correct way of conducting our meeting. We strictly adhered to his teachings.

The main purpose of our little club was to keep us close together, prevent drift and to initiate and enter into any kind of activity that would enhance our fellowship.

It was also our intention of amassing enough funds for an annual outing. Toward this end a fixed amount of money was to be a weekly contribution from each member.

At our first meeting it was unanimously agreed we would be different, have fun and enjoy ourselves in being so. This difference was to earn us the title of the "young eccentrics". The difference was, we would draw attention to ourselves, and at the same time behave as if all was normal. The difference also had to be cost free. Simple, attainable and of fun.

It was decided that on Wednesdays, Fridays and Sundays, when out of the house, in the street or anywhere in the village whatever we were doing or wherever we were going, we would wear or do something to our apparel that was odd, out of the ordinary or plain stupid..

For example the wearing of one brown shoe and one black shoe, or shoes on the wrong feet or one trouser leg rolled up or a handkerchief tied around the head and jaw. The different mode of dress was to be changed every week at our Sunday meeting, when contributions to the club and fines for not obeying the dress code were levied.

Non-conformance of the rules were ascertained by our code of loyalty and trust which had stood the test of time and flourished over the years. If a member was challenged by another as to the reason for not conforming to the current dress code, he would be reported to the weekly meeting and the culprit fined a penalty for each challenge. The whole proceeding, were of joviality and devoid of animosity or acrimony; we were a very happy bunch of young colliers.

There were numerous requests from other teenagers to join our select band of "eccentrics", but and because the original "thirteen" were of a long-standing cohesive group we decided we remain exclusive and not risk dilution.

We came to enjoy and revel in the local notoriety that followed our activities. On one occasion when the mode of dress was a walking stick and a chaplinesque moustache on the upper lip (boot polish) we were congratulated on our behaviour and innocent activities by none other than our old enemy, the helmeted terror – Bobby Beynon.

My job at the colliery was now of a routine nature, which I accepted as the norm, all my friends were engaged likewise. Making comparisons of a different lifestyle were difficult to conceive. Our vision was limited; we were destitute of knowledge outside of our own experiences. There was however a moment in my mining career, when the realisation that survival in one whole piece was of a necessity if I was to find a better, safe and easier way of earning a living.

My butty was doing his job of cutting coal. I was about my work of filling the box, when without warning the roof collapsed with shale pouring down upon us. There was no escape, we were trapped, we were buried.

My butty was knocked forward and unconscious with his body facing the coal seam. I knew he was trapped; there was no answer when I shouted and called his name. I feared the worst; I did not know how deep he was buried. I was trapped in a kneeling position, with my back against the coalface with the fallen shale reaching up to my shoulders almost to my chin. I couldn't move, my chest was tight; breathing was difficult but not serious. The only parts of my body I could control were my eyelids and mouth. I was upright, on my knees, with my hands by my side. Both lamps were under the shale and I was in the dark, I was on my own, I was terrified. I was sixteen years old.

After the shock of the initial collapse of the roof and my "burial" my thoughts were "Am I going to be totally buried or because all was now quiet had the roof stabilised?" We were lucky the roof had settled and I was safe for the moment.

Within a few minutes of the fall, I heard voices calling and shouting our names. I promptly answered and said I was alright but could not move and my butty was not answering me and I wasn't sure of his fate.

The reply came back not to move under any circumstances. I obeyed, I could not move anyway.

It took a great effort and in spite of the ever present danger of a further roof collapse to clear the shale and reach us. Shouting and encouraging me as they made way.

It seemed an eternity before I saw the first glimmer of light of the rescue teams, at the sight of which my distress abated.

We were eventually pulled free; my butty was in a bad way but alive. I was comparatively unharmed except for bruises on shoulders, neck and arms, and cramp in my legs, and frightened. After being pulled clear my immediate concern was my ability to stand, walk, stamp my feet and wave my hands. It was a great relief to find all parts of me working perfectly. My butty was carried unconscious on a stretcher to the pit bottom with me walking behind escorted by two miners.

The news of the accident had been communicated to my parents and also the fact that I was unharmed. On reaching the surface I was taken to the first aid room, where my father, together with my butty's relatives were anxiously waiting. The look on his face on seeing me was of joy and relief. He took my arms scanned the bruises, held them, looked straight into my face, as if he was searching the future and said "You are a survivor, Son". He quickly turned away, sat down and waited.

I was given a thorough examination by the "Black Doctor" and received a clean bill of health, with the proviso not to return to work for at least one week. My butty had already been seen and was on his way to the Royal Infirmary at Cardiff.

On the walk home by my father's side, I was greeted by the people of the street and especially by Priscilla who greatly embarrassed me with showers of kisses and hugs.

My mother, brothers and sisters were on the doorstep when we arrived. It was obvious that many tears had been shed at the news that I was trapped underground. The term used by my mother as she took me in her arms and almost carried me inside.

That evening I was visited by my friends and perforce I had to revisit the circumstances of the accident and its effects on me. They well understood the conditions I had encountered, and teased me that it was rather me than them who was buried. A further excuse for the visit was they wanted to test their newfound skills as chess players. They knew my father was a great chess player who had yet to be beaten by the valley's experts.

They cajoled me into asking him if he would play a game with one of them, in order that they could test themselves as to their capabilities. My father would have to be unconscious to refuse a game of chess. He took up the challenge and we proceeded to his study where he produced his chessmen and intimated that he would play the five of us together. Five young chess heads are better then one he remarked. The game took exactly twenty minutes, he mated in nine moves. My friends concluded we must have been very good to have lasted that long.

I could see that my father was pleased with this unexpected intrusion into his solitude; he seemed more relaxed than was usual. My friends who hitherto had been in awe of my father were also pleased at having played the game of chess with him.

My week of forced convalescence ended with my return to the pit, and against my mother's wishes. My butty was still in hospital recovering from his injuries. It would be a good while before he would be able to resume his coal cutting occupation.

Six o'clock Monday morning I tendered my check at the lamp room, I was given my lamp and told to wait until a Bill Simms came along. He was to be my new butty.

Bill Simms, my new butty, came along. A personality completely different to my old butty. Thirty years old bubbling over with enthusiasm and the owner of a big smile, accompanied by a hearty laugh.

Bill did not have a care in the world; he shook my hand, ruffled my hair and asked me how I felt about going back down after the accident. I replied "O.K. no problem". He then said "I have read many of your Dad's poems and if you can work as good as he writes we will get along fine".

I was sixteen and eligible for night shift work, which was now the case. Bill Simms, another man and myself were part of a team of four men and two boys now doing shift work. One week of days and one week of nights turn about. Our job was driving a tunnel (or heading as the miners called it) and extending it into the coal seam and the rock above the seam. The cutting of coal was of secondary importance. The rock above the coal seam had to be drilled, and explosive charges placed and detonated. The resulting rock falls and debris cleared. The tunnel made high and wide enough for man and horse to travel, and room for a railway to be laid. The new tunnel roof being held by the erection of stout timber supports with safety paramount.

The men were paid as a team and not as individuals. The money being calculated on the length of the tunnel's advance, the type and quality of the timber supports erected and the yards of railway laid down.

The explosive part of the operation was always and only done on the night shift. "Safety was the name of the game." The night shifts were mainly composed of the tunnelers and essential maintenance men.

The big ugly slag tips scarring the countryside around mining areas are the visible results of the tunnellers' efforts.

My wages paid by the Company was now, sixteen shillings, the standard rate for my age. With my new job there was a big plus. The pay of the men by result and as measured by the colliery surveyor was by nature of the onerous and precise work involved, equal to the effort and responsibilities.

The "boys" – myself and my opposite shift member would receive a bonus (voluntary) from our buttees as extra to our statuary wages. This averaged ten shilling a week and when accrued, my weekly pay was the munificent sum of twenty-six shillings.

Bill Simms despite his happy go lucky attitude was a disciplinarian of unusual severity. If he saw any of his team doing slip shod work or disregarding potential danger in the performing of the task set his voice would be loud and clear in his reprimand. Safety was his watchword.

The miner when at work is one of the most aware of persons, he is permanently in a situation of danger, all his instincts of self-preservation are on the "Que Vive."

His hearing is acutely tuned for a sound out of the ordinary. He will stop whatever he is doing and call for silence and advise his co-workers in the vicinity they too will cease their actions immediately and without question. The sound he might be hearing could be the creaking of timber supports or the grinding of rocks the prelude to a rock fall. This interlude would last for two to five minutes before assurance was attained.

His sense of smell is of a keenness of unbelievable sensitivity, the smell of gas emanating from a ruptured gas pocket in the coal seam, whilst rare, is of sufficient danger to vacate the place "pronto" until a fireman is called who will have various methods at his disposal for the dispersal of gas.

His eyesight quickly adapts to the perpetual gloom that surrounds him. He sees what he is doing with surprising accuracy and precision, his work of coal cutting.

His whole being is alive with all nerves on edge, and every instinct at colour red.

His survival and welfare is dependent upon these animal instincts and similar responses from his work mates.

The daily submission to these high nervous tensions subconsciously spill over into his non working and leisure hours, as well as into his thinking process.

A miner's actions and reactions will appear to be at odds at times to persons in other occupations where instincts have been tamed and domesticated.

I worked with the tunnelling team with Bill Simms as my butty for the next eighteen months. The work was hard and dangerous; it nevertheless was much better than coal cutting or coal boxing for the simple reason that I worked the full eight hours in the standing position and could walk about my job without bending, crouching or on bended knees. I was now six feet tall.

My butty was also a great pleasure to work with. He never imposed or set me a task that was difficult to accomplish or exposed me to anything that had a hint of some danger.

Bill made my final years as a miner a time of good memories of comradeship, coolness in times of danger and of his contagious optimism.

I am proud to have been a miner, and to have had the privilege of knowing Bill Simms and of being his butty.

The erection of the National Grid was complete. Thus enabling mills and factories to dispense with coal fired steam driven machinery and replace with the electric motor.

The Royal Navy had converted to oil and the Merchant Navy was now doing likewise.

The foreign markets were in turmoil. The signs that the predominance of coal was on the decline were visible and more so at the source of production

Pits were closing down seams, some mines being closed altogether, a great number of miners were only working part time, on three days a week.

My particular pit closed down two seams, and went on an intermittent regime of short time working.

Three of my best friends were sacked, now unemployed with a future undetermined.

Our exclusive club was no longer viable and sadly wound up. The funds withdrawn from the post office and distributed equally amongst the twelve. The total accrued was eighty pounds (six pounds a piece). The remaining eight pounds was unanimously agreed to be given in the form of a present to our dear friend and guide, the Librarian. The present was a fine quality "Plum" pipe and a tin of Franklyne Shagg. He was surprised we had considered him. He was very moved and delighted with our gesture. He was sorry – we were sorry – that our eccentric behaviour had ended.

Brinley joined the army and because of his trumpet playing abilities was sent to the Army School of Music.

Bobbie joined the Navy and was sent to Portsmouth. Dai and his family moved to another valley.

Billy, myself and four others were the only ones left of a friendship that had endured from infants to the "eccentrics".

The Wall Street Crash was having an affect on the dithering efforts of the government in their attempts of maintaining the orthodox economic policy of the Banks and the City, with the support of the economic dinosaurs and their masters resident at the Treasury.

This floundering in phoney economic theories whilst being advantageous to the City's bowler hat and pinstripe brigade was a punishment meted out to the growing army of unemployed, with another stroke of the lash in the form of cuts in dole money, and with Ramsay MacDonald's ideological conversion rubbing salt into the wounds.

People were being crushed without knowing why. Poverty and repossessions, the flavour of the decade.

One of the main beneficiaries of this misery and despair, were the court bailiffs. They worked overtime, especially in the mining valleys.

Restraining orders were everywhere, with eviction printed large thereon. My family were one of these unfortunate victims.

CHAPTER THREE

The Eviction

We were unceremoniously evicted on a Friday morning at nine o'clock. The children at school, me at work, my father in bed, my mother in hysterics. I came home from the pit at two thirty in the afternoon as usual, but this time I was met in the street outside the house by all my siblings jabbering away.

My mother was sitting on a chair in the backyard of the house, suckling her baby, a girl of two months. The last of the brood, "her nest" was empty.

I was all black and grimy and in my working clothes. She handed me a clean set of clothes. The bailiffs had allowed her to gather all the clothes she needed for herself and family.

With my bundle of clothes I went to a neighbours house, the occupants of which had prepared a bath of hot water for me to use and thereafter make myself presentable.

The coal miner in my day had to make do with a tin tub set down in front of the kitchen's open fire. While the ablutions were in progress all female members of the household would be banished.

It was a beautiful summer day in the middle of July. The eviction was the final blow to my mother's pride. In the backyard of the locked house, with all her children around her, a transformation took place. The safety and welfare of her family had become her first, last and only consideration.

She took charge, and in so doing she revealed an inner strength which hitherto she had either kept under wraps or was unaware of her possession of such an attribute. She devised a plan of action which would be put into operation on the return of my father from his mission of a 'cry for help.'

After the initial shock of the eviction, my father had gathered himself together sufficiently enough to weigh up his situation and that of his family and journey to another valley to appeal for help from some of his influential friends.

Meanwhile, my mother outlined her plan. Myself, my fifteen year old brother Glyn, and Tim our dog were to go to the home of my father's brother with a note explaining the reason of our visit and asking permission to stay a few days or until such time as she was reorganised. She would send a postcard to this effect.

Ethel and my three other sisters Olwen, age thirteen, Peggy, age eleven and Betsi, age eight, were to go to an address in Aberfan of one of my mother's sisters. They would also have an identical note of introduction.

My mother, father, young brother Arfon age four and baby Jean of two months would go wherever my father had succeeded in obtaining accommodation.

She emphasised come what may, she would have us all back with her within one week. The money for this exodus was forthcoming from my twenty-six bob pay, which I had received that afternoon.

The street was agog with the news that the "bums" had thrown out Huw Menai and his family. Sympathy and compassion was aplenty and sincerely meant.

Priscilla came on the scene took me aside and enquired to where I was going and would I be coming back. I told her I had my doubts about ever coming back to the valley. She burst into a flood of tears and cried most bitterly. I was very saddened and distressed by the thought that I had hurt our wonderful Priscilla.

Ethel and my mother eventually succeeded in pacifying her by saying I would write to her with the new address wherever it would be. This seemed to satisfy her.

She gathered my face into both hands, smothered me with kisses and with more tears welling up into her eyes, she ran out into the street. That was the last I ever saw of our wonderful Priscilla.

During our "eccentric" period, Priscilla was the thirteenth unofficial member of our exclusive club.

Priscilla for want of a more appropriate and kinder description, was akin to a camp follower. She was never far away. She was always our shadow. Our male company was her choice, in preference to the company of her own sex.

My best friends and one or two other club members will forever be indebted to our Priscilla. She was tall, jet black hair with the swarthy complexion and haughty manner of an Andulasian Senorita.

She was beautiful, and under different circumstances and congenial surroundings she would be a sight to race the hormones of any full-blooded male as she did us.

By the jealous and envious, she was whispered as of loose morals, and that she would drop her knickers for fourpence (old money).

This was nothing but malicious gossip; out of earshot, we would affectionately call her "our fanny fourpence", even though we knew the pecuniary presumption was not true.

We knew it as a stupid lie, however, suffice it is for me to say I was on her freebie list, being her most favoured suitor, as were one or two others of her favourites.

She was very selective, if she liked you she would honour you by bestowing her favours, which were gratefully accepted.

We were young teenagers, strong, healthy, and sexually aware, but with serious gaps in our knowledge. We knew the "what" but were woefully ignorant in the essential procedures and aspects of approach. We were not conversant with the timing of the "when" or the mechanics of the "how."

Priscilla to her everlasting credit rectified these gaps in our understanding of the female, during the mating embrace. She taught us the necessary techniques during our initiation, as well as the gentleness and tenderness required for the satisfactory consummation of that most intimate and fulfilling of human passion and relationship.

Our Priscilla had nothing to be ashamed of. She was of a polyandrous tendency and her liaisons with the "eccentric" friends of her choosing could be equated to the inherent polygamous tendency in the boys of her choice.

She was not in the least amoral as was supposed by those who tittle-tattled in the background. The boys may have bragged, boasted among themselves as to what they thought as conquests.

Deep down and to a "man", she was held in great affection and esteem by her twelve "eccentric" friends.

Introspectively, without our Priscilla, a few of us would have been sexually incompetent and fumbling idiots in our encounters and pairings later in life.

I thank you Priscilla, also the thanks of my lovely wife, when I confided in her of our experiences and juxto-positions in the long grass of Joby Henderson's meadow.

Her legs may have been askew, but her heart and beautiful smile was in the right place. She will always be remembered by those of us who were fortunate enough to have received the privilege of knowing her and of being willing subjects and recipients of her tutoring.

Promiscuity in the young is a perfectly natural phenomenon and should be left alone in its secret world where it rightly belongs.

A host of those who criticise the youth of the times, have indulged themselves at sometime or another, and are in no position to fault. The rest are simply jealous of lost opportunities.

This does not deny that precautions must nevertheless be taught and practised. Priscilla's lesson no. 1 was always be prepared, excuses were out of order, she was adamant. The availability of "French letters" or condoms as they are now currently called was always a problem, but somehow or other we managed.

My father returned from his quest for help from his influential friends with the welcome news, that a house would be available in another valley some fifteen miles distance away. But at the moment could only accommodate my mother, himself and the two youngest children. It would be another three to four days for full accommodation for the whole family to be arranged.

With this "good news" my mother's plan was put into action. Ethel's party was seen off, followed by my mother, father and the two youngest, with Glyn, the dog and myself the last to go.

The house where all eight children were born was closed, locked and barred.

The law was paramount, people are of no matter.

Uncle Jack and his wife welcomed us with open arms. They were distraught at the plight of my mother and her family.

I explained the position in regards to the new accommodation we were to occupy, and did not see any reason why our stay should be more than two or three days.

On the morning of our first night, Uncle Jack before setting off for work, (he was a colliery overman), let Tim our dog out of the house for his morning exercise.

After a while, he became concerned there was no sign of Tim returning, or sight of him in the vicinity. Uncle came to our bedroom and told us that he could not wait any longer for Tim; he must hurry on his way to the pit.

Tim did not return that day or the next. I was worried and gave him up as lost.

Tim was the most"beautiful" of ugly dogs imaginable. A mongrel completely non-descript. Chocolate coloured with one leg all white. His long curly tail half white and half chocolate. He was the most faithful of friends, docile, bright and intelligent. He was eight years old.

My family would have difficulty in forgiving of the loss of Tim.

The third morning of our stay at Uncle Jack's house, a postcard arrived from my mother, asking Glyn and me to return to the house from where we had been thrown out. To somehow break in and retrieve some papers of my fathers and a few special items of hers which she listed and to return to where she was now living.

Glyn and I planned our break in to coincide with the long twilight of the summer evening.

We arrived at the rear of the house unnoticed, with the exception of a very excited mongrel dog, jumping and wagging his long curly tail! Tim had found his way home from where he commenced his morning stroll at my uncle's house a distance of 15 miles by road. Over a mountain down a valley up and over a second mountain, a distance of about eight miles. I presume this was his chosen route. He was used to walking the mountains, with us lads during holidays and weekends.

We succeeded in prising open a small window at the back of the premises, retrieving the articles and papers specified by my mother. We also collected a few other items, piled them in suitcases, then crawled through the window, sneaked up the garden and on to the mountain; Tim following.

My mother's new accommodation was in a valley three miles distance over mountain paths, or fourteen miles by road.

Like Tim, we chose the mountain, wanted to be invisible and we knew the terrain.

We arrived at the new home sometime after midnight, tired and exhausted after humping two heavy suitcases over difficult country in the dark.

My mother gave Tim a bowl of water; he lapped it dry, slid down by the side of my mother's chair, and went to where dogs go when tired and asleep.

My father was in his usual non-communicative mode. He enquired if we managed to get the papers and the things my mother had requested. End of conversation. I could have lost my temper at this junction. I was fed up to the back teeth with his apparent unconcerned lack of responsibility. I bit my tongue and held myself.

With the exception of a bed and two chairs which had been given by my father's friends, the house was empty of furniture. Glyn and I for the rest of the night lay on the floor with Tim, we were all "dog-tired" and slept well.

I awoke in the morning with my mother handing me the Welsh national daily, the Western Mail, with the front page headline "Huw Menai and family evicted", with the ensuing story of the plight and dispersal of the family.

It was obvious to me that my father was behind the piece of news reporting which proved to be of immense value.

Furniture, beds, bedding, pots and pans and all the pieces that make a home were arriving donated and paid for by friends and admirers of his poems and other writings. The art and literary establishment had rallied around him.

Some of the furniture was new, and some secondhand. My mother was pleased and very thankful. Her family was together again.

A sum of money had been raised by a well-meaning group of Quakers many of whom were admirers of his works and poems.

This money made my mother independent for the time being, also a change in her attitude towards my father.

Her long-standing tolerance had been abused. She was becoming more assertive. She was no longer accepting that blaming her for all the ills and woes that had befallen him was a panacea for his failure to face reality. She had been deaf too long to his rantings and outbursts. Not anymore, enough was enough. Responsibility must be shared.

She was physically ejected from her old home, so be it. She was now mentally ejecting the past. A new valley, a new house, new trappings, a new beginning and a new goal. She was forty-one years old, my father of the same age. She was going to find it difficult to make him conform to her desire of making a new life.

His ability of blocking his mind from receipt of incoming unpleasantries was a major obstacle behind which he took refuge, in his pursuance of the mental luxury of living in the never-never land of imaginations and dreams.

His propensity of ignoring the immediate surroundings was breathtaking.

He was a wanderer in the universe of his fevered imaginations, where the centre is everywhere and the circumference nowhere. He was adrift from the real world most of the time.

I was young, impatient and on the side of my mother. I wanted what she wanted and she deserved to have it. My father, to my arrogant and pragmatic way of thinking at the time was a dead weight and would hold us all down, as was the case in the recent past.

In my mind he was partly responsible for the misfortune that had befallen us.

Four weeks after settling down in the new house and after the eviction, I could see my mother was reasonably happy with her new possessions and home. She was smiling and fully occupied arranging the new furniture, as well as organising the disposal of the surplus bits and bobs that was still arriving to a local charity. She was content and could at the moment pay her way. The literati had been exceptionally generous in her hour of need.

I was unemployed in a new valley and friendless, the making of new friends was a problem that was to be of a bother all my life.

I lacked the experience and know-how of making friends, as opposed to passing acquaintances - that was easy. My friends came with me the day I was born; they were with me at infant's school, at primary school, at play, at work and always the same. I enjoyed the companionship, the shared experiences, with the same group from day one, until the day I left the valley.

There was never a cause or need to make new friends. My friends came with the territory. We did not make friends we "were" born friends, we belonged to each other.

My little school was a shared home of learning, my terraced street was one big house, the doors of which were never closed. Where children were free to come and go and be mothered by all.

We were a belonging society where every mother's son and daughter was communal property.

I ventured out of this new valley where I now lived with the intention of visiting the local cinema, a mile distant up the valley. I eventually arrived to find a queue had formed at the entrance. I joined the queue and stood next to a pretty girl about my own age.

She struck up a conversation which I found very pleasing. We continued chatting, moving all the while towards the pay desk. Whereupon I timorously asked if I could sit with her inside the cinema, she agreed.

At the end of the film and on the way out, I volunteered to escort her home, which was a further half-mile up the valley. On the way, I said I would like to meet her again; without hesitation she acquiesced.

A day and time was arranged, I emphasised that because I had a long way to walk to the appointment. I would like to think that she would definitely keep to the arrangement. I would for sure be there and waiting.

That is precisely what I did, I waited and waited. I would not concede, one hour passed. She had let me down, my trust was misplaced, her promise was worthless.

This was a new experience. I was helpless, away from my old and trusted friends. I was learning the hard way, the pitfalls of trying to make new ones. I was seventeen years of age, naïve and trustful. I was left standing.

A feeling of inadequacy dented my pride. The sense of disappointment and mistrust was devastating. I was a novice in my understanding of human behaviour. I would not want this feeling of rejection and humiliation to befall anyone. I would always remember this incident.

On my solitary journey back home, I made a little vow; if ever I made a promise of whatever kind, I would do all that was in my power to keep it.

Hereafter, I rarely made a promise and then only if I was absolutely certain that the conditions were in my favour to keep it.

The insignificant incident with a girl I did not know, made me realise for the first time since leaving my old valley, that I was friendless, homeless and rootless.

I was unhappy, lonely and"very sorry for myself". The pain of adolescence is immune to treatment; its empirical advance to adulthood is remorseless and littered with heartaches and disappointments.

At home I was a misery, my old closed world, safe and secure was now a fairy tale of unbelievable innocence. Priscilla and the eccentrics had become tales of "once upon a time."

I was becoming the owner of memories. I must adjust to the loss of the past by looking to the future. My dissatisfaction with life at the moment was spilling over and affecting my relations with the family, snapping and unnecessary quarrels with my sisters, sullen with my mother and angry towards to my father.

The eviction and removal, its consequent domestic upheaval, the breaking of habits and routines had taken its effect. The loss of the only life I knew, coupled with the ignorance and arrogance of youth fanned the embers of rebellion. I was ready to break away.

I needed a cause and a reason. Both came sooner than I had hoped or expected.

My father had one of his meaningless outbursts of shouting at my mother. I lost my temper and told him to stop talking nonsense and to leave my mother alone, (typical youthful arrogance). This was the first time I had stood up in defence of my mother.

He ceased ranting and began to rave. I thought he was going to attack me as did my mother and sisters; they gathered around me as some sort of protection.

A split second of hormonal induced adrenaline released the dormant animal that is forever lurking beneath the surface of all men. In that same second, I had become a threat, an enemy adult invading his territory. His dominance was in jeopardy, his authority challenged.

"Get out of my house and out of my sight!" he shouted, and promptly vanished into his hide out.

"Get out!" is a howl of possession. I ceased to belong. I was given notice to quit. He had severed the family bond.

Within a minute of the ultimatum and in the quiet of his room, my mother and I knew that his remorse would be relentless, his torment pity-less.

There was not a thing I was going to do to ease his problem. I was the cause, he was the reason; I had to quit as soon as possible.

During my weeks of unemployment, I was ineligible for dole money. I was not yet eighteen. I could however have applied for work in one of the local pits. I knew on good authority that experienced boys were required in these local mines.

My four-week break from the coalface had brought about a once and for all decision. I was never going down a coal mine again. I was up here on the surface and in the sun, and that is how it was going to be forever.

My father had given me an escape route away from the straight jacket of parental control, and the responsibilities that I felt were being put upon me and also the possibilities of a road pointing in directions away from the coal field to places that existed only in my imagination and unknown.

The morning consequent to the spat with my father, sitting on my bed whilst dressing, I there and then without any thought whatsoever, impulsively decided to run away to London. That seemed to be the place everybody ran to. The six pounds share out from the "eccentric" fund I had squirreled away without the knowledge of my family I would use to pay my fare to the big city.

What I was going to do when I arrived there never even entered my befuddled brain. Running away to London was the only thought in my mind, irresponsible, clueless and hopeless.

I finished dressing, waited until the youngsters had left for school, went downstairs, and ate a small breakfast. I then left the house telling my mother I was going to the labour exchange to see if any jobs were available.

I went without a word or a goodbye; my mind was completely blank. My impulse decision was in control and senseless, with directions to London. I was on my way without as much as a toothbrush. I did however have six pounds.

From this moment on anything I did or anything that happened to me would be of a first time experience.

I had not been out of the valleys in my seventeen and a half years of existence.

I arrived at a bus stop, boarded a vehicle bound for Cardiff and from which I alighted outside the G.W.R. Railway Station. I found a ticket window and asked for a ticket to London. "You mean Paddington?" said the man, "No" said I, "I want to go to London." "Same place" he retorted, "Nineteen and fourpence"

Slightly puzzled, I tendered the fare; my next problem was finding the train. After much enquiring, questioning and deciphering of directional signs, I finally arrived at a platform from where I was assured my train would start.

Until this moment, the only train I had ever seen was two carriages and a guard van, pulled by a small tank locomotive and from which "boars and black doctors" descended.

The great beast rattled in, snorting steam, smoke and fire and pulling behind it what appeared to be miles of carriages. The thing stopped, I enquired of the man in uniform, was it going to London? "Yes!" he said, "Newport,

Swindon, Paddington".

By now I was beginning to realise, to the railway people, London and Paddington were synonymous. I boarded the train and was astounded to find myself in a corridor which traversed the length of the train. Most amazing! I averred to myself.

I settled for a carriage with five other persons. I sat next to a lady who asked me if I would like to sit next to the window; I said I would and we changed places. The train puffed its way out of the station, moving slowly, then gaining speed. I was on my way to London.

I looked around the carriage, surreptitiously glancing at the faces of my fellow travellers. They were all dressed up in their Sunday best and seemed to be engrossed in reading a magazine or newspaper. I removed my glance, turning my gaze towards the window, where I saw my image against the moving background.

The contrast to what I was seeing as myself in comparison to the sophisticated travellers opposite was disturbing and a jolt to my initial burst of bravado.

The excitement of my impulse, together with its anticipation suddenly receded into the distance. The light of common sense was penetrating my cerebral cavity and putting into motion the process of reassembling its befuddled and chaotic contents. Here was I, an immature pit boy, literate and numerate, but ignorant; intelligent but uneducated, on my way to a big city of which I had no conception or understanding and populated by those superior human beings sitting opposite. I wanted to run back home to my mam.

The train had only just cleared Cardiff Central Station.

Adolescent pride is unforgiving. I continued my journey to Paddington; the impulse of the morning had become the apprehension of the moment. Arriving at Paddington, and getting off the train, my first impression was of people in a hurry. Everybody seemed to be cantering, jogging and even running. My normal walk was a hindrance in the way of their objective. I was pushed, shoved with lots of "excuse mes" being bandied about. I followed a few of the passengers out of the station on to Praed Street where I stopped and took stock of my position.

I did not know which way to turn or what to do at that precise moment. It was four o'clock of the afternoon. I was hungry and thirsty, a small breakfast was my last meal. Opposite to where I was standing was a small café with a counter and stools to sit on.

I asked for a glass of lemonade and a doughnut. The man serving had a strong cockney accent. It sounded very strange to my sensibilities, which up to that moment was only tuned to the Welsh lilt. I realised I was in a foreign land with strange people.

Refreshed by my small repast, I returned to the street, looked around, felt in my pocket for the return half of the train ticket. Scanned it and pondered awhile, and placed it back in my pocket, at the same time telling myself that I wanted to get away from the valleys and pits. So get on with it!

I searched for a post office. I wanted to send a postcard to my mother telling her where I was and was all right and would write a letter later. The writing of this postcard made me aware of the selfishness and the enormity of my impulsive action of running away and breaking ranks with my family.

My mother would be greatly troubled with my sudden and unexplained absence, as well as being of concern to my siblings. I took comfort in the knowledge that they would receive the card on the morrow, thus alleviating to some degree their ignorance of my whereabouts and wellbeing.

The posting of this card was also a reminder to me that I was completely on my own; there was no fall back position. My physical needs came to the fore and were compelling. I needed the use of a toilet, I was hungry and thirsty. I also needed a bed for the night.

I went back to Paddington Station where I guessed there would be toilet facilities, and perhaps a policeman who would direct me to a place for a nights sleep. I found both. The policeman gave me a quizzical look when inquiring of the possibility of him helping me find a nights lodging. I told him I was a complete stranger in London, having arrived from Wales a few hours ago.

He took a piece of paper out of his pocket wrote an address on it, and said as he handed it to me, "Its not a very "clever" place, but its alright for one night; and its not too far away". He also gave me directions to its location. I eventually found the address, a charity-lodging house at the back of the station.

I enquired of a nights lodging. I could have a bed for one shilling and sixpence a night, from nine pm until seven am at which time it must be vacated.

The time stipulated seemed very odd but having no alternative I accepted. A night's accommodation secured, I felt more composed and with my anxieties also diminishing I would explore this part of the city of London where I now was and where I was going to be a temporary resident.

The contrasts of where I was that morning and where I was right now, was of another planet. Wide streets, endless flow of cars and buses, people in a great hurry, the men smartly, but quaintly dressed in a uniform of striped trousers with a bowler hat on their head, a rolled-up umbrella attached to one hand and a little suitcase attached to the other, all in great haste to get somewhere. Strange? I wondered if they worked for a living.

I walked down Edgware Road to Marble Arch, taking in and marvelling at everything I was witnessing. At the junction of Edgware Road and Oxford Street, I could see a lot of building work in progress. A cinema was under construction, as well as work on an underground station.

Where there is building in progress, thought I, there must be pick and shovel work that being the only "skill" I had. I decided that on the morrow, I would make enquiries on the site in the hope of employment. Encouraged by this hope, I wandered into Hyde Park and enjoyed the spectacle of the Speakers Corner.

Public meetings were not new to me; there were plenty of public meetings always in progress in the valleys, but never so many in competition and with so many hecklers in one place at one time.

I was thirsty and hungry, I crossed the road to the "Corner House Café" nervously entered, looking for and finding a vacant table. I sat down and was immediately attended by a young waitress (nippy) requesting an order. I was flummoxed and did not know what to order, how to order or the price of the order. To my great relief she noticed my dilemma and kindly suggested that I have beans on toast and a cup of tea. I promptly agreed and asked if I could also have a glass of lemonade. She gave me a beautiful smile and nodded her head. She quickly returned with my order including the lemonade and at the same time she made up the bill. Two shillings and three pence. That was the first time I had eaten beans on toast being served by a waitress and presented with a bill. My big city education had started.

It was dusk when I arrived back at the lodging house and presented myself at the desk, tendered my one shilling and sixpence, given a blanket and a slip of paper with instructions and the number four printed thereon.

I entered the dormitory; it was an awful smelly, dirty, shambles. Men lounging and laying on ramshackle beds, men in rags, men drunk, men with long beards, men shouting and cursing.

I found bed number four, sat down, judged my situation and concluded one night only would be the extent of my tenancy in this mess of a place, come what may!

I was very tired, took off my shoes, placed them under my pillow. I wasn't taking any chances, pulled the blanket over my head, in an attempt to shut out the noise.

My sleep was very cursory and intermittent, I would be glad to see the dawn. I arose from the bed as soon as the first glimmer of daylight appeared. I put on my shoes, went to the toilet, a place of indescribable filth, washed my face and hands, drying them in my handkerchief and hot footed it out of the place into the "fresh air" of the City. It was six o'clock in the morning.

I made my way towards the building site at the corner of Marble Arch. On my journey I was surprised to see so much activity so early.

On arrival at the site, I looked around for anybody or somebody who could help me. I was approached by the night watchman who enquired of my business. I explained that I was looking for work. He took me by the arm and guided me to the site foreman's office and suggested that I should return at nine o'clock and have a word with the foreman. I thanked him and left.

In my home valley a personal timepiece was a luxury more than a necessity.

The colliery hooter was loud and clear and marked the divisions of time for all essential purposes. It hooted for the start and finish of work, for all three shifts, also at twelve noon and midnight.

We did not look for or see the time; we heard it and we listened. The clock in the home was more ornamental than utilitarian. Here in London I must look for the time. I realised that a personal timepiece was an essential part of city-dwellers equipment. "Clock watching" was as vital to his wellbeing as any other function that made him "tick". I must get me a watch at the first opportunity.

To occupy the long wait before my appointment at the site office, I decided to walk and window-shop along Oxford Street. I was fascinated by the displays and variety of goods on view and for sale, and at the purchase price demanded. Four pounds, five shillings was my total wealth; it would not buy the necktie I was admiring.

I ceased window-shopping; I was envious of the person who could purchase that necktie without having to compare with the price of beans on toast. My walk continued down Regent Street on to Piccadilly Circus, where pin stripe and umbrellas were popping up from the ground in battalions, in great hurry either to get somewhere or away from something.

This continuous movement of so many human beings intent on some mission or another, was of a perplexity that rooted me to the spot.

This uncoordinated helter-skelter of people, dressed alike and vacant of expression must be the same people I had been taught in school who were responsible for governing the greatest empire the world has known. The welfare of its subjects be he a rickshaw 'coolie' in Hong Kong or a pit boy in South Wales was of their concern.

My teacher had told me London was the heart of the Empire. What she did not tell me was the heart was very sick.

At the moment I was marvelling at the brilliance and cleverness of these powerful governers, a band was playing a Sousa tune, and heading for Trafalgar Square with hundreds of bedraggled men marching in step with banners aloft declaring they were hungry.

I turned away, looked for the time and found it. I made my way back to the building site to the foreman's office.

The foreman enquired of my age and what skills I possessed. I told him. I was an unemployed young miner and capable and willing to do any labouring or manual work that was available, and that I had arrived in London yesterday.

He gave me a smile and said the contract was finishing in two weeks time but in the meanwhile I could have a job of tea boy to his workmen. The previous occupant of the job had absconded with the tea money and I looked honest enough to fill the vacancy if so desired.

I jumped at the chance even if it was only of a temporary nature. The work would entail making tea and delivering at any time for any one who requested it.

The men would each contribute one shilling and sixpence a week - for the purchase of tea, milk and sugar - I was to do the buying. Any monies left over at the end of the week, I could keep. It was also the custom of the men to tip the tea-boy.

The company would pay me twenty-five shillings a week. This arrangement was more than satisfactory, considering my wages as a miner was only sixteen shillings. I was to start tomorrow at eight o'clock in the morning.

Having clinched the job, I remembered that I had not found new sleeping accommodation.

I asked the foreman if he could recommend somewhere. He told me to wait while he went for somebody who could assist me.

He returned with a fellow in his twenties, who told me he was temporarily living at a Salvation Army Hostel, which was very good. He gave me the address and directions. The arrangements at the hostel were much better than I expected. I was put in a room with three other young men, two of whom were working. The hours and rules were not very restrictive; also provision could be made for accommodation up to fourteen days.

I struck up an acquaintance with one of the occupants, who was worldly wise, knew all the angles, ways and methods of survival on little money.

He took me to Petticoat Lane, where I purchased a towel, soap, toothbrush and toothpaste, for only a couple of shillings.

My tea dispensing duties continued uneventful and successful for the next fourteen days. My leisure time being occupied with visiting places and establishments I had read about. Museums, art galleries, famous buildings and especially Hyde Park's Speakers Corner, as well as looking for permanent lodgings.

My monetary situation was healthy. With my wages, tips and tea swindle money I had accumulated the sum of nine pounds and some coins. My fourteen days as tea boy, was good for my confidence as well as my pocket.

My job at the building site terminated on the Saturday. The next day (Sunday) I was informed by the hostel warden that I must move out Monday morning and look elsewhere for accommodation. This ultimatum was not a surprise; I had already located a few possible lodgings that were reasonable and affordable. I was also sure I could find another job with in a few days.

I was gaining in confidence and optimism and was capable of making my way in the big city.

Monday morning I awoke early to find myself alone in the room. The other three residents were up and away.

I washed and dressed and was preparing to vacate the premises, when I felt in my inside jacket pocket. It was empty; my nine pounds had been stolen.

It was a bitter blow. I sat on the bed angry and frustrated. Angry at my stupidity in trusting my roommates and in my lack of knowledge of the morals of slick city dwellers.

I realised that my life hitherto in the valley had been in the backwater of civilisation. Where open houses, reliance and trust of ones neighbours was the norm and taken for granted. I must 'wise up' and become aware of the city slickers up-to-date ideas of civilisation and take note of the differences.

My frustration was centred on the position now confronting me, stony broke, homeless, hungry and thirsty and what do I do now?

I bundled my few possessions in my towel, wrapped it up in newspaper and made my way out of the Salvation Army Hostel. On my way I mentioned to the Warden that I had money stolen and suggested my room companions. He commented that I should not have left it lying around.

My predicament was unenvious; I did not however feel any sense of desperation or self-pity. My thoughts went back to the valley and the Britannic Pit where I was buried up to the neck in coal and shale. The comparison had a salutary effect on my responses to the current situation now facing me. The few coins in my trouser pocket were sufficient for a cup of tea and a plate of beans on toast.

CHAPTER FOUR

The Army

I was young, healthy, "full of beans" and with a future untapped. Why worry, I am a survivor.

I began to walk in the direction that had become familiar to me, Oxford Street, Regent Street; on my way I decided I would like to see the Cenotaph.

I knew a great deal about the Great War, having read a considerable amount of literature on the subject. The book "All Quiet on the Western Front", by Eric Remarque made a lasting impression at the time on my young mind. Also I had many conversations with ex soldiers who had experienced the horrors of trench warfare.

The Cenotaph was a symbol I wanted to see, as well as being a target in my meandering. I cogitated a course of action I should take to resolve the difficult problem I was facing. As I made my way down Whitehall, "pin stripe and umbrellas" were cantering past in droves to finally disappear up steps through big doors. Part of the mystery was solved. I now knew where they went, but I still did not know from whence they came.

I arrived at the Cenotaph, was surprised by the beauty of its simplicity which emphasised its significance as a headstone on an empty tomb, waiting to be filled with the mangled bodies of a million young men who had been killed in a most horrific and unimaginable way.

I paused. I wondered. I walked on. My curiosity satisfied, I began to retrace my steps and return to nowhere in particular. At the same time admiring the imposing buildings on either side of the road.

On the top step of one of the buildings, was a tall man complete with waxed moustache, peaked cap, military uniform and a swagger cane.

At the bottom of the steps was a notice board with the legend that the building housed the army recruiting office.

The pressing problem of my uncertain future disappeared as if by magic.

I would join the Army. Bobby had joined the Navy, Brinley had joined the Army, why not me?

Bed and breakfast would be assured. Without further ado, thought or contemplation,

I mounted the steps, timidly approached the imposing figure in full regalia. He was ten feet tall, that was how he appeared to me at that moment.

He looked at me, scanning me up and down, measuring me, weighing me and judging me.

I was seventeen and a half years old, six foot one and half inches tall, weighing eleven stone four pounds.

I was naïve, and from the "hills". "Do you want to join the army?" He boomed, "Yes" was my timid reply. "Right" he said, "What regiment do you want to join!" "The Guards", said I. It was the only regiment I could think of at this most intimidating of moments.

"The Guards!", he boomed, only this time louder, which I was sure could be heard in Trafalgar Square.

"Come with me" he said as he ushered me through the big doors and down a corridor into an office. "Sit down!" he barked. I sat down. He also sat down behind a desk, shuffled some papers, glanced up at me as a fleeting smile crossed his face.

"How old are you?"; "Seventeen" I replied. His official veneer was dropping off, his attitude was showing signs of benevolence.

"Let us say you are eighteen" he said. I did not demur.

He then asked me where I was born and enquired a little of my background. He looked up from the forms he was filling, "Son" he said "I don't think you are tough enough for the Guards". He then gave me a synopsis of Guards training and discipline and ended with the definite statement that I was not Guards material and that I would be happier and more suitable as a soldier in the R.A.M.C.

I did not know what these initials stood for. I timidly asked him what kind of regiment it was and what did the initials represent.

His demeanour by now was completely at variance with his posture at the top of the recruiting office steps. With great patience he went into detail, informing me that the RAMC was not a regiment but a Corps and that the initials were Royal Army Medical Corps. He was quite sure that I would "fit in" and eventually enjoy my new career. Furthermore, the RAMC were very particular and choosy about whom they would accept. The preliminaries complete he told me I would have to wait an hour or two for the medical officer to examine me and if I passed I would then be inducted into the army. He then guided me into a canteen where there were a few young men sitting around. He asked if I would like a cup of tea. I answered "Yes, and could I have something to eat because I am hungry and broke".

"Certainly, son." he said "Don't you worry, I will arrange for you to have something to eat and drink." He then left saying "See you in a couple of hours".

Food and drink duly arrived, a cup of tea and beans on toast; both items were very welcome.

I was beginning to be very pleased with myself. The fact that I did not have to think about looking for work, or new lodgings was a relief. I could now relax and think of my family.

I must at the first opportunity send a card to my mother informing her that she now had a soldier son. I knew she would be annoyed and upset at this news. I also knew that her annoyance would be tempered with the knowledge, that there would be a permanence of my whereabouts and wellbeing.

I was joined at the table by a young man of fine physique and stature. He asked if I was joining the army. I replied in the positive, whereupon he volunteered the information that he had been accepted as a potential Guardsman and like myself was waiting for the medical examination.

He was a Yorkshire man, a miner from the age of fourteen until he was thrown out of work at twenty-four. His migration to London was in the hope of improving his chances in life. After three months of this fruitless search, he decided the army was his last chance.

We were both unskilled and had a common background. Our conversation was interesting and time consuming. I was nevertheless envious that he was to be a Guardsman. I was to be just an ordinary soldier. Little did I know then, I was the fortunate one.

My acceptance of the recruiting officer's decision to enrol me into the R.A.M.C. was to have a far-reaching effect on my life and future wellbeing.

My conversation with the Yorkshire man was abruptly ended by the entry into the canteen of an official looking character with a list in his hand.

He commenced calling names with instructions to stand up on being called. They were then "ordered" to follow him out of the room.

With the exit of these names the canteen contained only three people, myself, my table companion and a third person who came over and introduced himself, as a possible cavalryman. He was also waiting the attention of the medical officer.

He was twenty years old, and from the East End of London. He had been employed as a stable boy and groom to horses owned, on hire or loaned to the riders of Hyde Park's Rotten Row.

He enjoyed working with horses, but the hours were long, the pay poor and prospects nil. He had been sacked for protesting at the long overtime hours worked without extra pay. He liked the idea of wearing a cavalryman's uniform and having his own horse and being out in the open. He was a cheery and likeable person; I secretly hoped he would pass the medical test.

There we were, three youths anxious to forsake the freedom of civilian life for the disciplined uncertainty of a military life, where place of residence could be anywhere that was coloured red on the world map.

We were three disparate unemployed characters, taking refuge in the military machine, to escape the vissitudes of civilian life with the possibility that we might be ordered to die or "shed blood" for King and Country, in defending the Empire from its rightful owners.

The possibilities of such an eventuality was absent from our thoughts, reasoning, and our desire to be soldiers.

The Yorkshireman and I wanted security and bed and breakfast. The cockney wanted a horse. The medical officer arrived at noon and we were called in alphabetical order to the examination room. I was the last to be called (everything in the army seems to be done in alphabetical order).

I was told to undress "all off" by the recruiting Sergeant, who was the only person in the room – besides the M.O.

This was the first time I had been naked in front of people since my boyhood swimming days. I was not embarrassed or concerned. I was measured, weighed, pummelled, mouth open, tongue out, bend down, touch your toes, stand straight, hands out, eyes shut, touch your nose and finally out of nowhere the M.O. produced a torch, directed its light at my genitals, poked my testicles with a pencil at the same time asking me to cough. Then with the pencil in one hand, torch in the other, he began moving my penis from side to side, gazing intently at whatever he was looking at, or looking for. Now I "was" becoming concerned.

The examination completed I was instructed to dress, while so doing the M.O. informed me I was fit A1, whatever that meant.

I was then told to return to the canteen and wait. There I joined my two companions, who had also passed fit A1. We laughed and joked at our acquaintance with the M.O. and his pre-occupation with our genitals! To quote the Yorkshireman, "There weren't nowt wrong with my pissing tackle!"

The recruiting Sergeant all "ten feet" of him, in full regalia, peaked cap and swagger cane under his arm, stamped into the canteen, (the good guy back in the box), barked out to all in the canteen, and to the world outside, the message that lunch would be served and provided for with the compliments of the army.

He would return at 1400 hours for the induction ceremony.

He smartly turned about and marched out. We looked at each other and concluded that 1400 hours was two p.m. and we wouldn't move.

The meal consisted of meat, gravy and two vegetables. My best meal since leaving home, and was the first meal with fresh vegetables I had eaten in two weeks. It was followed by rice pudding and a cup of tea.

The lunch in the company of two amiable people, embued in me an optimism that had been absent a few hours earlier.

The immediate future was no longer threatening. I was committed to a definitive course of action since my initial impulsive urge of running away to London.

Fourteen hundred hours arrived on time. The man with the lists appeared. "I will call you in alphabetical order and each one of you in turn will follow me."

I was last, the other two having completed their ceremony.

I followed the man with the list as instructed into a large room where behind a big desk sat "Colonel Blimp" in person – and standing by his side was the recruiting sergeant.

"Colonel Blimp" read out my name, called me forward, instructed me to lay my hand on a bible which he was holding, and to repeat after him an oath, with something to do with serving King and Country and heirs and successors. I repeated the oath, a jumble of words devoid of meaning to me.

"Sign here" was the next command, and I did. "Return to the canteen" said the sergeant.

Back in the canteen were my two companions and our conversation was occupied with what was going to happen next and how long was it going to be.

Our wait ended with the Sergeant entering the canteen, minus peaked cap and swagger cane. He pulled up a chair and sat down. I sensed that the "good guy" was in ownership.

He immediately put us at ease. He was very fatherly and informative. Further in the building where he would show us was a dormitory with six beds. There we would stay the night, then early the next morning we would be given railway warrants and travelling instructions to our individual destinations. Transport would be provided for the journey to the railway station.

In the meanwhile we were free until 2200 hours when we must return without fail. "You are now soldiers in the British Army," he said.

He produced from his pocket a handful of coins and a sheet of paper. He gave each of us five shillings commenting it was a gift from the army's benevolent fund. He assumed we were "broke" and a few shillings would be of use if we left the building for the evening.

We signed for the monies, and followed him to the dormitory where we would stay the night. He shook each of us by the hand and wished us good luck. That was the last I saw of this complex man.

The dormitory was empty; we had the choice of beds. We chose three beds next to each other and promptly spread ourselves on top to relax.

It had been a strange and stressful day. It was five p.m. I rested quietly, lost in thought.

I was brought back to reality by a shout from the young cockney that he was hungry and wanted his dinner. I responded by saying that we had dinner earlier this afternoon, but it was teatime. I also could do with something to eat.

On hearing myself saying this, I realised that the eating habits of the people I would henceforth be consorting with were different from the customary ways of the Welsh valley people.

Breakfast, dinner, tea and supper was to become, breakfast, lunch, dinner and a cup of cocoa. I must get used to the sophisticated regime.

To assuage his hunger, our cockney companion suggested that we make our way to Soho where he knew of a "joint" which provided a good "nosh" for two bob. I readily concurred, likewise the Yorkshire man.

We found the "joint"; a scruffy little place at the back of one of Soho's side streets. It was full of smoke and noise with a long counter and stools placed at intervals.

Our guide did the ordering, there was little choice. A plate with chips, beans and two sausages, together with a knife and fork was slapped down in front of me.

The "joint" might have been primitive, the meal was anything but. It was delicious and worth every penny of the two bob asked. A cup of tea served afterwards was threepence extra.

Hunger satisfied, we had time to spare. It was agreed we take a walk and see some of the life of Soho.

The cavalryman would show us the way and what to see. He appeared to be at home in this particular part of the city. He was full of wit and endless patter as well as being nonplussed at my lack of knowledge of what I was now experiencing.

He was continually teasing me over my ignorance as he explained things that aroused my interest and curiosity.

As the evening wore on, the Yorkshireman proposed that we locate a pub to slake a thirst he was enduring.

Our guide knew the exact place where a suitable pub was, which, like his eating "joint", was full of smoke and noise. I had never been inside a pub. There were two in my home village, where drinking by teenagers was frowned upon and not the done thing. Myself and friends had far more interesting pursuits than wasting time, sitting, drinking and smoking with old fogies.

I informed my companions that I didn't drink beer and furthermore I was not yet of age to enter a pub. Howls of laughter and scurrilous suggestions emanated from them making me feel very embarrassed and immature.

I went into the pub with them. I was asked, "What was I drinking?" This was the first time I had ever heard that request, I said, "I didn't know." Before I could enlarge on this comment, the Yorkshireman said "Have a shandy" I knew what that was, it was a relief to answer "yes" at the same time I proffered some money to pay. He told me not to bother as he had more money than me. "I was to have it on him".

Looking around a thought crossed my mind. If only my friends could see me at this moment. With strangers, laughing and joking with a half pint in my hand, inside a smoky pub somewhere in a back lane in London's Soho district.

Thirst quenched, our guide suggested that we wander over to Piccadilly and have a "gander" at the girls. I posed the question what did he mean by "gander" and also what girls. He stopped me in my tracks looked at me in astonishment. "Don't you know anything or are you bloody stupid altogether?"

I replied that I knew quite a lot but what I was seeing and experiencing at the moment was out of the ordinary and all new to me.

He then went on to explain that the girls he was alluding to were prostitutes and did I know what prostitutes do? I said I had a vague idea, but this was the first time I had ever seen a prostitute in the flesh or in action.

"Have you ever had sex with any girl?" His terminology was direct, explicit and in the vernacular.

I understood the question; I was not however going to divulge to him my cavorting with our Priscilla in the long grass - that was our secret.

I answered in the negative. "Gor blimey, you are green, aren't you? What the hell do you do in those caves up in them Welsh hills?"

By now I was feeling a little bit out of my depth with this "wise boy". But I still wanted to learn and was curious.

On the Regent Palace Corner were two girls. They were a tawdry looking pair and not what I imagined prostitutes to be. Two young girls on display, sex on the hoof, commercialised with a price tag. The idea was abhorrent and left me cold.

Our polyandrous Priscilla was for free with those she liked and chose for her gentle loving"unadulterated" sexual favours and forays with us teenagers in the seclusion of the long grass. She was in a different league and bore no resemblance to what I was now witnessing.

These girls were flaunting their considerable female assets in the hope of tempting a 'purchaser', who would no doubt subject them to all manner of indignities to get value for his money.

I pondered what circumstances or aspects of their lives were conditioning or were driving the young females to so blatantly and publicly demeaning themselves.

The mantra that it is the world's oldest profession, begs the question. It could be that they enjoyed their work.

My sheltered existence in the valley did not prepare me for the bizarre and seamier side of life.

It was obvious to me that I was involved in one gigantic learning curve, which would turn full circle a few years later.

My preconceived notion of human behaviour was of a biblical interpretation based on the "tale" of two lumps of stone with inscriptions engraved upon them and carried down a mountain by a big strong man with a grey beard. Some three thousand years before the moon landing, the Internet, or the bomb.

Within the inscriptions were ten or more sets of behavioural instructions, a hotch potch of"thou shalt's" and "thou shalt nots".

Thou shalt not covet thy neighbour's arse, his wife, daughter or Mercedes Benz!

Thou shall honour thy father and mother or thou wilt receive a clout across the earhole, so on and so on!!

Thou shall not kill, other than by the millions.

These dos and don'ts sublimely pervaded and conditioned the natural curiosity of the youth in our non-conformist valley. Leaving us high and dry when confronted as I was, with real live people behaving in contradistinction to the words engraved in stone of thou shall and thou shall not.

I was bemused and fascinated by the panorama of events in which I was a willing spectator without the least idea of what it was all about.

It would therefore be remiss of me to be either critical or judgmental of the Soho scene.

I knew I had to grow up and learn a great deal, to form an educated opinion relevant to the behaviour and habits of the "human animal", during the frequent bouts of sexual incontinence.

The night was ending, our civilian life was closing. Tomorrow we will be in the relentless grip of the military machine, which would begin immediately the transition of civilian to soldier, with its humourless efficiency, merciless precision and institutionalised indignities.

The walk down Whitehall to the dormitory was leisurely, the conversation dwelling and speculating on the days that were ahead, and the commitment we had undertaken. Anticipation with a tinge of apprehension was evident. We were volunteers and fear of the unknown was inclusive.

I was tired and exhausted, it had been an eventful day littered with surprises.

I slept soundly throughout the night, to be awakened at dawn by the 'follow me man' who always seemed to have a list in his hand. "Wakey Wakey!" he hollered.

"You will wash, dress and retire to the canteen, where breakfast will be served, after which you will stand by for further instructions. You will not move from this canteen."

An order had been given. The military machine was being cranked up to receive its new victims.

It was eight a.m. when the man with the list reappeared, ordering my two companions to follow him. They went without question, or a goodbye and disappeared forever.

I was alone at the table, I surmised they had received their travel warrants and were on their way to their respective training establishments.

It was my turn. The 'list man' with his now familiar cry of 'follow me' came to the table. This time the 'follow me' ended at the desk of a mature lady who bid me sit down, while she explained the procedure.

I will be given a train travel warrant and two shillings for bus fare, also written instructions of train times and buses, as well as a planned route of where to change and most importantly the time I should arrive at my final destination, where on arrival I must report to the guard room who would be aware of my pending arrival.

Transport was arranged for me to proceed immediately to Waterloo Station.

She handed the relevant documents in an envelope. The Railway warrant and the two-shilling piece separately. She pressed a button on her desk, in came the 'follow me' man, this time it was to the entrance of the building and down the steps into a waiting taxi which immediately took off for the station. (Another first, a ride in a taxi and a London cab to boot!)

On my arrival I made straight for a bench or seat in order that I could examine and read the instructions in the envelope.

I was to board the Southampton train which stopped at Basingstoke, there I would disembark and catch a train for Fleet, where I would get off, exit the station and catch the first available bus to Crookham Village. Get off the bus and walk the remaining distance to Crookham Camp. I should arrive at the guardroom by 1300 hours.

The bus stopped within fifty yards of the camp's entrance. I presented myself to the soldier standing outside the guardroom. He escorted me inside, where a sergeant demanded my name. He looked at some papers in front of him, called a soldier from an inside room and ordered him to "march" me to the Company Orderly Room, some distance away.

There I was handed over to another sergeant sitting behind a desk who "demanded" (my days of being kindly asked were over!), my name and religion.

At the preliminaries before my induction into the army at Whitehall, I was asked my religion. I answered "Christian". "I know that," said the officer sarcastically, "What I want to know are you Church of England, Church of Rome, or any other kind of Church?"

I was completely ignorant of religious differences. Everybody in the Valley went to a Chapel. As far as I was concerned at that moment I could be a member of the church of Turkey, but common sense prevailed. I said that as a boy I went to chapel.

"Right" he said, "Methodist", and so I became a Methodist or as I learnt later, a member of "the other denominations." The preferred title given by the army to other religious groups, all under the one banner and designated by the soldiers as 'odds and sods.'

The sergeant shuffled some papers, produced a file in which he wrote down all the details I had been asked at Whitehall which I now repeated.

He stopped writing and looked up with an official stare as if he was about to pass sentence of death or some other diabolical punishment. He pronounced my army and R.A.M.C. number 7261377, with the rider 'Remember it, as part of your name. You will be in serious trouble should you ever forget it.' (I have never forgotten it).

This seemingly innocuous statement by the sergeant stripped me of my civilian identity for the next three years.

The army has an abhorrence of Christian names. Henceforth I would be 7261377, Private Williams, my pro-names were redundant.

Soldiers compensate for this deficiency by the use of nicknames or regional identifications. The whole of my army life I was called 'Taffy' by my comrades, others were Jock, Paddy, Brummy, Geordie; all Millers were Dusty, all Wilsons, Tug, short soldiers, Tich, tall soldiers, Lofty.

"You will be billeted " continued the sergeant "in Hut 4, C. Block. You will be a soldier of a squad in A Company."

"The escort will take you to the stores, you will be issued with uniform and full kit. You will be taken to the shower room. You will shower and dress in your army clothes. You will then be taken to Hut no. 4 and handed over to a senior soldier, who will show you what you must do and how to do it."

"March him off to the stores!", shouted the sergeant to the escort, who was waiting outside the Orderly Room door. At the stores, I was asked my height, what size shoes did I wear? I answered and was given a jacket, "Try that for size". It seemed to fit in places. "Good" said the issuing Corporal, "if it is a bit too big or small, take it to the camp tailor, and he will make it fit."

The full kit issue now began. It was put on the counter piece by piece, as separate items, handed to me by the escort to be placed in the kit bag now in my possession.

The full kit comprised the following as called, and handed out by the corporal.

Cap, badge, shoulder and collar badge, button stick, knife, fork, spoon, razor, comb, lather brush, toothbrush, hairbrush, holdall for same. Two boot brushes, one tin of boot polish, one tin of brasso, one button brush, one bar of soap, tea mug, complete uniform, puttees, brown fatigue jacket and trousers, clothes brush, forage cap, peaked cap, pair of size nine boots, pair of gym shoes, two pairs of gym shorts, two gym vests, three underpants, three pairs of socks, two leather boot laces, three towels, one brown cardigan, great coat, ground sheet, one white ceremonial belt, 'housewife' (a small holdall with needles, thimble and a few brass buttons, wool and cotton thread), gloves and braces.

The battle webbing of backpack side haversack and water bottle completed the issue.

I signed for the kit. The soap, brasso, boot polish and toothbrush was demanding a second signature because they were initial issue only, replacements were my responsibility to be bought and paid for by me.

With my kit safely in the 'bag' the escort conducted me to Hut no.4 in C. Block, where I was handed over to the senior soldier, who immediately took me to a bed and space, my home for the next six months.

The hut held thirty men; the senior soldier, better known as the old soldier, mentioned that all these men like myself were new recruits who had arrived from all over the country these past two days and it seemed I was the last arrival of this particular intake. We would, with men from another hut form a squad of forty.

I looked around and was surprised to see lots of men sitting on their beds working hard at polishing boots.

My escort was dismissed. The old soldier emptied my kit bag on to the bed, sorted out the soap, towel, uniform trousers, shirt, socks, underpants, and gym shoes, handed them to me with the instruction to follow him to the shower room.

I stripped and took a shower for the first time in my life, emerged and dried myself. The old soldier handed me my army issue of underpants, vest, shorts, socks and gym shoes.

The donning and feel of these strange garments was a traumatic jolt. I was shedding the old and familiar for something new and uncomfortable.

Up until this moment being in the army was unreal, "airy fairy", an adventure, a refuge, with bed and breakfast. The implications and seriousness of my Whitehall, impulsive decision was confronting me. My immaturity and unworldlyness was now self-evident, the consequences of which I would have to live with for the next three years.

My civilian clothes together with my persona were being discarded for a uniform that would identify me with the rest of the squad as a candidate for the sadistic arm of the military system of conditioning and rebranding of a civilian to the army's own specification of obedient, unthinking, ask no questions automaton.

From today forward, I will be prevented from thinking for myself, or arriving at my own decisions.

The army will take over and lay claim to my thought process and my physical movements. I will be under orders with sanctions for disobedience attached.

I will be told when to sleep, where to sleep, when to wake up, when to wash, when to shave, what to wear, how to wear it, when to eat, what to eat, when to have a haircut, what style, what time I can leave barracks, what time I must return.

It was called disciplinary training – "bullshit". It was a euphemism for conditioning and brain washing. The name of the game is unswerving obedience to orders.

I will be conditioned during the months ahead by a process of studied humiliation and degradation. My dignity will be assaulted, my parentage questioned and ridiculed. I will be publicly called a "stupid, silly little man" and "a Welsh twit."

My will to resist will be under great strain; my urge to question will also be tested.

"You are a silly little man, what are you?" "A silly little man Sergeant." My progress to abject servility and obedience will be ruthless and relentless.

Marching up and down, "Left turn, right turn, double quick march, slow march, left, right, left, right, halt, look to your front, stand still, you silly little man!"

The will to resist is one of nature's tools in the struggle of survival and self-preservation. The army must deny these basic instincts, by subverting and attempting to eliminate them.

The will to obey is "Sine quo non". "You will do what you are ordered to do, you will obey without hesitation or question. You will poke your mother's eyes out if ordered. Only after the order is obeyed will you complain if you think the order was wrong."

"There is one thing in this world more wicked than the desire to command, and that is the will to obey."

That quotation, which I remember from some reading, is a terrible indictment upon which the shades of the crucified youth in the wars of my century shall pass sentence.

I enquired of the old soldier about the disposal of my civilian clothes. He informed me while I was under training at Crookham Camp, I would not be allowed to wear civilian clothes. I would however, after finishing training at the camp and posted elsewhere be able to receive permission to wear them after duty hours. Meanwhile I had the choice of sending them home or hiding them in the bottom of my kit bag. I chose the latter option.

Back at "Hut no.4, Block C", feeling uncomfortable and itchy in my clothes. I sat on my bed, listening to a recitation of dos and don'ts, given by the old soldier to the huts' occupants, some of whom came and sat on the bed with me, a kind of welcoming party.

A few of them had arrived an hour or two before me; others had been here since yesterday.

We were all new, all strangers, wanting to pool our apprehensions.

Geographical locations of our homes were exchanged, information of our trade skills, or lack of skills were swapped.

Social intercourse with a group of men (I now included me in this category), with whom I was going to be in close contact was a necessary adjunct in easing the gruelling, teeth clenching months of conditioning and rebranding to the military's specifications that lay ahead.

The old soldier gave us a resume of our duties for the morrow, starting at 0600 hours with the bugler sounding reveille.

We would get up, make our beds in the manner prescribed by the manual, we must wash, shave, dress in full uniform, minus cap and wait for the bugle call of "Come to the cook house door!"

"You will then form two lines on the road outside the hut, where you will be joined by new recruits from other huts. Forty of you in total".

"The squad will be taken over by your appointed Sergeant instructor"".

"Now you must prepare for the morning. Buttons to be shining, cap badge to be polished and inserted in the cap, the same with shoulder and collar badges. Trousers to be creased, boots polished with a sparkling shine on the toe cap. You will be inspected by the Sgt. Instructor, so be prepared for some unwelcome and sarcastic remarks".

"You will be marched to the dining hall for breakfast. So make sure you are in possession of your knife, fork, spoon and mug".

"After breakfast you can saunter back in your own time as long as you are in the hut by 0715 hours".

"At eight o'clock the bugler will sound "Come on parade!". You will line up outside, as you did for breakfast".

"The sergeant instructor will take over and thereafter lavish all his loving care and attention on you ("Ha ha!") until you pass out as fully trained soldiers of the R.A.M.C. You will no longer be in my charge. My responsibilities will be with the next intake. Right now I want you to get your eating utensils and follow me to the dining hall where a meal is prepared for you".

I was hungry; in fact I was hungry everyday of my transition at Crookham Camp. I was a growing lad.

The meal comprised, mash potatoes, (soggy) cabbage, carrots, meat of some description, gravy and a slice of bread. We stood in a queue at the serving counter, plate in hand, rations slapped on, which was not over generous. There was no second helping.

The dining hall was a long hut, empty of furniture, except the trestle tables and wooden benches. A most spartan and unwelcome setting in which to enjoy ones food.

It was patently obvious this decrepit camp was a forgotten relic of the Great War. Yet to be either modified or demolished and replaced with conditions of a more humane kind.

The huts we lived in were devoid of any comfort. A trestle table with two benches one either side of a coal-fired pipe stove in the centre of the hut was the only furniture.

The ablution facilities were of a primitive nature. A long slate bench fitted at intervals with cold-water taps with galvanised iron bowls underneath, which after use were emptied into a nearby drain. Washing and shaving was done in cold water.

Hot water was available from 18.00 hours to 20.00 hours and only in the shower room.

The personal toilet arrangements were only slightly more civilised. The cubicles were minus doors and toilet paper, or hand washing facilities.

Both these indispensable buildings essential though they were, for some perverse reason were hidden in a far corner of the camp, a walking distance of three to four minutes from the living areas. It was necessary therefore for a routine to be established for the placing outside each hut, a large bucket for the bodily function of its inhabitants after lights out.

The nightly placing of the bucket and the morning slopping out was a weekly turn about duty for those named on a roster, maintained by the "old soldier who lived in the hut."

We returned after the meal to an evening of "brassoing", polishing and shining in preparation for tomorrow's meeting with a "rebranding" expert.

I was tired, the last two days was a revelation, a realisation of my ignorance.

I was a world away from my valley and its very ordinariness, away from my friends. Everything was different; in habits, in style, in speech, attitudes and in food, as well as the topics discussed with sex the predominant subject.

I was homesick. It was 22.00 hours and we must be in bed before lights out. I welcomed the end of this particular day which over the years has petrified in my memory, every incident as it was, and how it was.

The bugler sounded the last post and lights out. The old soldier obeyed, flicked a switch. It was dark and sleep came swiftly.

We awakened to the sound of reveille. The routine as laid out by the old soldier the previous night was altered to accommodate a medical inspection immediately after breakfast, which consisted of porridge, a slice of bread and margarine, a kippered herring and a mug of tea. The tea was dispensed from what was purported to be an urn, but looked like a converted oil drum with a tap attached. The tea also tasted if it had come out of an oil drum. My first army breakfast was definitely not a gourmet delight.

Meal consumed, back in the hut, preparations in train for the medical inspection.

The sergeant stamped into the hut, bawled out "Stand by your beds!". In came the M.O. with a member of his staff. "Drop your trousers and underpants to your ankles" ordered the Sergeant.

Throughout my time in the army, this exercise was carried out with meticulous precision and timing at intervals of three months.

Twenty to thirty men lined up in a barrack room, standing to attention eyes front, their trousers and underpants down to the floor with their appendages at ease, without the hint of a smile on their faces, waiting for the M.O. with his little spatula and torch to bend down, touch 'it', move on to the next man and continue on down the line without a word being spoken.

This solemn and humourless military pantomime is a sight to behold of unbelievable incongruity.

The purpose of this genitals ritual and probing is not always obvious. I have never been given a reason or received an official explanation for this unseemly exercise.

I have often speculated if the officers underwent this same insensitive public assault on their dignity and decency as did their men.

Inspection over, "Adjust your dress", ordered the Sergeant. Trousers and underpants hoisted into place, dignity restored. "Fall in outside!" yelled the Sergeant.

"This morning you lot, (we were always 'you lot'), will be given basic training in army deportment and military courtesy, the interpretation of commands and the carrying out of these commands".

"Right turn! Quick march! Left, right, left, right". Without further comment we reached the square where other squads were marching up and down in their various stages of training.

"When on parade you will always stand to attention, unless ordered otherwise" said the Sergeant. Square bashing was in its preliminary stage.

"Attention means feet together at an angle of forty five degrees, arms at your side, in line with the seam of your trousers with thumbs pointing down. You will stand perfectly still, eyes facing front, you will never talk, whisper, speak out of the side of your mouths, or look sideways at me".

"On the command stand at ease, you will move your right foot to the right in one quick movement, to a distance of eight or nine inches. The rest of your body will remain at attention."

"On the command Stand Easy, you will not move your feet, you will relax your body without visible movement."

"Right you lot, we will begin. Attention! pause, "stand at ease", pause, "stand easy". Pause.

This went on for one hour non-stop after which a break of ten minutes was given. A N.A.A.F.I. trailer was situated in a corner of the parade ground, where we were allowed to purchase a cup of tea and cake for fourpence if we so desired or could afford.

After the break, another hour was devoted to the practice of saluting with cap on and with cap off. With cap on, your right arm well fully outstretched, brought sharply to the temple, with palm open, fingers and thumb closed and tight together. Then in one movement your arm brought sharply straight down to your side. Saluting without cap, the head and eyes are sharply turned in the direction of the officer. This salute is only done when on the move, your arms stiffly at your side.

At the end of this particular lesson there was again a short break for tea and cake. After which we lined up for inspection of a personal nature.

The Sergeant asking each in turn our surname, and official army age, as well as commenting on the way we were dressed and the way he would like us dressed. As well as telling us, as a squad to either get our hair plaited or cut. He would prefer cut "if we didn't mind". He would make sure the camp barber was in our hut at 1900 hours. "He will give you the regulation short back and sides."

"You Williams, when did you last shave?" "I have never shaved," said I. He almost threw a fit. "Well make sure you 'scrape' that bum fluff off your baby face before the next parade." he shouted. (I was embarrassed), "and when you speak to me, call me Sergeant." "Yes Sergeant."

The last lesson of the morning was how to "fall out". "On the command 'dismiss' you will turn smartly to your right, and break away."

Training given at the morning session was to be repeated ad nauseam.

Before the final dismiss of the morning was given, the sergeant informed us the afternoon session would be of movement, how to march, how to line up in size and how to form fours.

We were then marched to the road outside our hut where we were dismissed followed by the long dash to the toilets at the far end of the camp.

We were able to relax for a half-hour after the morning session and before the bugler sounded 'come to the cook house door'. Then there would be the usual mad scramble out on to the road to line up and be greeted by the Sergeant shouting for attention, "Stand still, look to your front." Short pause, "Right turn, quick march, left, right, and on to the dining hall outside of which was a bench with two large buckets of warm water. A very 'hygienic' facility for washing and rinsing our knife, fork, and mug after a meal.

The afternoon training lesson started with sizing.

"Tallest on the right, shortest on the left, in single rank size. That is the command. The two ranks will break away and form one line, in order of height, making sure that the man on your right is taller than the man on your left. You will move quickly and quietly, without fuss, whilst shuffling yourselves about. The line will end with tallest on the right, shortest on the left."

I was six feet two inches, the tallest man in the squad, and inevitably ended up as marker, a position I hated. It becomes a pivotal role in C.O's inspections and ceremonial parades.

We practised this exercise, until we got it right, with plenty of encouragement from Sgt. Ryan.

The next part of this drill was to reform the single sized line into two lines and in size.

"You will number off. Then on the command, 'even numbers one step back march', you will take one step back and stand still". Both exercises were repeated all that afternoon, until and with lots of encouragement again from the Sgt. We got it right; precise and spot on.

During this part of our training, it was a great relief to have marching lessons. Every now and then the Sgt. would halt the stationary training drill and march us around the square, barking out orders and commands; "Right turn, left turn, forward march, quick march, march on the double, about turn, halt, attention, stand still, look to your front, stand easy, stand at ease!"

This was square bashing in style. I enjoyed it, I was in the open in the fresh air and having plenty of exercise, and a relief from the stand still type of drill training.

The routine of on parade and marching to every meal, was the 'square bashing' exercise I found most irksome and pointless.

The humiliations and degradation heaped upon us by the instructors soon wore off. Their rehearsed remarks and wisecracks lost their sting with repetition. I took refuge from their witticisms by adopting the attitude of a spectator at a music hall performance and secretly enjoying the antics of these uniformed clowns and comedians. That I was a fall guy and butt of some of their jokes was of little consequence. Always at the back of my mind was the niggling thought that I was a willing recipient of whatever the army chose to throw at me. I was a volunteer.

I joined the army of my own free will. I did what I was ordered to do. It was not a problem, I was pliable. I was not going to break.

There was no respite from the "square bashing". Every day a repeat of the previous day. At the end of our training, like Pavlov's dogs we had been conditioned to react to stimuli.

The sight of three stripes on a sleeve and we would spring to attention, stand still, eyes front. We became perfect in every respect as laid down in the manual of Military Training and by order of Sgt. Ryan.

We were also exceptionally healthy. The marching and stomping exercises for six months in the open air had advantages especially for me. I had spent three of my most important growing years, underground, covered in grime and breathing dust.

The drill and square bashing component of the training syllabus was comparatively easy and to me a welcome diversion from the barrack room "bull shit", which was a good fifty per cent of the course and always ongoing.

The pettifogging harassment of grown men with the menial tasks we were ordered to undertake was to me (but not to the military), unnecessary. Many hours in the evenings would be spent using all kinds of methods to obtain a sparkling shine on the toecaps of our boots. We would debate and argue over the qualities of various brands of shoe polish, Kiwi, Nugget, or Cherry Blossom. The consensus was Cherry Blossom.

Everyday there would be an inspection of one kind or another. Kit inspection was very popular with most officers.

There was a sadistic tendency to spring this inspection on the Squad with very little notice.

A kit inspection is a highly organised event with the usual precision. The kit and equipment has to be spotlessly clean, all brasses polished, all webbing blancoed and laid out on the bed in a planned order and position, button stick, knife, fork, spoon, razor, comb, lather brush, toothbrush, socks, boots, shirts and so on. All folded neatly in the prescribed manner. Every item placed in a measured position on the bed.

Barrack room inspection was on a weekly basis, table and benches scrubbed almost white; slop bucket polished inside and out, stove black-leaded, its brick base whitewashed. Beds in line with blankets folded correctly, bed space clean and without a speck of dust. With inspections and preparing for inspection, time to relax was at a premium.

The C.O. weekly inspection was an elaborate affair exhibiting the discipline, precision and efficiency of the men and the awesome power of command and obedience. The squad would assemble on the road outside the hut, be inspected by the Sergeant when we would be reprimanded for not being up to the standard demanded. This tirade was a weekly occurrence. It never changed.

The order "Right turn, quick march!" is given "Left, right, left, right!" and on to the parade ground. "Halt!"

"Tallest on the right, shortest on the left in single rank, size! Two ranks form! Attention, stand still! Look to your front!"

The position of attention is maintained, all the while as the camp's R.S.M. and a Sgt. would walk up and down the ranks of all the squads on parade. Passing comments on hair, boots, brass work and demeanour; these comments were written down by the Sgt. After the parade, they would be handed over to the instructors who would berate us with their full armoury of wise cracks and sarcasms, personal and otherwise.

Every soldier and officer not on essential duty would be on the C.O.s parade.

After the R.S.M. inspection, the squads would be placed at "easy". The Sgt Major would retire to the side of the square, where a portable platform had been erected and besides which was the Military band.

Long pause, silence with the exception of the breeze and chirping birds.

There would be movement coming from the building near the square where the platform was sited. The C.O. is on the move, with a retinue of officers. As they approach the platform the stentorian boom of the R.S.M. calls the parade to attention. The band strikes up a tune.

The Sergeant Major makes his way to the front of the platform and the band ceases playing. He salutes, about turns and halts. The officers leave the platform and march to the front of their respective squads, at the same time, the Sgt instructors about turn and marched to the rear of their squads. Long pause, and silence.

The commanding voice of the R.S.M. reverberates across the parade ground and the little village of Crookham. "Parade, by the right, quick march!"

In line abreast we set off to the tune of the regimental march played by the band, marching past the C.O. on the platform.

The officer leading the squad gives the command "eyes right", all the men's heads and eyes turn sharply right, with the exception of my head and eyes.

I am the front rank marker; I look straight ahead. The command "eyes front" is given. The squad, now out of the corner of their eye, dress by the right and keep the rank straight, we marched and saluted in close formation, open formation, quick marched in columns of four, all to the music of the band.

On these occasions new recruit squads are excused, until they are proficient, which is about six weeks from commencement of square bashing.

When I entered the army, my head was empty of any preconceived ideas of military discipline. Indeed it was almost empty of everything unconnected with my life in the valley. In this new life, it was akin to a sponge, ready and wanting to absorb and hold what was available for soaking up.

The skills acquired during "square bashing", with its physical movements of timing, precision, and repetition is identical to the skills of cycling or swimming.

Once taught and mastered it is never forgotten and will always be capable of doing.

My ability to recall in some detail this period of the past is therefore not remarkable. What, however, strikes me as odd and remarkable is that I cannot remember the name of the C.O. or any of the Commissioned Officers.

The name Sgt Ryan, the instructor, is tattooed on my brain and immune to eradication.

The officers, senior and junior were overtly public school, had seen action in the Great War. The ribbons on their uniforms were evidence of their meritorious service.

The handling and treatment of the private soldiers in their charge had been learned in that great conflict and it was now being taught and passed on at Crookham Camp.

The trench mentality prevailed. Their war had been fought and won in the trenches and the next war was to be fought, where it left off.

The Blitzkrieg and the Panzer divisions were only nine years in the future and we were being taught how a trenching tool could be used as a defensive weapon.

Facilities at the Camp for intellectual pursuits were minimal. Board games were unavailable; there was no camp library or reading room. The N.A.A.F.I. was the only place where a newspaper or periodical could be found.

Leisure was of a physical kind, consisting of inter squad boxing, inter-company football matches, and gymnasium exercises.

I enjoyed boxing and was co-opted into the Squads' Team trained by none other than Sgt. Ryan. He was an excellent coach, whose mannerisms and attitude whilst coaching and at the ringside was in sharp contrast to his histrionic parade performances. His squad won more contests than they lost.

I was in the welterweight class and quite good, I too won more times than I lost, but only just!

My first leave or furlough, the term preferred by the military was Christmas - one week. I was issued with a free travel warrant, given a weeks pay in advance, two shillings a day. I purchased a suitcase from the N.A.A.F.I. wherein I packed my civilian clothes and personal effects; I had no intention of wearing my uniform when at home.

My family were overjoyed to see me and also pleased to see me looking a picture of health. My father gave me a hearty greeting; I sensed he was more than pleased. On demand of my sisters I was compelled to parade up and down the living room in my uniform, demonstrating some of the drills I had been taught. It was my pleasure to see them laugh.

Other times I was asked endless questions by the whole family, as well as giving an account of my adventures, trials and tribulations during my five months absence from home.

I made enquiries of my friends and their welfare. I walked the mountain to my old valley to visit the few that were left and together we gathered in a local pub. We were all grown up and of age (I was two months short of eighteen) where a glass or two of shandy was in order.

We laughed over our recent past and joked about our activities and especially with our confrontations with Bobby Beynon. We also expressed our sadness and sorrow that the world had moved on and dragged us along with it. I was loath to leave.

A Christmas card addressed to me was delivered by the postman. It was from our wonderful Priscilla, from an address in Slough. I made a note of the address and promised myself I would write her a letter in the near future.

Back from leave to the camp's routine of inspections, boot polishing, blancoeing and shining of brass work.

Square bashing for the squad was confined to mornings only. The afternoon being dedicated to stretcher drill.

How to put a wounded soldier on a stretcher and place him in a position relative to his wounds. How to lift and carry a loaded stretcher without further damaging its occupant.

This like all other drills was repeated until it was perfect and to Sgt. Ryan's satisfaction.

We were also given very detailed instructions by numbers for the assembly of a "Thomas Splint" to a wounded leg. I have forgotten all the numbered instructions but for some reason or another I do remember instruction no.9, "The Spanish Windlass".

The splint exercise was also repeated until perfection was attained and Sgt Ryan satisfied.

Why this heavy cumbersome metal splint was so important has always eluded me. After leaving Crookham Camp, I never again saw this splint in practice or in use. My expertise in fitting one was never tested for real.

The syllabus was changing daily. Military drill and square bashing was limited. Most of the day was given over to elementary first aid, and camp fatigues. Gardening, white washing, sweeping and cleaning toilets.

The squad was the camp's handy men or "charwomen". These domestic chores were a pleasant interlude. We were free from the watchful glare and verbarian skills of Sgt. Ryan. We were also free from his orders, albeit temporary. Kit inspection, hut inspection, c.o.'s inspection and all the "kinds of bull" were ongoing.

Everything was easier, routine had set in, habits were forming. The repetition of drill. The clocking and timing of every movement of our daily lives had become automatic, everything was in order, and done to order. "Trousers and underpants down to your ankles!" "Stand still! Look to your front!" This was simply another drill movement, our sense of fear and foreboding had disappeared as well as our dignity. We had become obsequious, capable and willing. Our independence, self-reliance and self-assertion were forfeit.

Rebranding was complete, but as far as I was concerned, only the packaging had been changed. The contents remained the same. My civilian persona was intact. I was more mature, healthier, wiser and more knowledgeable going out of

Crookham Camp than when I was coming in and now I was shaving!

The travails and indignities we endured together gave me hope that I could conquer my insularity and difficulty in making new friends. I was unsuccessful though most of the squad were very friendly and I know that one or two counted me as a friend, but unbeknown to them it was all one-sided. They were nice people, and good acquaintances, but they were strangers to me, not friends. I could not bring myself to confide or express my innermost thoughts to strangers.

I knew I had this problem; which was unimportant. It affected no one other than myself.

The final days of our training were very relaxed. The end was in sight. Squads were disbanding. The men posted to different parts of the country and empire.

Soon it would be the turn of our squad. I wondered to where I would be sent?

A week before the passing out parade, we were given an aptitude test and intelligence tests.

Prior to these written tests, we were issued with an abridged version of Robinson Crusoe, to read and on which to write a small essay, and answer questions about its contents.

I knew every detail of Defoe's classic; I was presented with the book by my headmaster as a prize for five years of unbroken school attendance. I was thrilled as a young child with the story. I read and reread it half a dozen times for the next three or four years. For me it was "childs play" to write an essay on Robinson Crusoe.

The test overall was somewhat difficult. I was a complete duffer in respect to maths. However I was surprised when the results were handed out. I along with three or four others were given the army's first-class certificate of education. This classification was of advantage during the next phase of my career in the R.A.M.C.

The date of the passing out parade ceremony was promulgated, as were the destinations of our individual postings. My posting was to the Military Hospital at Edinburgh Castle. I was overjoyed. I could not have chosen better if that opportunity had been available.

I was about to travel the"world", I knew my geography, I knew where it was. That was the sum total of my knowledge. Of the city, the castle, I was ignorant.

At the end of the passing out parade, we were given a "pep" talk by the adjutant praising our precision and efficiency and that we must maintain this standard throughout our service and be proud of being a soldier in the R.A.M.C. We marched back to the road outside the hut.

"Halt! Left turn! Stand at ease! Stand easy! Look to your front!" Other than "dismiss", these were the final commands thrown at us by Sgt. Ryan.

His parting words "You lot are the best squad I have ever trained, and I wish you all well and the best for the future."

It can be safely assumed that this was his standard goodbye for us, and all who had gone before, as it would be for the future recipients of the ferocity of his methods and the authority to behave accordingly. All would eventually succumb to the classic hate syndrome of "loving" the sadistic bastard.

Dates and times of our individual postings were displayed on the company notice board, with instructions to report to the orderly room to collect the necessary documents and railway warrants.

My journey was to start at Fleet Station on to Kings Cross, where I would board a train for Waverley Station, Edinburgh, to arrive there early the following morning. This arrival day would coincide with my eighteenth birthday.

I was to travel in full battle dress, knapsack, haversack, water bottle, worn as a harness "minus the bit" and with my kit bag chock-a-block with all my regulation gear and my civilian clothes tucked away carefully at the bottom.

There is no hand carrying attachment to a soldier's kit bag. It has to be slung over the shoulder or carried awkwardly under the arm. Suitcases are not regulation, therefore not allowed.

It was departure day, a typical February day, snowing and bitterly cold. I and three other postings presented ourselves on time in full battle order to be inspected by the orderly officer of the day, outside on the road near the guardroom.

It was cold, it was miserable, making the inspection a speedy and cursory affair.

We boarded a waiting truck to be taken to Fleet Railway Station, leaving Crookham Camp to the tender mercies of Sgt Ryan and the like.

The time of my residence at the R.A.M.C. training base was my first experience of close living with people of different backgrounds and interests to mine. It was in stark contrast to the sheltered, isolated, parochial life in the hollow of a small decaying mining community in hills back of the beyond. Where the valley was my world to a new kind of life where the world is my valley.

At fourteen the only attainable ambition was to be a miner, at eighteen I was on my way to take up residence in a castle. Carefree, with determination to meet the future on its own terms.

Sgt Ryan's "Look to your front" will resonate for many years to come, as from now, I was not looking back.

I entered the train at King's Cross, struggled with my kit along the corridor looking for a suitable carriage. I found one with three occupants and an empty window seat.

After a struggle I placed my kit bag on the rack. As I undid my webbing belt to relieve myself of the knapsack and haversack, the gentleman in the corner came to my assistance and made it easier for me to divest myself of the equipment. This I also placed on the rack together with my great coat.

I sat down; the lady opposite gave me a smile and remarked that "It must be a relief to get all that stuff off you". I smiled back and nodded my agreement. The couple in the other corner were well acquainted with each other as they were in deep conversation which continued with interruptions for most of the journey. The train was moving and taking me to Scotland. As it clanked its way over the points and crossings, the lady opposite enquired of my destination. I told her Edinburgh. She volunteered the information that she also was going to Edinburgh; it was her home. She was a woman I judged to be in her early thirties.

I sensed she was curious and wanted to question me. I had no objection whatsoever. I eased her difficulty by telling her that I had never before been to Scotland, and was looking forward to the experience.

I opened the door, the questions came flooding in. I answered them all and was pleased to do so.

She asked me where in Scotland I was going to be stationed, I told her the military hospital at Edinburgh Castle.

Her face lit up, "I only live a street away from the Castle," she said "and insofar as you are a stranger, once we are off the train, I will be your guide."

I thanked her for the offer of help. She asked my age, I told her eighteen today. "You are young aren't you, and a happy birthday to you."

I could feel the blood rising in my face; a physical disability I had suffered with for years and which I thought had disappeared for good. I had not had any occurrence all the while at Crookham Camp.

I was blushing; she assured me with a big smile that my age was nothing to be ashamed of. "I was eighteen once" she said.

My journey to Scotland in the company of this nice lady made it an event of great pleasure that shortened a tediously long journey.

On the train's approach to Waverley Station, with the help of this lady, I donned my "battle dress", pulled my kit bag from the rack, retired to the corridor and waited for the train to pull into the station.

I had arrived in Scotland. The nice lady was waiting for me on the platform. I eventually disembarked; she was carrying a small suitcase and bade me follow her out of the station. It was pitch dark, and was snowing heavily; the streets were deserted. It was 05.00 hours. I was thankful that the lady was showing me the way, otherwise I would have been in some difficulty. I walked beside her as she pointed out some interesting features or building. It was very cold as we plodded on through the snow.

We arrived at a crossroads, and stopped. She pointed to the road in front and told me to continue walking that road for about ten minutes and I would then see the castle.

She bid me goodnight and good luck and I gratefully acknowledged and thanked her for her help.

There was not a living thing to be seen. The snow had a deadening effect, all was silent and eerie.

The castle loomed large out of the darkness. I reached the drawbridge and crossed it to come up against the massive doors which were shut.

I was very cold and wet, my pack was getting heavy. What now, I thought? Doors shut, what do I do?

I was getting irritable. I walked along the length of these massive doors. Lo and behold, at the end of one of these doors, was a small wicket with a bell push at its side, which I promptly pushed. Immediately a voice which I was not expecting, called out from the other side, "Who goes there?"

I was baffled. I had not been briefed for this situation, however I took a chance and shouted back "Williams, I have just come off the train and I want to come in". Slight pause, "What is your company?" asked the voice from the other side. "I don't have any company, I've come to work in the hospital." Another pause. The wicket door opened and standing in full uniform, rifle, kilt and sporran was a soldier of the Argyle & Sutherland Highlanders. The first kilted soldier I had ever seen.

I entered the castle and followed him to the guard room a few steps away, wherein was a large fire grate with a roaring fire burning. The Sergeant of the guard rose from the table, looked at me and said, "You must be cold laddie!" in a broad Scots accent. "Go and sit by the fire and I will get you a mug of tea to warm you up."

Those were the kindest, most meaningful words from a voice of authority since my induction into the army, and they were directed to me because he cared. I was going to like Scotland, and it was my eighteenth birthday. In the far corner of the room were three other members of the guard, sleeping or snoozing, waiting their turn to guard the drawbridge. The Sgt. handed me the hot mug of tea. He asked me about my journey, how long had I been in the army, how old I was (I must have looked young, as everybody seemed to be interested in my age!). He had noticed my Welsh accent, and asked what part of Wales I hailed from. He also informed me that the R.A.M.C. Orderly room would be in operation at 07.00 hours, but I would have to wait with him in the guardroom until then. The orderly room was only a short walk away.

At 07.00 hours, (you will have noticed by now that my times are military!), in full dress I presented myself to the orderly Staff Sergeant sitting at a desk with another soldier close by.

"Help him take that stuff off", ordered the Staff Sgt. to the soldier.

The gear off, the Staff told me to sit on the chair by the desk. He then ran through all the details of the routine and regime that I was now entering.

I would draw blankets and sheets from the store; they were to be changed every fourteen days.

I would be issued with a white pair of plimsolls. These were to be worn everywhere, when on duty in the hospital and associated buildings.

My putties could be put in the bottom of my kit bag for the duration of my duties at the castle.

One shilling and sixpence would be "voluntarily" deducted from my weekly pay as a contribution to Mess Hall and dining facilities and for laundering on a weekly basis of two shirts, two underpants, two pairs of socks and two towels. The laundry was collected on Friday and delivered back on Tuesday.

"You will be seen by the Personnel Staff Sgt. after breakfast. You will remain in the dining room until called".

"Herchal, (the name of the other soldier), will escort you to your room and bed space, which is room no. 4 where there are two empty beds. You will make a choice. He will also introduce you to the other soldiers in the room."

With Herchal's help I collected my kit and followed him out of the hospital compound, into the staff living quarters, which was on the Prince's Street side of the castle, with a fantastic unimpeded panoramic view of the City of Edinburgh and the Firth of Forth.

The room held eight beds and was windowless. The entrance to the room (there were six such rooms) was along a wide veranda, built into and overhanging the castle wall.

The rooms were part of the castle's original architecture. They looked like dungeons of a sort, which had been modified, modernised and made comfortable with central heating.

The opening to the room was by a door, let into a huge lattice of glass which filled the curved opening and gave plenty of light. Most of the rooms' occupants were doing their morning ablutions in preparation for inspection by Cpl. Fogarty.

I was introduced to a soldier who by the number of stripes on his right arm was of long service, he also had two red rings on the wrist part of his sleeves which denoted he was a first class nursing orderly, which in those days was equivalent to a S.R.N.

This soldier, Thompson by name, helped me sort my kit and instructed me in the correct and prescribed manner of storing my battle webbing. At the side of the bed was a hook on which to hang the kit bag containing my issue clothing. At the front or the bed was a large box with clasp, in which I deposited my cleaning material, brushes, brasso, boot polish, "housewife" as well as mug and eating utensils, and personal private property. Everything except kit bag, greatcoat and best uniform had to be out of sight. These items were folded neatly and correctly and placed on a shelf at the head of the bed.

I was the new boy on the block. Thompson placed me under his wing. The men returned from their toilet, to whom I was introduced as Taffy Williams and that is who I was for the rest of my service in the R.A.M.C.

I chose the empty bed next to the door and on the right. The bed next to me was in the ownership of a fellow as tall as me, which was a change. Up to now I was always the tallest in the squad. He went by the name of Higgins and for some unknown reason he was always referred to as Topper Higgins. He was a trained cook, having been to the Army School of Cookery at Aldershot; he had also been trained in special diets for hospital patients.

I immediately took a liking to Topper, our personalities "clicked". We became the closest of friends. He was the one real friend I made in the army. He was three years my senior and had seen two years service to date.

Thompson suggested that I follow him down to breakfast. I made for my mug and eating utensils but he said they were unnecessary. The dining table would be laid out with knives and forks. It was so, including tablecloth and side plates. I was amazed,

I was not expecting this. The dining room resembled a restaurant with all modern conveniences.

The upkeep, cleaning and service were on a roster basis and my turn for duty would come sooner than later.

Breakfast, was eggs, bacon, sausage, bread, and a cup of tea, served from a hot plate by the duty waiter.

All very civilian without a hint of the military, even the soldier diners were in white gowns and white plimsolls.

Crookham Camp and its spartan regime would hereafter be a forgotten and unpleasant preliminary to what was happening to me right now.

After breakfast, I was summoned to the office of personnel administration, where a Staff Sgt. with his breast full of medal ribbons, greeted me.

An authoritative figure, married with children, and billeted somewhere in the city. There were no married quarters for N.C.O.'s and other ranks at the castle.

He welcomed me to the hospital unit and hoped I would enjoy my stay.

My initial training and educational record had been marked as very good. On this basis, he would recommend me for further training as a nursing orderly, which would commence in the kitchen at 06.00 tomorrow and where I would be employed for one month. Thereafter my status would be reviewed every month for three months.

I progressed from cook and pan cleaner to hospital cleaner, to office boy and finally to the wards as trainee nursing orderly. All the time I attended classes of one and two hours twice a week, where lessons were given on the skeleton, anatomy, first aid and related subjects.

Notes were taken, reading material given relevant to the status as a beginner or advanced student.

Most of the NCO's in the hospital unit were timeservers, survivors of the Great War, married and living in the City.

The affect on my young life by these NCOs was minimal. There were however two corporals and one Sgt who I look back on with some nostalgia.

Corporal Fogarty, the ward master and hospital disciplinarian was the military rulebook incarnate. He was also a highly decorated soldier of the War. It was his duty to see we were properly attired and groomed, short back and sides, clean, and on time. Each shift would be paraded, and inspected before being dismissed to their duties. He was also the instructor on the bi-weekly refresher drill parade, which was routine and perfunctory. It pleased Fogarty.

The parade ground was a small piece of tarmacadam road at the rear of the hospital.

Cpl Fogarty was a person to be avoided whenever possible. Cpt Walsh was a gentle, cultured person and a lonely man. He was in charge of the stores for both hospital and the RAMC personnel requirements; he slept on the premises.

On the morning of my arrival at the castle, I went to the stores to draw my sheets, pillow and blankets. He was most courteous and solicitous of my well-being. He asked me if I required any personal material, brasso, boot polish or toothpaste. I said I was all right at the moment. He then mentioned that if ever I ran short of this kind of material, he would unofficially let me have it for free, thus saving me a few shillings.

I recounted this incident to Thompson when in conversation with other members of the room.

They laughed heartily, at the same time advising me that whenever I went to the stores for anything, to walk out backwards.

I did not quite see the joke at the time; my naivete was showing, I was growing up.

I knew Cpl Walsh for three years and not once did I hear, see or know of any untoward incident associated with him. Rumour and innuendo can be very hurtful in restricted surroundings. It did not seem to affect him; he was a nice, charming N.C.O. with a double row of war ribbons, who supplied me with cleaning materials for free.

Staff Sgt Clutterbuck, unmarried, and living in a room in the administrative part of the hospital. I leave it to the imagination the connotations in the vernacular that was associated with his name and which he was called out of earshot. I am certain he knew all the connotations and permutations his name inspired.

He was a pre-war soldier coming to the end of his twenty-one years service. He was the only N.C.O. I know of who was genuinely loved by the troops. He apparently did not care for authority or military discipline, yet he was particular in his duties of a clerical mature attendant on the efficiency and administration of things clinical and medical appertaining to the hospital. It was an unwritten rule amongst us ordinary soldiers that an eye is kept on him, on the odd weekends, that he emerged from his room. He had a habit of periodically going on the "binge" or as he called it "whoreing and boozing." We knew his usual haunts.

The castle gates were closed at midnight, a special pass had to be obtained beforehand if the intention was to stay out after midnight. This was rarely given and then only in extenuating circumstances. We always made sure that Sgt. Clutterbuck was home by midnight, and more often than not supported on his way by his watchers on either side.

My duties in the Castle Hospital were periodically interrupted by relief duties at the locations of various Scottish Battalions. A month in Fort George with the Camerons, a month in Aberdeen with the Gordons, also at Maryhill barracks, Glasgow with the H.L.I. and at Stirling with the Black Watch, as well as summer camps with the Universities and Colleges O.T.C.'s, at Blair Atholl, Peebles and Kirkcaldy. Duty at these O.T.C. camps was a holiday in beautiful country, and living under canvas. A medical officer, a Cpl. Nursing Orderly and me (dogsbody!) were in attendance for emergencies, which were rare.

The normal surgery consisted of cuts, abrasions, bruises, stomach-aches and the occasional broken limb. The catering was done by a civilian staff; meals were served in a large marquee.

Myself and the Cpl, as common soldiers dined with the civilian staff after the O.T.C. and officers had been catered for. We dined and ate in style. The waitresses saw to this. We were treated by them as special.

Sgt Ryan and the Crookham experience was a price worth paying for the freedom, company and enjoyment at these summer camps, with good food aplenty, congenial surroundings, discipline on the back burner and dozens of beautiful young Scottish waitresses to converse and stroll with along the banks of the Tweed or at "Salmons Leap" at Blair Atholl.

I had completed two years service; there was an examination to assess progress and capabilities of the Trainee orderlies. A lot depended on the success or otherwise of these exams. An increase in pay and the possibility of progress up the ladder.

I passed the examination with good marks. I became a Second Class Nursing Orderly, with a shilling a day rise in pay and the privilege of wearing a single red band on my sleeve denoting my new status.

I quietly thanked the Whitehall Recruiting Sergeant for his rejection of me as a potential guardsman and placing me instead in the part of the Military which was giving me possession of the best moments of my young life so far.

I was twenty years old, terminating my teenage and adolescent years in an environment totally foreign to the environment at the onset of my adolescence.

The blinkers on my vision of the world had been partly removed, but my knowledge of the lives, habits, idiosyncrasies and the understanding of people was still abysmal. My yardstick of human behaviour was formed and limited to my valley, my friends, their parents and my parents, and on which I would judge and assess other people.

The disdain and ridicule heaped upon Corporal Fogarty; the rumour and innuendo around Cpl Walsh; the affection and solicitude shown to Sgt. Clutterbuck. There were wisecracks on my Welshness and immaturity, all being bandied about in a jocular fashion, and passed off as normal barrack room intercourse.

To me these were new situations and emotions that were absent from my standard scale of values. I would have to adapt to the new standards by discarding the old.

My appreciation of the army and in particular of my unit, was also undergoing modification.

Sgt. Ryan's bullying and his philosophy of "Obey, do and die", I was finding unethical and inconsistent with the caring training I was now receiving with the emphasis on the rights and wrongs of one's moral duty and obligations to the sick and wounded of the army.

A good part of my leisure time was used in exploring the castle and its environs. I was a resident of the castle and was free to explore without the restrictions placed on visitors and sightseers.

The castle was "my home" and no part of it was out of bounds. There was not a nook or cranny anywhere in the castle or its grounds that escaped my attention.

Likewise the City of Edinburgh, in the company of Topper Higgins, I visited all sites of historical interest from Holyrood Palace to the Forth Bridge.

After being hemmed in by mountains in a narrow valley, and spending part of my teenage years working in a dark hole in the ground, to arrive in this beautiful city and live in a castle overlooking it, and to have successfully made a real friend, was fantasy posing as reality.

Having obtained my Second Class Nursing status, my duties on the wards became more onerous. I was also now available for night duties.

Amongst the complement of the hospital staff were six female nurses, members of the Queen Alexandra's Imperial Nursing Service or Q.A.'s, as they were more commonly known.

The hospital matron was a middle-aged motherly person and addressed as Sister Dorrell. Her red cape sported a fine array of Campaign ribbons. For some reason or another she took a great deal of interest in my wellbeing and when on duty would always talk to me, and occasionally would on some pretext summon me into her office where I would be invited to partake of tea and biscuits.

The favouritism shown by the matron was the source of much merriment and speculation by my roommates. The attention by the matron, I attributed to the fact I was the youngest member of her staff. I also looked younger than my age, evoking in her the mother instinct laying dormant in her spinsterhood.

The female nurses were of officer status and to be addressed as ma'am. I respected and worked well with all the female staff, with the exception of a twenty year old student Q.A. She spoke with a cut-glass accent, and pranced about the wards with an air of superiority. Whenever I had cause or reason to talk to her, she would adopt a patronising and condescending attitude towards me.

There was once an when occasion I invited serious trouble for myself. She interfered with my "expertise" and questioned my knowledge when I was changing and dressing a nasty gash on the leg of a young soldier.

I told her I knew quite well what I was doing and it was not the first time I had changed a dressing, and perhaps I could teach her a thing or two about the skills involved in the dressing of wounds.

She was taken aback by my riposte to her questioning and appeared to be very hurt. She turned and walked away in silence.

She was a Q.A. nurse, with the status of an officer. For the remainder of the day, I was on tenterhooks wondering if she had reported me to matron or the personnel officer.

The afternoon of the following day, I was again changing the same dressing, when the young Q.A. came by, stood and again watched me. On completion of my task, I started to walk past her, she touched me on the shoulder; I turned to face her, whereupon she said she was very sorry if she had upset me yesterday. That was not her intention.

I replied to this gentle apology by saying I was slightly upset, but it was no excuse for my rudeness towards her. We looked into each other's eyes and smiled. This was my first encounter with a girl from a different background to mine. My prejudices and indifference went up in smoke. I liked her from that moment, and I knew she liked me.

Our mutual antipathy at the time was of a subconscious social and class basis, creating an invisible barrier which we both crossed by the spontaneous act of humility in acknowledging our faults, together with the realisation that first impressions can be woefully misleading.

We became very close friends both on duty and clandestinely when off duty. Our ranking positions and the officer mentality of the military hierarchy precluded us from openly pursuing what I am certain would have been a very rewarding relationship. I was sorry and unhappy to see Audrey Featherstone leave the castle after six months, to continue her training elsewhere.

I recall this episode to remind me that people are not always what they seem to be.

It is the nature of youth to yearn and seek the company of the opposite sex. Wile, guile and lies are the tools used in pursuit of the quarry.

Whereas I was not a novice in the resulting climax of the chase, I was very much an amateur in the art of the hunt. There never was a need to chase Priscilla; she was always there and ready for the asking.

My friend Topper was a craftsman of some repute in the methods of approaches to girls and bade me to learn the craft from him when out and about on the hunt.

Having been brought up in the company of five sisters, I was always happy and comfortable in the presence of girls. For me to follow Topper's example of some kind of "ad hoc" relationship was quite out of the question. For me it was all or nothing.

My "eccentric" days and nights involvement and intimacy with Priscilla was the touchstone of my future behaviour and conduct when associating with members of the opposite sex.

I would seek their company, enjoy their closeness and conversations, with the thought of sex forever present. The act or any attempt of fulfilling the act was always absent. My libido was in suspension and would remain so over the decade to come, or until a girl with my ideal of Priscilla's characteristics, personality and charm would appear.

The smell of crushed grass beneath a soft, warm yielding body, the sensuous pleasure of adolescent love furtively tasted in Joby Henderson's meadow would linger on awhile.

My curiosity had been satisfied, my desires put on hold.

Subconscious celibacy was the mood of the decade, and would prevail until my ideal woman would make an entry into my life.

The cultural side of my existence as a young miner was varied. The valley was very conscious of its geographical isolation. It compensated for this by creating a number of self-financing, diverse activities available to all. Choirs, drama and elocution classes, a well-stocked library, chess clubs and debating societies.

There was enthusiasm and encouragement from parents and teachers. The youth become active participants in these ventures which were seen as educational and uplifting, as well as a diversion and release from the routine labours of a precarious existence.

I was an avid reader of the library's books, and a member of a chess club and debating society.

We may have been cut off and unworldly, but we were certainly not by any stretch of the imagination a crowd of cave dwelling philistines.

My cultural education in the army was non-existent.

Thinking for oneself was not allowed, politics and religion were taboo subjects, books and newspapers were invisible. There was no room set aside for quite contemplation or relaxation.

The soldier's physical wellbeing is the predominant factor in the army's curriculum. That his mind is being atrophied in the process is of little consequence.

Once when my room mates were teasing me about life in the "caves" up in those Welsh hills, I blurted out the fact that most of my "cave" friends were good chess players and could quote the classics, and in a moment of pique I posed the question, "how many of you can play chess or quote the classics?"

Silence reigned, the reply to my question went unanswered, the teasing continued.

A few dates later Thompson and Topper said they would like to learn the game of chess and would I teach them the rules. If I agreed, Thompson would approach the welfare officer with a view of obtaining a grant for the purchase of a chess set and placing it in the recreation room.

I agreed, Thompson true to his word succeeded in obtaining a first class set of chessmen and board. Thereafter I spent many happy hours with Thompson and Topper, teaching them the rules of the game. They were both very keen, and eventually became good players, especially Thompson; he was a natural player. On many occasions he proved to me that I was not such a good player as I thought.

My Christmas leave was a welcome break, also a relief to get away from being called Taffy and to hear my correct name being used for a change.

I had not been some since last Christmas - a whole year.

Everybody had changed except my father. He was still chained to the world he had created inside himself. Withdrawn, introvert, and moody, with only an occasional attempt at showing some interest in regards to the health, welfare and education of his offsprings.

Ethel was away from home and a nurse. Glyn was an apprentice carpenter, Olwen and Peggy in grammar school, Betsi and Arfon in Elementary school, Jean the baby, toddling and chattering.

My mother had adapted gracefully to the unperceptable changes taking place in her family.

I walked the mountain with Tim by my side, to the old valley in the hope of meeting some friends of "yesterday."

I was disappointed; most of them had moved to new locations and new occupations.

The valley was dying; only one pit remained working, part time. Its closure was imminent.

My five "best friends" were scattered around the country, with the ubiquitous Christmas card keeping us in touch, which we exchanged without fail, with little snippets of personal information within the greetings.

Priscilla had renounced her polyandrous inclination and became a trainee officer in the probation service. Bobbie was radio telegrapher in the Royal Navy; Brinley was a top trumpeter in the Military School of Music. Dai had moved with his family to another valley and was still working in the pit. Billy was somewhere in London, living rough with no fixed address.

During the Christmas leave my sense of belonging became a puzzle. I knew that I could never take up residence in any of the valleys or work there again.

Rusting pithead gear, ugly slag heaps, and dilapidated terraced hovels, were not subjects for my nostalgia.

The mountains, the ponies, the secret hiding places, the long grass of Joby's meadow, my lost friends, my extended family, will be sorely missed and the cause of some melancholy.

My military career was coming to its end. The Whitehall recruiting officer had signed me on for three years in the regular army and seven years on the reserve. I looked forward to my reversion to civilian status, without the slightest trepidation.

My three years security in an ordered regime of precision and disciplined routine, of passivity, devoid of decision making was to be exchanged for the chaotic uncertainties of a "normal life".

My release from submissiveness and servility to the freedom of making my own decisions, right or wrong, offset any lingering doubts I may have had about my pending discharge. I would decide whether or not I needed a shave.

My service in the R.A.M.C. and absence from my extended family was a period of profound change in my perception of people and things.

The army I found to be an organisation with hidden socialist tendencies, and of comradeship, where Dumas's cry of his musketeers, "one for all, all for one", is encouraged in its recruits.

The disciplining of all for the protection of one is an essential part of military doctrine.

This teamwork combined with the dubious principle of invincibility and the conviction of each soldier of his own immortality drives armies of men forward to their mutual annihilation and the destruction of everything that impedes their progress.

One for all, and all for one is a commendable aim. The methods used in teaching and maintaining this formula, I declare, is undignified and primitive.

This organisation is also coy about defining the gory details behind the glamour of uniforms, marching bands, parades with flying colours and the cheers of the crowds.

It is only when the soldier discovers the realities behind the glamour, of mean fear, servility, bombs, bullets, flies on jam, corpses on the parapet, men covered in lice and blood and the machine of which he is but a cog crushing people and rolling on, will the diabolical absurdity of the whole thing infuriate him. His life ending in rat holes, blood, and stinking chemical and napalm atrocities.

Being aware of these potential horrors did not impinge in any way on my consciousness.

The army's training and preparation for these horrible eventualities is always ongoing. Whereas at the same time for fear of its negative effects, nothing is ever done or said to counter the denial syndrome, that part of a soldier's psyche that sends him to his death.

The trained soldier brushes aside as a delusion the probabilities of him becoming a victim of napalm incineration or of his disappearance in a bomb blast.

This denial is endemic in all armies and is the oxygen of war.

Another feature of the army's dichotomy I found intriguing is its absence of hate in the training programme.

A soldier is trained to be aggressive before, and during the kill, but he is not required, neither is he instructed, to hate those "whom he is about to destroy."

It is only after the politicos designate an enemy and truth is derogated to the bottom of her well, that hate is manufactured and purveyed with glee by the press and radio. With regards to soldiers during events of peace, it is my experience to have listened to, and seen more hate and calculated xenophobia in ten minutes of civilian life than in my years of services.

These disciplined men ignore the mob-ridden tabloids, and the tabloid-ridden mob. They will hate when they are ordered to by their C.O., until then a pox on both their houses.

The armed forces during "events" of peace, (these events were short-lived in my century), is a benign monster. Caring for and nurturing its own as it quietly goes about its business of training in preparation for war.

The service man after the completion of his repackaging and conditioning is like a coiled spring, harmless, unobtrusive and quiet. But on release his power, ferocity and will for destruction is terrifying.

He is disciplined and conditioned to respond on command, to place his fore finger on a little red button, and "press", and at a distance of thousands of miles, obliterate people he does not know and cities he has never seen. Without pity and imagination.

My service in the R.A.M.C. was during peace; therefore there was no reason for me to suffer or participate in this dark and sinister side of the army's "raison d'être" This was to be in the future.

It was chance, and a kind recruiting officer, that enrolled me into the army's medical service and not into the guards or a line regiment. One of the results of this fortuitous happening, was during my training where I became very domesticated. I could make beds, cook, launder, clean house, and was proficient at all domestic chores.

The training also gave me knowledge and awareness of my body. How to keep myself fit and healthy by good food, exercise, and normal living, and not to abuse it by laziness and carelessness.

Above all it taught me the skills of first aid and nursing and gave me the opportunity to see Scotland, be a resident of a historic castle, overlooking a beautiful city.

The effect on me of the Medical Corps semi-civilian status and of the life I was living, was of a positive nature outweighing the petty regulations, personal indignities, and inability to complain.

My perception of daily life and of the people I was coming in contact with was also being reassessed.

Calloused hands, scarred with broken fingernails, had been the accepted cost of my working life. Not any more. The carefully manicured hands of the "counter jumpers", the genteel office clerks, penpushers, and nursing staff I was witnessing and working with was a model for my hands, which over these past couple of years had become unscarred, smooth, and well cared for.

I often glanced at them to compare with the hands of not so long ago; that scraped coal into a box, shoved it along a dark tunnel, and concluded that penpushing in the sunlight of day in a comfortable office was a better and easier way of earning a living, than pushing coal in dim lamplight along dark and dangerous places. It was also patently obvious that clean and well-manicured hands were of greater value in price, social esteem, and respect than hands with scars, callouses, and broken nails, from honest hard work.

The circumscription of my life to the cul-de-sac of a small mining village with its community in the midst of nowhere was at an end.

The runaway London impulse, was the key that opened the way to a new kind of life. A time of excitement adventure, pain, terror and finally to great happiness.

It was also the same key that locked away the past, of a blighted valley where a free and happy childhood, the sympathetic and passionate friendships of innocent adolescence was endured and strengthened in conditions of extreme deprivation and harshness.

Three years exactly from the day I was inducted into the army, I was instructed to report to the orderly room. There I was informed of the procedure for my transfer from the regulars to the army reserve.

At the end of the process I was given a discharge book with details of my service and reference to my character written therein.

With this document in my possession, I ceased to be a soldier in His Majesty's Regular Army. Although I was "still one of his subjects", I was no longer under constraint to jump on command immediately, and on the double. I could also reclaim my ability to talk on equal terms with authority without standing to attention with eyes front.

I was re-classified as civilian with permission to revert to type, wander back to the crowd and on to the dole.

Corporal Walsh wished me good luck as I handed back my uniform, battle kit and bedding.

I then returned to the orderly room to collect a railway warrant, my army pay and money in lieu of civilian clothes.

Topper Higgins and my room mates were on duty, our goodbyes having been exchanged at breakfast.

The only pang of regret I experienced was of leaving Topper, the only friend I had succeeded in making during my years of service.

CHAPTER FIVE

Civvy Street and its Perils

My train was leaving Waverley Station at noon. Waiting on the platform, my thoughts returned to the day I arrived in Scotland. A dark, cold, snowy February day and my eighteenth birthday.

Here and now I was leaving Scotland on a warm sunny August day and not yet twenty one years old, with a future undetermined and no idea of what I would do back in the village.

The nursing and domestic skills I had acquired were of value only in the army's male environment. In civilian medical establishments, nursing was very gender orientated as female only. A male interloper - in such a closed female profession at the time would have been as welcomed as a dose of syphilis in a nunnery.

I would have to forgo any hope of work where my R.A.M.C. expertise would be valued.

Coal mining was for me the only alternative method I knew of earning a living in the valleys, and that most definitely was a non-starter in my book.

I would sign on the dole and wait for something else to turn up.

I arrived home, three years and two weeks from the day I ran to London. A much changed person in every respect, after my peep over the horizon to the view of the wider world.

I knew of a life of possibilities if given the opportunity and my willingness to take advantage when the time came.

I signed on the dole, was registered as an unskilled labourer and ex-service man. The official at the desk informed me in a most patronising of manner, as an ex-service man, I was a prime candidate for government jobs that gave priority to ex-service men, such as postmen.

I had no intention of being a postman, or any kind of government man. I told the official clerk he must be joking, grinned and walked out into the fresh air.

My time whilst waiting for something to turn up was spent in enjoying the freedom and loosening the shackles of three years of tight control over my destiny.

I walked the mountain, visiting childhood haunts admiring the views of afar, and only now noticed by me for the first time.

Up here with the munching sheep and the song of the ascending skylark, I was on familiar territory. Where hopes and adolescent fantasies were wished and conjured up.

Down there in the world of people, I was living in a state of uniform dullness, broken only by the tedious routine of artificially stimulated excitement, where tabloid man and that embodiment of the mob "the man in the street" with their chattery and smattery and sham gentility roamed, and polluted everything they touched.

My re-classification and re-entrance into civilian life I found to be an almost identical pattern of conformity as I had left.

Years of tight discipline, with an emphasis on "You will do whatever you are told to do!", during the mental conditioning, was also flourishing out here in "civvy street."

I was perplexed by the disciplined mass mind, the phenomena of its divorce from the human mind and its propensity to conform. I was seeing mass man, "Tabloid man" as a mirror image of military man without uniform. I knew exactly what he is going to say because like his mirror image he is not allowed to think.

He responds and obeys the organised and fallacious cliches, half-truths and catchwords that are continually pumped into him. He is a kind of incarnate headline. He does not talk, he rustles like the leaves of a newspaper. I was at home up there with the sheep.

My second week of signing on the dole, a fellow in the queue asked if I was "new around here?" I said I was. We talked and he told me his ambitions. He was married with one child and had been out of work for six months.

Some of his spare time was taken up in attending classes sponsored by the W.E.A. (Workers' Educational Association) I told him that I too had lots of spare time and would like to join the W.E.A. classes. Arrangements were made to meet whereupon he would introduce me to people who would facilitate my entry.

In the building which held the W.E.A. classes, I was ushered into an office where a very severe looking man was sitting behind a desk, laden with books and papers of all kinds. He had the look of my old headmaster in appearance and manner of approach. He enquired of my reason for wanting to attend classes.

I told him I had been in the army and was out of contact with civilian life and would like to catch up. (I made that up as I went along, I could not tell him that I had time on my hands and was bored). He did not fall off his chair or look upon my earth-shattering reply with much enthusiasm. He simply mumbled "Oh yes! Give me your name and address and we will contact you."

I said my name was Alun Menai Williams. Before I could go any further he asked if I was any relation to Huw Menai the poet. I said he was my father. This time he nearly did fall off his chair. He stood up took my hand and said "This is a surprise. I know your father very well; your family and their troubled past, and I heard them speak of you. My name is John Noble; tell your dad that you have been speaking to me."

With that I was immediately enrolled as a pupil in classes of the Workers' Educational Association.

He advised me what classes to attend and what subjects to study; he also piled me with literature relevant to the W.E.A. and its objectives.

When I arrived back at the house, I told my mother that I had enrolled into classes of the W.E.A. and that John Noble the Principal, knew my father.

"Yes, he was a great help when we were evicted and in trouble and has been so ever since. He was mainly responsible for obtaining the house we are now living in. Your father and John Noble have been friends for many years" she replied.

This friendship was to my advantage in the weeks that followed. Secret nepotism resulted in my application to Coleg Harlech being accepted.

I was to become a resident student on a four month course in political science and economics. All fees including dole contribution paid by the W.E.A.

This was a very rewarding four months. My communal living experience hitherto was of regimentation, precision, order and discipline. It took me a few days to get used to and settle down to a free-for-all chaotic and unruly way of living, in a dormitory full of young intellectuals, pseudo and genuine.

The radicalism of my formative years in the valley with my friends and at the coalface with my butties, had become dormant by the repackaging and subsequent servility by the army.

It was now being awakened by the revolutionary and conspiratorial fervour by many of my new companions of the "left."

The atmosphere of the Coleg was of a pervading sense of urgency, in the educational attainment of its students.

Books, newspapers and periodicals of every political persuasion were freely available. Lost opportunities sidelined in favour of new opportunities now available to enhance one's potential in a setting of geographical beauty with the adult teaching and learning facilities.

I could do no other than compare my presence in this establishment of learning where mental exercises and intellectual stimuli were pursued with great gusto and purpose. There was such a contrast with my past years devoid and barren of mental effort in favour of the physical and brutish impulses encouraged and strengthened by the teachings of Sgt. Ryan.

During this particular period of "my century", anti-fascism was a "crank" "ism" practised by intellectual crackpots and communist sympathisers, and to all intents and purposes a waste of time on a lost cause. Benito Mussolini and his fascist movement was of little importance to the "masses". To the inner circles of the political elite and the press barons it was an Italian state supporting an official anti-communist movement and not to be discouraged, even if it was state controlled capitalism, and anti-parliamentarian. Mussolini's rubber truncheons, purgative treatment and imprisonment of the opposition was of concern to me and my fellow students.

My increased awareness of fascism with its destructive and insidious ethology of ethnic superiority, was being reinforced by the revolutionary and conspiratorial theories of the company I was now living with. We were a bunch of active anti-fascists long before the country and most of its people were awake to what Hitler and Mussolini were plotting and preparing.

I finished my course at Coleg Harlech a much wiser, more educated and mature person than on entering.

Six months later, Adolf Hitler became Chancellor and Dictator of the Third Reich.

The portrayal and characterisation of Hitler and Mussolini in the press of the day was as a Chaplinesque idiot and Italian buffoon. As subjects of ridicule this was symptomatic of the official garbage portrayed by a perverse coterie of compliant journalists at the behest of newspaper barons.

These two characters became the greatest mass murderers, rapists and pillagers the world had ever witnessed, who at the onset were known by the brave few for the potential catastrophe that lay ahead if their twisted philosophy prevailed.

These few were ignored by the many at the cost later of millions of lives and the destruction of priceless treasures.

The portrayal of these monsters as jokey figures of fun, not to be taken seriously, but ridiculed and laughed at, was seen by the antifascists as journalistic obscenity. The majority were deaf to the cries of the suffering victims of these evil men.

My four months acquaintance be it of a fleeting kind, with Adam Smith's 'Wealth of Nations' and David Ricardo's 'Principles of Political Economy' whetted my appetite for more.

It was not to be; my time of learning in the company of experts was at an end.

Back to the dole queue, and the inevitable waiting for something to turn up, or perhaps more to the point of a positive move by me to make it turn up.

My return to the domestic scene and my continual presence in the vicinity of my father, was a cause of some unease. I was having difficulty in suppressing my disgust and anger with the periodical outbursts of blame and fault that he still heaped upon my mother without reason or rational explanation.

I was also very aware that the notice to quit and my subsequent skedaddle had not been rescinded by gesture or innuendo. Furthermore I appreciated if this father-son antagonism was left to fester, it would contaminate the family. Sides would be taken and quarrelling would ensue. To me there is nothing in the world so silly as quarrelling. I would remove myself from the danger as soon as possible.

The house now occupied by my family was not my "home." I had lived there only for four weeks before I left for London. My "home" was away in a valley some three miles walk over a mountain where resided my extended family and friends, and where lingered my memories. I was a stranger in my parents' house, henceforth my home would be wherever I pitched my tent. My parental home emptied of me to return only as a visitor to the house they called their home.

During my absence the family had adapted and adjusted well to the post eviction hassle. My absence was taken for granted, I was the elder brother living away from home, unknown to either their new friends or neighbours.

Not long after my return from Coleg Harlech, a notice was displayed in the dole office, inviting applicants to apply for training in a variety of industrial skills. A choice of trades and location of the training centres was also listed and including the provision of free board and lodging. One of these centres was at Letchworth, the other at Park Royal, London.

The opportunity to move had arrived. I applied for Park Royal; the London magnet was irresistible. The problem with this option was all courses with the exception of precision fitting were complete. It was precision fitting at Park Royal or bricklaying at Letchworth. I wanted London so I became a precision fitter trainee.

Board and lodging was in a house close to Wormwood Scrubs prison and within walking distance to and from Park Royal training centre. There were five other occupants, all trainees, in the lodgings. Sparse but clean and comfortable, ample and wholesome the food.

I did not have a clue of what precision fitting was or entailed. My first day of training was all the education I needed to know that precision fitting was not my metier. I was given a piece of steel about eight inches long by four inches wide and directed by the instructor to a bench fitted with a vice, whereon the piece of metal was placed and clamped. I was handed a file with which the instructor had demonstrated the correct way to file a piece of metal to size. Steady one directional movements deliberate and with slight pressure. With the perfunctory lesson finished he went to the next pupil. I filed the steady one directional movement for the remainder of the day by which time the steel bar had been reduced to seven and half inches by three and half inches, with the sides neatly rounded, as instructed. This kind of activity was a daily routine, interspersed with lessons of how to read and manipulate a micrometer, the qualities and capabilities of different files, and the importance of precision measurements for the correct functioning of mechanical movement.

The weekends from Saturday noon until Monday morning were free. Some of this free time I spent in the company of other trainees exploring the city, learning to smoke cigarettes and drink beer. Other times I preferred my own company, enjoying the antics of speakers and hecklers at Speakers' Corner and attending various left wing meetings and anti-fascist rallies whenever the opportunity occurred. The radicalism of my adolescence which had been quiescent too long after its awakening at Coleg Harlech was now sitting up and taking notice. This London environment was right, the times were right.

During one of my trips to Hyde Park, I revisited the site of my tea boy labours, to admire the beautiful Gaumont Cinema now attracting crowds of filmgoers and which I had a hand in building. At least I kept the sweating brickies thirst assuaged with tea and biscuits as they piled together the bricks and mortar. Looking at the building I found I was also looking at myself. The naivete, ignorance and innocence of youth during my first London excursion, was inexorably moving away and being replaced by a sense of disbelief at the self interest and lack of social awareness and responsibility I was encountering during my daily intercourse with people. The vulgarity, cheap cynicism and sneering selfishness of a grab and cheat system of values. Where snobocracy ruled and where the main aim in life is how to get money and more money, where to spend it, how to avoid the consequences of having less, where to put it so that nobody else could get at it. How to die with plenty, and live with little. During these past few years my education from ignorant pit boy to a sophisticated city dweller was progressing apace. I now possessed a wrist watch and was a cheat.

My training course was scheduled to last six months, without a guarantee of a job at the end. I lasted four weeks. I had no intention of becoming a precision fitter, filing away behind a bench in a dirty, noisy factory and measuring lumps of metal to size.

I was twenty one years old with a yearning for freedom of all restrictions and restraints. I was not yet ready for industrial or commercial imprisonment.

During the walk back and forth from the lodgings to the Training Centre, a short cut was made through and across the forecourt of a petrol station at Gypsy Corner. One day I saw a notice on the window of the petrol station "Pump attendant required." I applied and as reference or background were of very little importance I was accepted on face value. The wages were two pounds and ten shilling for six days with alternative Saturdays off. With split shifts of eight am to five pm and two pm until ten pm. After my acceptance of the job I enquired of the landlady if she would keep me on as a paying lodger independent of the Training Centre and the price for my board lodge. A satisfactory arrangement was agreed of twenty five bob per week for bed breakfast and evening meal.

My job at the petrol station was in the company of a wide cockney boy of my age. Six pumps were manned between us and we were together on both shifts. The pumps were modern for the period and hand operated. A two gallon glass tank was on the top of each pump, which were filled by the pumping action of a handle at the side of each pump. When the glass was full the delivery hose was inserted into the car's petrol tank and gravity fed.

The glass had to be pumped full every two gallons.

The amount dispensed was shown on a clock face meter on the front of the pump. After each sale was completed, the meter was turned back to zero.

My cockney companion had been with the garage and on the pumps for eighteen months. He was quick, efficient, and friendly with a quirky sense of humour and a "crook".

He had discovered a method of manipulating the pumps to the disadvantage of the garage owners and to the advantage of the pump's operators.

For his system to work without fear of discovery he was obliged to take me into his confidence and split the proceeds of his swindle, which on average on a weekly basis came to twenty five shillings each.

I accepted this illegal bounty willingly, without a qualm, even though I knew I was cheating and the accomplice of a cheat.

I excused myself and took refuge in the knowledge that the "pin stripe" umbrella and his ilk in their exclusive West End Clubs, relaxing in their Chesterfields, sipping gin and tonic, and smoking fat cigars were "respected" cheats on a grand scale.

Robbing nations on the pretext of Empire Trading, swindling each other with their secret deals and insider trading and back-stabbing each other in the most gentlemanly of ways.

I was a bumbling nobody amateur without emulative aspirations in comparison, whose illegal gains were less than the price of one of their banded Havana cigars.

The price of petrol was one shilling and sixpence a gallon for Benzole and Ethyl and one shilling and threepence for R.O.P. (Russian Oil Products). This cheaper brand was the fuel of the few working class and secondhand car owners. The majority of customers were the well-heeled city types, entrepreneurs and commercial tycoons. In their Humber Hillman's, Armstrong Siddleys, Austin Saloons and Rolls Royce's. A good proportion of the Rolls Royce's were chauffeur driven and in the ownership of persons in the entertainment, show business, and theatre world. A few were generous in their tipping, "Keep the change, lad", was a pleasant sound.

Our duties as well as servicing the vehicles was to collect payment, take it to the office and return with the change, if any. The customer remained seated, he rarely stood outside his car.

There were exceptions, one such chauffeur with his Rolls Royce and passenger in the rear seat, would always select me for the required service.

The car would pull up at the pump I would be operating at the time. The passenger would vacate his seat, stand outside the car and chat to me about generalities as I went about my business of filling the car's petrol tank. When full, the chauffeur would lean out of the window and hand me the money. I would return from the office with the change and told to keep it.

After the completion of the transaction with the driver, the person with whom I had been in conversation would give me two half crowns and a complimentary ticket to the theatre where he was performing at the time.

Ivor Novello then bade me a good day, entered his car and drove away. The routine with this gentleman never altered during my time as a petrol pump attendant at the Gypsy Corner Garage on Western Avenue.

At times of inactivity on the pumps, I learned to drive a motor car. Tutored by none other than my cockney companion. I also obtained a driver's licence which cost five shillings and no test. Thereafter I was free to drive a motorbike or a double decker bus.

I enjoyed my job as a petrol pump attendant. I liked the open air and the rain on my face. I liked meeting people and the freedom from authority. I liked the money, I no longer liked my mate as he was getting greedy.

The thought of Bobby Beynon waiting around the corner with bread, water and dangling handcuffs ready to pounce was a daunting and terrifying prospect, demanding of a solution.

I gave one week's notice and quit. After six weeks of a pleasant undemanding occupation I had become a victim of the grab and cheat ethics of a society in which I was becoming part of and embroiled in.

The economic depression was gaining momentum, unemployment was becoming institutionalised, with poverty endemic in the industrial heartland and the coal fields.

It was extremely foolish of me to quit a reasonably paid and secure job in the hope of finding an alternative.

The main motive for what seemed an act of crass stupidity, was of a moral concern at the time with my conduct in the unusual and criminal situation in which I was involved, as an active participant.

My natured behavioural conduct was finding its self at variance and out of "sync" with my perception of city behaviour. Where amorality and normality were inclusive without any blurring at the edges.

I was unemployed, my funds were running low and I was ineligible for the dole. I had left a job of my own accord without reason.

I applied for a variety of jobs without success. I was desperate; if I did not find work soon, I would be thrown out of my lodgings.

Scanning the vacancy columns in the Evening Standard, I came across an advert. The London Passenger Transport Board wanted men of certain specifications as 'platform attendants.'

In my desperation I applied. I fitted the required specifications. I was accepted; the compulsory medical and intelligence tests were in my favour.

Within days, I became a trainee of the L.P.T.B., complete with uniform, free travel pass and instructions to report at eight o'clock on Monday morning at the Station Master's office at Marble Arch Tube Station.

During the past ten weeks, I had travelled on the underground trains, waited on platforms, and negotiated the stairs and escalators all very natural and problem-free.

The first few hours of my first day's work at Marble Arch Station was trouble-free of incidents.

I did all I was asked to the best of my ability. I swept, polished, emptied bins and swilled the toilet floor. As the day wore on I found I was avoiding people. I wanted to be quiet with a great desire to be on my own. I was becoming agitated and anxious without cause or comprehension.

I took to a bench at the far end of the platform, sat down in an attempt to "pull myself together" and away from a mental process taking control which I did not understand.

My attention was suddenly drawn to the rumbling noise of wheels on metal, of a train pulling into the platform and the ensuing rush of commuters in and out of the carriages.

My eyes strayed and fixed on the tunnel from which the train had emerged, then switched to the tunnel at the other end and into which the train was now entering. It was all so familiar. I realised that I was once again working underground and that this was the cause of the awful sense of feeling of insecurity that I was now experiencing.

The afternoon wore on with my imagination and its hallucinatory element playing tricks on the environment I was in. Transporting me into another dimension with Marble Arch Station becoming an exact replica of the pit bottom of the Brittanic Colliery with its lights, noise, smells and steel beamed arched roof, all there and with the coal face at the end of the tunnel. By the end of the shift I was almost in a state of panic.

I clocked off, raced for the escalator, reached the surface, looked up at the sky, gave a sigh of relief and walked the three miles back to my digs.

The long walk was of a dream quality. My mental processes being engaged in self analysis, and calling into account my irrational behaviour of the day. I knew the trigger that set off such behaviour, but I couldn't fathom out why the smallest of similarities between the bottom of Marble Arch Station and the pit bottom of the Brittanic Colliery should evoke such strange emotions. I was neither claustrophobic nor fearful. That I was working underground and the irrational consequences emanating from that fact must have a Freudian explanation, because common sense was telling me loud and clear in the words of Sgt. Ryan. I was a silly stupid little man to succumb to such irrational and infantile behaviour.

I was late arriving back at my lodgings, nevertheless the landlady had kept a lovely meal for me which I ate with great relish. I had not eaten a morsel since breakfast. I took a bath and a change of clothing and went out for the evening feeling refreshed, slightly euphoric and amazed at my mental aberrations on the first day as a platform attendant.

During my session of self analysis I concocted a plan to test if I was "barmy", "going barmy" or just plain silly without cause. I presented myself at Acton North Central Line Tube station and produced my train pass. I was going to indulge in the time-honoured practice of re-visiting and repeating the offending incident. I boarded a train headed for Ruislip, disembarked at Marble Arch, walked along the platform, sat on the same bench as before, looked around and waited for the next train which I entered on its arrival, and continued the journey to the end of the line at Ruislip, where I remained on the train for the return. I again got off at Marble Arch repeating the platform exercise. I boarded the next train to South Woodward, where I remained seated for the return journey back to my starting point of Acton North and home to my digs.

I spent an evening travelling with the courtesy of the L.P.T.B. on its trains looking for dragons to slay and devils to exorcise. All in vain, I did not find a single one. There wasn't any. Instead it was a ride of curiosity, enjoyment and personal satisfaction, proving my trauma was a one-off, never to be repeated. The whole unpleasant episode was lacking for want of a logical explanation or a Freudian psychoanalytical interpretation.

I have a penchant for and a willingness to embrace the chaos theory of the Amazonian butterfly and its possible effects on my odd behaviour. The flitting of this beautiful creature, with its iridescent wings glinting in shafts of jungle sunlight, is a prettier scenario and has the same value in my book as the Freudian "mumbo jumbo" or any other interpretation of the nebulosity and intricate machinations of the human mind.

The next few weeks as an employee of the London Transport Board was trouble free. Educationally interesting and undemanding. I learned a great deal about the system, its operation and most importantly its users.

Part of my contract of employment was a requirement that I serve at any station as and when necessary. I did one week at Piccadilly Circus, where the herding instincts of "Pin stripe and umbrella man" were manifest. His upright posture, measured walk, glazed eyes, clenched teeth, sealed lips, bowler hat, umbrella, monogrammed attaché case and London Times tucked underneath his arm, is a slightly bizarre spectacle on the surface.

Down in the underground in the hurly-burly jostling, shoving strap, hanging, diverse crowd of overalled craftsmen, unkempt labourers, pretty female typists, staid office female secretaries, pimps and prostitutes, he is a walk on extra, on the wrong set.

Another oddity of the tube's conditioning effect is the classless phenomena of more worthy observance and the cause of much amusement to me. This was the resolution and ability of the commuters to avoid and resist any attempt at conversation or eye contact.

I was not aware of signs or notices forbidding this most human of human attributes talking, or a sly wink at a pretty girl.

Poor dumb, blind London commuters. Talking with anybody and everybody and winking at all the pretty girls was rampant where I came from.

It was not my intention of making a career in the transport system of the metropolis. I was always looking for a job I might be capable of doing in clean conditions and with prospects. I was certain I could do a 'pen pushing' type of work if given the opportunity. That was my aim and hope.

Eight weeks of platform attendant cum-janitor, was now broken by one day a week of shadowing the train guard (and his shout - "Mind the doors there, please"). This was a welcome and pleasant change and preferable to what had become a tiresome chore of platform sweeping and standing around looking important.

The novelty of the job had worn off. Routine and repetition was taking a grip. I was ready and anxious for a change.

The job market for young unskilled men like me was limited. The pool of both skilled and unskilled men was increasing at an alarming rate.

A change of occupation under these circumstances was out of the question. However boring or routine my workday, I was secure with bed and board assured, with wages to pay for the same.

I was a loner without any commitments, I could if possible postpone any change until a favourable opportunity presented itself. Fate would decide otherwise.

Friday evening, drawing wages and clocking off, I was told to report Monday morning for duty at Waterloo Station. This was my first stint at this station. It would also coincide with my last stint as an employee of the L.P.T.B.

I reported to the Station Master's Office as was usual, and interviewed by the Asst. Station Master, in his full gold braid uniform, who asked how long I had been with the board, my reply of nine weeks was greeted by a sarcastic "You are wet behind the ears aren't you?". I could feel the blood rushing to my cheeks, I was blushing, I was embarrassed. There were young female workers within earshot of this most unnecessary remark.

I was annoyed; my demeanour registered this fact . With a smirk on his face, he instructed one of his minions to take me to the platform foreman.

I did not like the Assistant Station Master; I was not going to like the Assistant Station Master. I had a suspicion he reciprocated my sentiments. His remarks and tone of voice with the titter at the end, plus the female audience was not conducive to a good master-servant relationship.

The foreman greeted me "nicely" by presenting me with a bucket and mop and a "Follow me" to a flight of steps at the station entrance. With instructions to mop and clean them down and when finished to report back to him.

Of late bucket and mop had become the tools of my trade, I was an expert in their use. Mopping and cleaning steps with people traipsing up and down is a difficult and frustrating operation, which over the past weeks I had learned to cope with in a reasonable and efficient manner without complaint.

I leisurely went about my duties of mopping and cleaning with my standard apologies of "Excuse me" and "I'm sorry" directed at the steps users who were on their way to kicking the bucket or impeding the actions of the mop.

With the last step cleaned to my satisfaction, I repositioned the bucket, placed both hands on top of the mop handle and looked back to admire my handiwork.

The bumptious gold braided little officer of the metropolis's underground rail network crept to my side and enquired if I had finished. "Yes" was my reply. Without further ado he commenced walking slowly up the steps, on reaching the top, he reversed and descended at the same pace, until he reached the bottom. He stopped looked down at his feet. "Those steps are not very clean, do them again", he said.

This was the second time in the space of a couple of hours, this dressed up 'ninny' had interfered with my circulatory system, I could feel the blood rising and this time in my whole body, from the tips of my toes to the lobes of my ears.

He was slightly below average height. I raised myself to my full six feet two inches, looked down on him and posed the question, "Are you asking me, or telling me to mop the steps again?" His answer was "I am neither asking you or telling you, I am ordering you."

The blood reached my eyes, I saw red. The dam burst, the bomb exploded, the balloon went up, all hell broke loose!

Up to this split second, I was a highly trained disciplined and conditioned individual. Programmed to take orders, obey and respect authority.

This little pip squeak released me from years of restraint. He had misjudged and breached the fine dividing line between the exercise of authority and bullying. I would disobey, I would resist, I would answer back which I did with pleasure and elan.

He shifted his gaze from his foot inspection, looked at me, mouth agape partly in shock and partly in terror, when I told him in my best army vocabulary and in the vernacular that he could anatomically dispose of my job. At the same time, I flung the wet mop at his chest, kicked the bucket of water over his feet, gave him the obligatory two finger salute, smartly about turned and marched triumphantly up the offending steps with pride and dignity intact, and mighty pleased to boot.

I was glad that my underground railway experiment had ended. It was for me an odd experience both physically and mentally. I was also pleased I had terminated the whole miserable episode on my terms.

My public display of anger and intemperate verbalisation on the concourse of Waterloo Station is one of the most cherished moments of my life.

My respect for the London Tube workers is boundless. It is an unenvious occupation, which bequeathed me with memories of an ambivalent nature.

Unemployed and on the dole was becoming a habit to which I had no fundamental objection. Other than the perennial necessity of bed and board and the predilection of the landlady in her demand for monetary recompense for these services.

The search for work could wait. I would take a holiday, see my mother, brothers and sisters. The few pounds I had saved together with my quarterly army reserve pay of £15 would see me through a couple of weeks.

I packed my railway uniform into a neat parcel labelled it with my name and clock number and packed a suitcase with all my worldly possessions. I thanked the landlady for her kindness, and made my way to Acton North tube station where I dumped the uniform into the care of the ticket collector and proceeded to Paddington Station for my journey to Cardiff and the Rhondda Valley. My mother and siblings were happy to see me as I was to see them.

Everyday I was being asked "How long will you be staying?" And every day I would reply, "Until you get fed up of seeing me around."

My father, I am sure was very pleased to see me, but was very circumspect in other ways. He never personally questioned me about my life since leaving home, or how I was managing to survive. He would however be very attentive at meal times when I was questioned and teased by my mother and sisters.

His "tantrums" were now subdued and of less frequency according to my mother. She had also arrived at the stage of accepting her life being played out day by day with some days good and some days not so good. She also told me his writing had increased and more of his work and poetry was being published, especially in the Western Mail, with the odd cheque coming in the post.

CHAPTER SIX

Pimps, Prostitutes, Drop-outs and Anarchists

I walked the mountain to my old valley with the intention of calling on the parents of my friend Billy in the hope of being furnished with his last known address.

They were pleased to see me. I answered endless questions about myself, my mother and father before I could make my request regarding Billy's life and where he was living it.

They told me that Phillip had been discharged from the army and was now with his brother Billy somewhere up there in the "smoke". The last card they received some three to four months ago was without a return address.

I was disappointed with that information which was slightly alleviated when she mentioned that Ifor, one of the thirteen of my eccentric days was visiting his mother, (Ifor was the club's Treasurer).

She had been talking to him; "He had a good job in London," and she gained the impression he had seen Billy a few times, but was not sure where he lived. I said my goodbyes to Mr & Mrs Davies, and promptly made for Ifor's house some three to four minutes walk to the end of the terrace.

The front door was open, I stood at the entrance and called out Ifor's name, "Good God, that's Alun. Come on in!". He met me at the entrance, and we shook hands, pleased to see each other.

He took me into the little living room wherein were his mother and sister. We were not strangers, we had everything in common.

The conversation for the next hour revolved around a series of "Do you remember?", and where was who and who was doing what, and who with.

Ifor looked well, he was tall and good looking, with an infective smile and a wicked sense of humour, like other members of the "eccentric" club - a loyal and dependable friend.

Trust without question was one of the unspoken intangible assets. It was this which was missing in my life on leaving the valley and a possible cause of my inability to make friends. I was completely at ease with Ifor, likewise he was with me.

He suggested we take a walk to the local inn and talk about ourselves over a glass of beer.

He was smartly dressed in a well-cut bespoke double breasted suit, with a button through shirt, quiet striped tie, trilby hat and patent leather shoes. The acme of a typical prosperous business man visiting his poor country relatives.

I congratulated him on his sartorial elegance and opined the fact he must have a very good job to afford such expensive attire.

"I'll tell you all about it when we get inside the pub," he said.

He commenced his oral biography with a bald statement. He was one hell of a liar to his parents, his relatives, the neighbours or anyone else of a prying tendency.

He purported to be the manager and part owner of a lucrative bookmaking business in London's East End. He also admitted the only thing he knew about book making was when he gambled on the dogs at White City which he said was his pastime, work, and hobby.

"OK!" I replied, "But what exactly do you do for a living?" He looked at me straight in the eyes and with that infectious smile breaking out, he said "I live with a prostitute. I am her pimp, she earns big money and she shares it with me."

I was surprised, slightly shaken but at the same time very impressed by this forthright revelation.

My knowledge of the seamy Soho scene and the seedy hidden side of city night life and its "knocking shop" image of pandering to the whore-mongering extra marital proclivities of the respected family man, or the rampant incontinent promiscuity of the young man, had come a long way since my early and naïve encounter with prostitutes in the company of a Yorkshire Guardsman recruit and a wide cockney boy cavalry recruit.

During my work on the Tube, I was occasionally on speaking terms with some of these "fallen" girls, especially on my turn at Piccadilly Circus. Beneath the economic confusion which existed, there was an ongoing malaise infecting the moral development of the nation, of which the politicians were either blind or did not care. The depression's momentum had spawned a situation where the difference between the individual and the community was becoming acute.

A society maintained upon gross inequalities, the distribution of work, enjoyment and the decencies of life was coming apart at the seams.

It is therefore no mystery that the moral chaos of the period was the mother and father of the sexual anarchy, where the bed became the work bench of hundreds of young girls and women, upon which they laboured "under" lubricious and inauspicious circumstances to maintain their husbands, children and pimps.

Ifor was only one of the many taking advantage of a prosaic decaying system, where love, beauty and romanticism is sidelined to the dreary sordid commercialism of a natural imperative.

We were living in a period favourable above all else to Ifor's way and view of life. He had become a successful entrepreneur- a money maker. He was my friend, trustworthy, loyal and dependable. I was not going to attach horns or hooves to his extremities. Ifor, myself and millions like us had become automatic products of a system of grotesque anomalies. Crying out for a change we hoped would not be impotent or destructive but of thought, attitude and values.

I responded to Ifor's declaration in a matter of fact way. The 'Thou shalt nots' of the regimen of totem and taboo of our upbringing had long ago been consigned to the bin marked "All balls", as excess baggage, not wanted on the voyage in a leaky ship of state, sailing in muddy and discoloured waters, where morality was cast adrift, when the pragmatic opportunism of the grab and cheat came aboard. Ifor was happy and content; I had no problem.

He explained in some detail his ascent or descent into his chosen profession. The difference is academic. Ifor was a procurer. His protégé was a high class 'hostess'–euphemism for an expensive prostitute.

His job was marketing her services by bribery and connivance with hotel porters, headwaiters and the like who introduced her to rich clients who enquired of the possibilities of the services of a 'hostess'. She would also be passed on and recommended by satisfied 'customers.'

I eventually got around to the question of did he know where Billy lived? The last time he saw Billy was a few weeks ago, selling the Daily Worker at the back of Paddington Station. They retired to the nearest pub where they had a long talk. According to Ifor, Billy was up to his neck in politics and obsessed with Moseley and his blackshirts. Otherwise he was fine, the same "eccentric" that we all knew and liked.

It seemed to Ifor that Billy lived not very far away from his place at Warwick Avenue, Maida Vale. He gave me his own address and insisted if or when I came back to London, I must stay with him and until I was fixed up with a place of my own. Also he had an idea where Billy lived and where I may be able to contact him.

Our confidences, personal idiosyncrasies and dark secrets safely locked away, we made our way back to Ifor's home, where a little meal had been prepared by his mother and sister, which I enjoyed, the company being the main component, after which I wished his parents good luck and goodbye. Ifor escorted me to the bus stop where he brought out a wallet bulging with notes and offered a "few quid", if I so required. I was tempted, but I said I was alright at the moment. He was disappointed at my refusal. I eased his mind by saying if I come to London, I may "bum off" him until I was settled in a job. That pleased him. He gave me his wicked smile, shook hands and a "See you again". As I boarded the bus, I had a distinct feeling it would not be too long before I would see him again. I had been home four weeks, and was getting bored. My time I used in walking the mountains, lounging around the house, visits to the local library and attending political meetings and gatherings of which there were many, and always on my own. These sedentary activities though pleasant and undemanding were no substitute or palliative for the feeling of discontent and dissatisfaction with myself. I was hankering for some kind of action and excitement. Since leaving school at fourteen my life was of hard physical work with danger, change to a regime of discipline and restraint, change to a climate of hopes and ambitions, and now freedom, unlimited, no commitments, no baggage, no job, no money but full of fanciful ideas of hopes and pie in the sky.

I would return to London; two of my best friends were there. I had Ifor's address as a base to do but of which I did not have a clue of what I was going to do or wanted to do.

This in itself was exciting enough to kid me into making a return to the city when as a young runaway with hopes, my initial perception was that Sodom and Gomorrah was just a rude musical hall joke in comparison to a corner of London Town designated as an unofficial open air brothel. Where all sexual preferences were catered for, at the cost of a haggled fee.

The next eighteen months was to be the most strange, exciting and mixed up time of my life.

I would be part of a homogenous group of people, where everyday was different, where the zest of life and the determination of its continuance involved the dislocation of tested patterns of behaviour and the denial of a substitute and amoral lifestyle.

We would be selfish, altruist, especially to each other; dishonest, cheats, charitable, and unscrupulous.

A schizophrenic attitude to this new and novel way of living prevailed. It was essential we were neither good or bad. We were victims, scavengers in the breakers' yard and scrap heaps of a sad, corrupt and bankrupt economic system of which the opinions of the financial gurus of the day had promulgated as under production or over consumption, either of which, take your choice.

The depression, boom and bust of an alternating "status quo", Poverty and plenty, turn about ad infinitum, was the political and economic climate of the day.

The phenomena of the poor, the unemployed and dispossessed accepting this situation was odd, to say the least. The dumb acquiescence to imprisonment by poverty without hope of escape or the will to resist is a typical British disability.

Token resistance was ineffective. It only served to bury aspirations of release deeper in the slough of despair.

The blaming of the all powerful "They" and the self-absolution by the impoverished of their sins of omission and inaction, was to a great extent a contributory factor in the maintenance of the misery. Myself and my contemporaries were not prepared to accept the system's attempt of our immolation in sustaining a fictional "status quo."

As the man said "If you can't change it, join it." We would attempt to do both, with one to sustain the other.

We would play the system's own game and become petty operators of the successful grab and cheat values of the major players and grab a few crumbs of the cake being withheld from us, in order to survive until the coming of the next "status quo."

I became part of this survival tactic by a conscious decision driven by circumstance and partly by the company I chose to be associated with, and my great pleasure to know, Billy, Ifor and a host of pimps, prostitutes, political activists, anarchists and drop-outs.

Paddington and its vicinity of Maida Vale, were the homes, apartments, lodgings, and hangouts of a wave of unemployed South Walesian migrants of both sexes. Sons and daughters of the poverty-stricken miners of the valleys. The majority of these young men were workless and on the dole, such as Billy and myself. Or itinerant waiters, labourers, buskers, scroungers or pimps like Ifor.

The young girls were skivvies, house maids, servants, waitresses, nannies or prostitutes like Dilys. Casualties of the depression determined to survive in a hostile environment and dubious culture. Free from the Welsh Chapel morality and parental guidance.

There was a part of Hyde Park, not far from Speakers Corner, and near the site of the Tyburn Tree, where every Sunday evening a crowd of Welsh expatriates would congregate in a nostalgic ritual of Welsh hymn singing and folk songs.

This particular part of the Park known as the "Welsh Corner", was where friendships were made, old ones revived, liaisons formed and where the "Hiraeth" for the homeland was expressed in their singing and choice of songs.

These impromptu open air concerts with impromptu conductors were also enjoyed by a large audience of onlookers.

To Billy and I and many more like us, it was a refreshing interval in the daily chore, of milking, cheating and using the system that was denying us the opportunities and chances to which we were entitled and our right.

My mother was somewhat perturbed with my intention of returning to London. What job would I do; how long would it take to get a job and how was I going to manage on seventeen shillings dole money?

When I told her I was going to live with Ifor, (who she knew had a good job), until I was on my feet, she was relieved.

I did not inform her of Ifor's profession; this incident always makes me smile when I think of it.

It was past noon when I arrived at Ifor's house, a two storey building converted into two self contained flats. Ifor was living on the ground floor. A young girl of average build, good looking and blonde hair came to the door.

I said "I would like to speak to Ifor Jenkins."

She answered by saying that Ifor would not be back for a few hours, "Can I give him a message?"

I replied" I would like that. Could you tell him that Alun called, and that I will come back later."

She looked at me, beamed a sign of recognition and said "You must be the Alun from his home, he has done nothing but talk about you and your family since he returned from his small holiday."

I answered "Yes that's me alright." She caught me by the arm, "Come right in and wait for Ifor."

I entered, complete with suitcase and was shown into a tastily appointed living room, and invited to sit down and relax with a hastily rustled up cup of tea with ham sandwiches.

I felt very welcomed and thereby at ease. She was very interested in my friendship with Ifor, and wanted to know how it came about. I explained that we were friends as babies, and grew up together with a few other such friends.

At the beginning, the conversation was lop sided, I was very wary of asking of her family and home, until she introduced herself as Dilys, "but people call me "blondie" as you can see!"

"That is a very Welsh name but you don't sound Welsh. Are you from Wales? Apparently her parents originated in Ammanford, a West Wales mining village. They then moved to the Kent coalfield when she was a very small child.

Her mother died when she was twelve years of age, leaving father with her and two small boys. She had done well at school and entered grammar school, but left at seventeen, taking a position as nanny with a family at St. John's Wood. She changed the conversation at this point, on to the subject of books, entertainment, politics, all of which she was up to speed and very articulate. I could understand Ifor's interests in this fascinating person.

I was keen to know more about her but withheld my curiosity. I would tackle Ifor at a later and more opportune time.

Ifor eventually arrived, surprised, but very pleased to see me.

I told him I had come to London hoping that he would put me up for a few nights, until I found a place of my own.

He exchanged a few words with Dilys whereupon it was decided I could sleep in the spare room as long as I so wished.

Dilys went about the business of preparing a meal, while Ifor explained the domestic set up. Dilys would be leaving for her "work" around eight pm, and would return by taxi anytime after midnight. He would leave the house at the same time to pursue his hobby of gambling on the dogs at the White City Race Track. "Here is a spare key for you to come and go as you please; you are on your own."

During the meal I asked Ifor if he had seen Billy of late. He had seen and spoken to Billy and his brother Phillip at Hyde Park Corner, where they were selling the Daily Worker, with Billy "spouting" his anti-fascist views.

Dilys chipped in with the information that she often saw Billy at a café in Praed Street, where she occasionally visited.

Ifor suggested I go to Hyde Park some time tomorrow and maybe I would be lucky enough to catch up with him. That is exactly what I did. I got to Hyde Park around noon. I saw Billy and his brother by a small stand selling the Daily Worker.

I went over to Phillip (we were strangers as he was six years my senior) proffered him sixpence for the paper, held my hand out for the change at the same time turning my gaze on to Billy a little distance away, dishing out handbills.

The look of astonishment on his face at the sudden appearance of his best friend was a sight to behold. He grasped me by the arm and we moved away from Phillip and the little stand. He then took hold of both my hands with the question, "Where the hell have you been these past few years?" He then returned to his brother telling him, he would be with me for the rest of the day; and would see him back at the lodgings later that evening. He whisked me over to the "Corner House" found a vacant table, and ordered cups of tea and beans on toast!

Our past four years were then reshuffled, face up, with Billy's lifestyle revealed.

He was a political animal with strong convictions, a keen sense of injustice and a desire to rectify the perpetuation of a system that allowed its continuation.

His active participation in this seemingly hopeless struggle was the cause of many confrontations with authority and police during a multitude of demonstrations he attended. He had been jailed, fined, beaten, threatened but never deterred. He enjoyed his mode of life on the dole, with handouts, the odd job, and meeting like-minded anti-fascists and dissidents of the present "status quo" like himself. I told him that I had arrived in London yesterday and was in accommodation with Ifor. He questioned my knowledge of Ifor's "occupation" and lifestyle.

I explained I had recently met Ifor back home in the valley and how he had told me all about himself and his 'profession'. "But did he tell you," said Billy, "of the greyhound racing, the betting and the company he's keeping." "Yes", I replied, "He told me all that". "Well you must know", said Billy, "That Ifor is rolling in money and only one step ahead of the police."

On the odd occasion he met Ifor, Billy became richer by five or ten pounds and like me was not prone to moralising the source of the handout, and especially in regards to one of our best friends.

"I want you to come and live with me and Phillip" said Billy. " There is plenty of room and the landlady I am sure will organise a camp bed or something if I ask her. We will go right away to Ifor's house and collect your things".

I said there is no particular hurry because Ifor didn't mind me staying there. "But I do", said Billy. "Where the hell is your commonsense? Ifor could be picked up by the police at any moment for living off the immoral earning of a prostitute and if you are in the house, you could be suspect also. How dumb can the pair of you be?"

I acknowledged his wise counsel and with Billy in tow, promptly made repair to Ifor's house.

Ifor was there on his own, Dilys was shopping.

A mini reunion over cups of tea took place; with laughter and touches of sadness, spicing the conversation.

I had, on entering the house intimated to Ifor that I was moving in with Billy. "You are not going right away?" "Yes!" I said, "better now than later." He was slightly taken aback, but not offended. That word was not part of our lexicon.

He did not ask the reason for my hasty departure. If he had, I would have told him. Suitcase in hand I made my way to the door, he called Billy back, talked for a second, then ushered us off the premises with the exclamation "Don't forget I am always here when you want me."

Billy's abode was a ten minute walk and on the way, he opened his hand and showed me a wad of pound notes that Ifor had pressed into it, with the request to share. There was twelve pounds - a lot of money indeed. The landlady agreed without hesitation to fix up a camp bed in the spare room with Billy and Phillip with the same condition of a rent of ten shillings a week. The room was quite large and on the second floor, with table, two chairs, three camp beds, a sink with cold running water, a gas fire for heating and a tabletop gas ring for cooking. Toilet and washing facilities were along the landing and communal with other tenants on the same floor.

The gas for cooking and heating was paid for in a small satellite slot meter in a corner of the room. The meter did not register the amount of gas consumed. It would take only shillings which when inserted would automatically turn the gas on and when a predetermined amount was used the meter would automatically turn the gas off. Phillip had found a method of unlocking the money container on the meter without any trace of tampering. This resulted in the same shilling being inserted and retrieved as often as required. A shillings worth of gas normally lasted about three days. Our shillings worth lasted fourteen days or more!

The landlady emptied the container once a quarter and there were always a few token shillings inside. Her suspicions were never aroused during my stay at the lodgings. This deception was used only when we were in financial straits, and cold, (which was very often).

Our domestic arrangement was very simple. Of the dole money of seventeen shillings, ten went on rent, four shillings into the communal kitty for food, with Phillip in charge. The remaining three bob was for "luxuries" such as coffee, toast, and a bacon sandwich for breakfast at Joe's café.

Once a quarter, we struck rich, the communal finances were "unlimited". Phillip, an ex-soldier had been repatriated from India with suspect sun stroke, and discharged with a small pension paid quarterly. This together with my quarterly reserve pay and the occasional largesse from Ifor, kept us away from begging, busking and thieving.

Our diet was varied consisting mainly of food purchased at local street market stalls, of broken biscuits, damaged tins of beans and tomatoes, dented tins of sardines and corned beef, cracked eggs, stale bread; all very cheap and suspect, with food poisoning for free.

Billy had been living in London the past four years and had established a pattern and routine of living, where the idea of gainful employment was a chimera. Looking for work that wasn't there was a waste of time according to him. Over the coming months, like thousands of my countrymen, I would also find it a waste of time.

Joe's café was a small restaurant in Praed Street, and not far from Paddington Station. It boasted a long counter with stools and ten tables. Its clientele were mainly labourers, the workless, scroungers, pimps, prostitutes, Billy and myself. It was open twenty four hours a day. It never closed. Its night customers were as many and varied as by day.

The choice of food was simple and limited, but cheap and wholesome. The place was always clean. Its main attraction was one could for the price of a cup of tea, sit and stay as long as one wished.

Joe was very tolerant of his customers, and had a good understanding of human frailties. He also ran a very profitable under the counter sideline in accoutrements, toiletries, condoms, quack reliefs and potions for abortions at discount prices for the many prostitutes who frequented his café. He catered for all their professional requirements. This café was where I spent a lot of my time with Billy and others of like mind. Politics discussed, tactics on demonstrations proposed and opposed. The best way to put the world to rights was argued with Billy's pet hate of Mosley and his blackshirts always to the forefront.

Breakfast with a greasy bacon sandwich and a cup of tea, one shilling, was the standard morning fare. One morning I was sitting there on my own, Billy having gone to King Street to collect his pile of Daily Workers, when Dilys came in and went straight to the counter, she glanced around, saw me and gave a wave of recognition. A couple of minutes later she sat by my side with her cup of tea, pleasantries exchanged. Then with a shy look and a tone of embarrassment said, "I expect Ifor has told you what I do for a living". Not wishing to embarrass her further, I told her he had given me all the details of both their lives and as such there was no need for her to be uncomfortable with me. Ifor was my friend and if she too would like to be my friend, I would welcome the privilege. She relaxed, looked relieved and was pleased with my invitation.

She then explained her main reason for visiting Joe's. He knew her method of earning a living, thus easing the embarrassing difficulties of obtaining the "necessities." Also on occasions it was a meeting place for friends of her profession. "On the game" the preferred terminology of its practitioners.

The ice was broken, my curiosity was aroused, and prompting me to ask the question of the circumstance of her meeting with Ifor; and the close relationship which now existed between them.

"Now I know you better, be curious no longer" she said, and with that she related how at seventeen years of age, she came to London to fill the position of nanny. She became pregnant by the father of the child she was looking after.

Thrown out by irate wife and mother, helpless and homeless, she was directed by a friendly policeman to a women's hostel, where she stayed for a while, until she eventually found work with a catering organisation as a casual waitress. A job in which she was continually being propositioned by the male diners. She was pregnant, she needed money, so what the hell!

Ifor was employed by the same catering company also as a casual waiter. Their duties brought them into close contact with each other, and as time elapsed, Ifor noticed her body slightly changing shape, he had previously noticed her "overtime activities." He broached and discussed both subjects with her.

They were in agreement; he would arrange a "back-street" abortion and find suitable accommodation for them both, and if she chose she could carry on what she was doing, he would look after her.

As she said, "All quite simple, nobody gets hurt, only me. Ifor is my "agent".

He cares for me and I care very deeply for him. I was in big trouble and Ifor helped me." (And in so doing I thought also helped himself). "There is nothing I wouldn't do for Ifor."

She continued the summary of her drift into prostitution with the statement of fact. She was once seventeen years old, naïve, and for free to the takers, but the price paid by her was rapacious and unjust.

She doubted if her body would ever again be capable of bearing a child. She was no longer for free, men would have to pay big money for 'cold lamb' made up to look appetising. I liked this sad, intelligent girl of twenty two years, the same age as myself.

We were interrupted by a young girl who was a "workmate" of Dilys's. I was introduced as Dilys's friend and a long standing friend of Ifor's. She purchased a cup of tea and sat down with us.   She gave Dilys a quizzical glance who responded by saying, "He knows we're on the game, so don't worry." Thus I became friendly with most of the prostitutes that passed through Joe's café, likewise Billy and our particular crowd of 'odd bods' and political activists. They respected us for our strange ideas and 'barminess' and we in turn respected them as nice ordinary girls who had made a choice. We had no cause or reason to moralise, or the right to do so.

Many times while drinking tea or lounging in Joe's café, one of the girls would give me a packet of cigarettes with some wisecrack or another and walk away. Invariably the packet would contain a ten-shilling note hidden amongst the cigarettes.

My particular acquaintances of the time accepted, and treated the girls as normal as they would treat other girls. Sexual advances or sexual overtures, or any untoward behaviour was not part of our code. The girls knew this and acted accordingly. This mutual respect was never breached by them or any of my political friends, of this I am certain. We were always strapped for cash; our female admirers knew this, hence the odd ten bob and packet of fags. They also - in a strange way - associated with us in our identification with those oppressed by fascism, and the inequalities of a revolving "status quo".

My evening and nights were spent in a myriad ways. In Joe's café (incidentally, Joe was Italian and one of Mussolini's early socialist casualties - he escaped!) Listening to the hecklers and speakers in Hyde Park, an occasional visit to a cinema (my only luxury), and numerous rallies, meetings, and demonstrating wherever there was a blackshirt presence.

Billy and I would sometime saunter on our own, down Oxford Street, Regent Street to Trafalgar Square, participate as recipients of a mug of soup and a slice of bread and dripping, handed from a trailer positioned on the Square, by a charitable affair known as the "Silver Lady." We were never in need of this gratuity but we found a certain satisfaction of joining a queue of down and outs to receive something for nothing. We also enjoyed the long walk together, with the mug of soup a welcome target.

Once when on this walk my mind turned to a time, now long long ago, when I stood outside the Regents Palace Hotel in the company of a cockney cavalry man, who insisted on making fun of my lack of knowledge of the purpose of two girls parading up and down and how confused I was at their reason for the commercialism of their female assets.

Once again, I stopped outside the Regents Palace Hotel, the time with Billy, to talk and tease one of the girls plying her trade. I knew her well, she had often given me a packet of cigarettes as I drank tea and lounged at Joe's.

My world had turned full circle. Here I was laughing, joking, teasing and being teased by a charming generous girl whose life I once marked as tawdry and degraded, shame on me!

Billy was full of hair-brained schemes of cheating the system, and those he identified as collaborators. He had learned that a vacuum cleaner company had a new model that was to be launched on the market, and required door to door salesmen to push the product. The potential salesman would be given a week's intensive training in salesmanship and in the operation of the new machine.

The sum of two pounds and two shillings, plus a midday meal would be the recompense for such efforts paid at the end of the course. Whereupon the door-to-door work would begin with a retainer of one pound per week, plus fifteen per cent commission on every sale of a machine.

The brainwave was to apply for the course and if successful to do the training and the door-to-door work for a week or two at the same time drawing the dole.

The logistics of signing twice a week at the labour exchange and drawing dole money and breaking off in the middle of a training session was according to Billy a minor obstacle, which we would overcome by telling a tissue of lies when the occasion arose.

We presented ourselves at the vacuum cleaner sale headquarters in Oxford Street, dressed up in the best that our wardrobe would allow. We were potential vacuum salesmen, washed, shaved, clean, tidy, and ready to sweep the town.

We had previously arranged our own personal sales pitch and background, with actual and fictional details if required.

The office we entered was festooned with posters and notices setting out the 'delights' of being a 'Hoover' salesman, with the opportunities of earning fabulous amounts of money, and advancement in the organisation. There were many applicants, besides Billy and me, waiting for interview and a chance at the stated bonanza.

Those were the days before C.V's for workers was dreamed up and when labour was cheap, casual and plentiful.

My turn for the interview came. A perfunctory affair; age, married or single, any criminal record, present address.

The interviewer then went into a long spiel about the duties of door-to-door salesmen, especially of the vacuum cleaner type, and what was expected of us after the expense of training. Appearance and personality was of major importance.

I would receive a letter within three days informing me of the success or otherwise of my application. "Thank you for coming."

Billy received identical treatment and we left with a "couldn't care less" attitude of the success or failure of the interview.

I left Billy with his brother Phillip at Hyde Park corner, where he carried on doing what he liked best, selling the 'Worker' and handing out anti-fascist literature.

I then went on my way to Joe's café and a threepenny cup of tea and conversation with whomsoever of my many odd acquaintances, who would be doing likewise, after which I would return to my digs, and read a book I had previously purchased for sixpence from an excellent second-hand book shop located in the middle of Praed Street, of which I was a frequent visitor.

Our applications were successful and it appeared to me that everybody else's also were successful. The drop out on the first day of the door to door selling was a good fifty per cent, Billy and me included.

The week's training was fine, informative, friendly and monetary rewarding. There were no recriminations or questions asked about our lateness on two occasions. We apologised for our laxity, as did quite a few others on different days of the week.

The first day of door to door selling was at Romford. We were transported there with four other salesmen and half a dozen vacuum machines. The theory was that a salesman made a sales pitch to the customer and if he or she showed the least interest he would dash to the van collect the machine and little bag of dried saw dust and give a practical demonstration of the machine's efficiency.

The street that Billy and I were operating in did not appear to have lino on the floor let alone carpet. After one hour of negative responses we called it a day, and made our way to the nearest tube station and back to Joe's, together with a demonstration machine which we deposited later into the local pawnshop.

Door to door salesmanship of any description was like precision fitting, platform attendant, petrol pump operator, miner, soldier, all added to my ever growing list of failures in my search for a viable, stable employment and future that did not curtail or diminish the kind of freedom I was now enjoying on the dole, with the anticipation and excitement engendered by the social and political agenda now being pursued. In particular to the laissez faire attitude, and in some instances hidden respect towards the fascist menace now threatening Europe. The iniquitous household Means Test which was driving thousands of young men and women out of the parental home was also of my concern.

From now on, at least for the next ten months, I would avoid wasting valuable 'agitating' time in looking for work that wasn't there. I would busy myself with tea drinking at Joe's, conspiring with my companions, long walks with Billy to Trafalgar Square and a mug of soup, quiet reading in my digs, the bi-weekly dole signing ritual, attending and heckling fascist meetings (Billy's favourite), chatting with and teasing Joe's female customers and scrounging and cheating the system at every available opportunity. My days were full. I was very aware of my surroundings and the company I was consorting with and also of the circumstances that perpetuated and reinforced the survival instinct in this hostile environment.

During this time with pimps, prostitutes, political activists, layabouts and dropouts, I was privileged to meet a strange cross-section of humanity and listen to individual tragedies, misfortunes, mistakes as well as the highs and lows of their lives.

One of these characters who fascinated me and all who knew him was John Blackmore, of thirty years of age, with a stubble beard and raincoat always buttoned up to the neck, of superior intelligence, self taught, a walking, talking, encyclopaedia of global politics, especially of the U.S.A. He had been a very active member of the I.W.W. (International Workers of the World), commonly known as the 'Wobblies.'

A deck hand of seventeen years of age on a cargo ship, he was bound for New York where he jumped ship. He wandered around scraping a living, until finally settling in Detroit, where he became an employee of one of the General Motors assembly lines.

Over time, he became involved in union matters and its organisation. He took part in the local politics and became a prominent member of the 'Wobblies.' His vociferous condemnation of the methods used by the corporate strike breakers, brought him into confrontation with the police and company guards, when picketing a strike bound factory. Many were the occasions he was beaten up by these 'thugs'.

John was articulate and precise in his language. His detailed account of the Sacco and Venzetti injustice and political execution was as if he had been a prime witness of this judicial atrocity. It was obvious to me and others who listened, that he was hurt at the time; his description of the Wall Street Crash was illuminated with humour and sarcasm when he made mention of millionaires throwing themselves out of skyscraper windows.

The 'Wobblies' were eventually proscribed and he was thrown out of the country as an undesirable foreign national.

John Blackmore was a man of immense stature, integrity and of compassion for his fellow man. The so-called philosophical conundrum of the glass, half full or half empty, was to him humbug and nonsense.

His simple mantra of 'It is' or 'It is not' was the guiding principle of his thought processes.

Is it right or is it wrong? To John there was no middle way. If it was right he would fight to defend it. If it was wrong, he would fight to put it right. He saw compromise as the coward's way.

With Billy, he was an early volunteer in the Battalions of the International Brigade, fighting on the side of the government in the Spanish Civil War, and was one of the many volunteers killed at the battle around Cordoba. My friend Billy was wounded in the same battle.

John Blackmore lies in a grave somewhere on a dusty Andalusian plain without a marker of where he lay, or a sign that he ever lived and died for what he thought was right.

Il Duce and his fascists declared war on Abyssinia.

The Democracies donned their blinkers, whilst making token and half-hearted attempts to persuade the Italian Dictator to desist. A continuous, optimistic approach was employed. The switching and bribing of other peoples' territories was tried without success. The bombing and gassing of a barefooted rag tag army continued. The League of Nations with Britain in the lead went into appeasement mode. The foundations for World War Two were being laid.

Hitler sensed this democratic prevarication. He teased, kidded, and fooled the government into a full-blown appeasement policy. A smoke and mirrors trick of unparalleled audacity bedazzled the foreign office and its masters. They lost the plot.

CHAPTER SEVEN

Holding Hands on the Banks of the Nile

Mussolini and his Libyan garrisons were a potential threat to the Suez Canal, which was now being used to the Italian's advantage and without hindrance, to transport his troops to his war in Abyssinia.

I was on the army reserve list; a partial mobilization of a specialist force was promulgated.

I was called up to become a member of the 13th Field Ambulance Unit of the Royal Army Medical Corps bound for Egypt, and the Canal Zone. This event brought to a sudden end to many months of absolute and unrestricted freedom and my education, where the curriculum was set by anarchists, "crazy" political activists, pimps, prostitutes and dropouts. All experts in their respective and chosen fields.

I left this "school" a complete person, and; with the knowledge that good people when confronted by adversity and injustice will adopt a communal attitude and lifestyle as a protection against the difficulties and dangers surrounding them.

I enjoyed the protection of the disaffected and was pleased to be of this community; I left with regrets. My call up papers included a railway warrant to Crookham Camp and a week's notice for compliance. Billy and my fellow conspirators were sorry that I was leaving their company and wished me well. My friend Billy was also visibly upset when I showed him the official letter on the morning of its receipt. He was for tearing it up and vanishing. I wouldn't do that, I couldn't do that. I saw it as an opportunity for another change, another adventure, another experience.

The fascination of the unknown has its own logic and my inherent curiosity and restlessness was equal to the challenge. I would find out why the country needed my services in such a hurry. Up to now it did not care if I had starved to death. I had no idea as to the reason for the"call up" or my eventual destination.

I packed my case at which I was now an expert and made my way to the Rhondda Valley and my mother.

On my way to Paddington Station, I called on Ifor at his home. Dilys came to the door; they had heard that I had been called back to the colours, and were pleased to see me before I left. I thanked them both for their past kindness and hoped that one day I could return it.

They thought the remark was unnecessary; they enjoyed my company on the rare visits to their home.

Dilys kissed me on the cheek. Ifor took me by the hand and true to form pressed a few pounds notes into it.

I never saw them again!

These two nice unique persons made an indelible mark on my memory and another incident to cherish and add to my collection.

I had not been home for eighteen months. I did not want to return to the army without my mother knowing the reason why.

I also had the notion that I would be going overseas and I knew she would be very cross and hurt if I had left without her kissing me a goodbye.

My mother was surprised to see me, I did not as was usual, send a postcard forewarning of my impending visit.

She was however overjoyed to see me and was curious as to the reason for such an unannounced and sudden visit. She did not like my answer, but accepted that it was inevitable that I had been called up. The three days I was with the family passed quickly.

I prepared to honour my railway warrant to Crookham Camp, wished everybody a goodbye and "See you all as soon as I get back from where I am going!" A big hug from my mother with tears. I was on my way out when my father appeared at the door of the hideout (study), with the look on his face that I last saw on his greeting me in the first aid room of the Brittanic Colliery some years ago. He took my hand exactly as before and said "You will be alright son, but look after yourself; we will all be thinking of you."

I was grateful for these sentiments, my dormant respect for him was aroused. He was concerned and had expressed it. I said "Thank you Dad, I'll be alright, no need to worry." I did not know what else to say. I left the house in the company of my favourite sister Olwen, who insisted on accompanying me to the bus stop. I left her crying when I boarded the bus.

Crookham Camp was exactly the same, nothing had changed; everything was still in place including the slop bucket. There was, however, a marked difference in the treatment handed out. I was an 'old soldier' with experience called back to the colours to do a special job. A softly, softly approach was adopted by those in authority. They were dealing with civilians in uniform 'press ganged' back into service. The sergeant of the guard was most welcoming. The Orderly Room Sergeant was questioning in a civil manner. I was getting embarrassed. This did not feel or seem right. I was prepared for the standard wisecracks and indignities of yesteryear and being bullied by any soldier with stripes on their arms.

After the routine of kit issue and of uniform, followed by a shower and the discarding of civilian clothes, I was taken to a hut where "B Company" was residing.

This company was the designation of the unit that held all personnel being posted abroad. Placing them in squad formations and giving refresher courses in discipline, square-bashing and reminders that we were soldiers under orders. The dining facilities were separate. We were also segregated from the training, shouting and bullying of new recruits.

I entered the hut, all very familiar, as if I had never left. Men sitting on beds, men sitting around the stove (it was winter), but this time they weren't brassoing or polishing, they were talking, smoking, joking and laughing.

I was looking for an empty bed when a voice shouted out "Taffy Williams!" It was Topper Higgins a friend of my 'castle' days. Besides Topper there were others of my old unit also here, some time servers like Topper and Herschal and reservists like myself.

It was evident that a formation was being assembled of well trained qualified men, who at some time or another all worked together as a cohesive unit, and were again being brought together for an emergency and where further training was unnecessary. A total of forty men excluding officers and N.C.O.'s of which there were two sergeants, and a Quartermaster Sergeant. With the exception of one sergeant they were strangers to me. The Quartermaster Sergeant was a short stubby man with a prominent paunch and small beady eyes. Q.M.S. Roberts was saddled with the nickname 'Piggy Roberts'. He was the senior NCO and boss of the whole outfit.

The other Sgt. I knew only too well, Corporal Fogarty with stripes, three in number, on his arms and a full chest of campaign ribbons. The Martinet, the Military Manual incarnate was now Sgt. Fogarty and in charge of training and discipline. I wondered if the extra stripe had mellowed the man. Time would tell!

It was good to talk to Topper once again; we had a lot to tell each other. He was now a fully qualified army cook and a specialist in invalids' diets and was expecting his promotion to corporal to be promulgated in the next few months. Herschal was courting, engaged to be married in the summer; he hoped he would be able to fulfil that commitment.

They were all curious as to what I had been up to in 'those Welsh caves', since I was discharged. I gave them a synopsis of my activities. They were surprised, especially when I said I had spent the last eighteen months in London, consorting with pimps and prostitutes and taking part in political activity and demonstrations. I embellished and exaggerated my story, they took it all in. Their attitude of yore changed; they could see I was no longer the naïve immature teenager that was easily teased! I was fully grown, confident, worldly wise and in a position to tease them for a change.

The following few days went quickly and trouble free. Sgt. Fogarty enjoyed himself in brushing up our rusty drill. He paid particular attention to the half dozen or so reservists in the ranks. Reminding us that we were soldiers again and 'Don't forget it!' Also 'Get that hair cut!'

The drill sessions were interspersed with parades, and in the medical officers hut for a series of vaccinations and injections, which to honour the saying, left my arm 'like a pin cushion.' There was also the genitals ritual of "Trousers down to your ankles, stand still; look to your front."

Preparations were well in hand to 'package and despatch' us to a destination of which we could only guess. The consensus was Aden, with the odd one giving Egypt as a possibility. Overseas kit was issued, khaki drills, with short and long trousers, long socks with turn ups, a topee and a mosquito net. This last item being the greatest invention since the wheel, as far as we were concerned, on arrival at our destination.

Twenty four hour passes would be issued to those who applied. There was a 100% take up and pay parade was later that day. We knew the moment of our departure had arrived, we safely assumed it would be the day after the return from the twenty four hour leave.

Topper, Herschal and a few other of the Scottish lads had never been to London. After listening to my dubious city activities with their sexual connotations (which I had exaggerated), they were quite anxious to visit the city in my company. The twenty four hour pass was from noon on the day of issue to noon of the following day. Regulation dress to be worn, civilian clothes not allowed. I would have preferred to have used the 24 hours relaxing on the camp and with a visit to the local cinema at Fleet.

I was going to live and be in close contact with these men for some time to come, I did not want to be unfriendly or off hand. Furthermore, Topper asked me to come along.

My conversations with him was on a different level to what I had been used to of late; where thoughts and attitudes were tuned to the chaos of the depression and the struggle for some sort of existence. He had been, and still was under the all enveloping protection of the military umbrella sheltering him from the vicissitudes of a society of which I had been on the fringe and which was beyond his ken. I could not turn his request down. I would show five of these young soldiers including Topper, the 'low life' of Soho and its environs, as well as the 'working' locations of one or two of the girls, but they would have to do their own introductions and bargaining. I would then leave them to visit some of my own friends.

I had no intention of visiting anybody. I would however, return to the Railway Station and catch the first available train to either Basingstoke or Fleet. All went to plan. I left Topper and the other four soldiers in a small pub off Soho, well briefed of the how and the where to obtain the 'object of their desires.' I arrived back at Fleet in time to see the feature film being shown at the local cinema. After which I walked the half mile back to Crookham Camp alone, with my thoughts.

I returned to "B Company" hut around 22.30. There were four or five others already there from the 24 hour leave. They had passed most of the day in looking around Fleet and in the local pubs. It seemed that the majority of the men had either gone to Basingstoke or Aldershot. A few along with my five had gone to London.

The return of the mass of the 24 hour pass recipients was desultory, continuing through the night until 10.30 the following morning, with the return of Topper and a half dozen other overnight revellers all looking the worse for their carousing.

After the midday meal, the whole of "B Company" was ordered to parade at 1500 hours in best dress, buttons and boots shining.

That was the first time we were on parade as a complete unit with officers and NCO's. We were addressed by the Camp Adjutant who informed us that we were now soldiers, part of the 13th Field Ambulance Brigade of the Royal Army Medical Corps and bound for Egypt and the Canal Zone. At last we knew for sure our destination. He wished us a safe journey good luck and "God save the King." We then marched passed the C.O. on his saluting base, 'eyes right' to the beat of a single drum.

After the parade, a notice was posted on the company notice board giving details of times and method of movement. We were to parade complete with kit at 0630 and move off at 0700 and march in formation to Fleet Station, where we would board a train for Southampton.

The remainder of the day and evening was spent in marking our kit and labelling every item with army number. All clothes, uniform and such with stencil and black marking ink. All brasses and metalwork the number hammered on with a metal die stamp.

The spectre of the unknown was hovering around the hut's occupants. The mood was of quiet contemplation, anticipation subdued, excitement in abeyance, apprehension in abundance. Slop bucket collected and placed outside the hut, the bugler sounded the last post. 2200 hours, lights out. Forty men took to their beds to lay their head on the pillow, full of thoughts, of fears and hopes of what the morrow and the days ahead would bring.

Reveille sounded at 0500 hours. Sgt Fogarty stomped into the hut on time, bawling and banging a dustbin lid.

I leapt out of bed, as did everybody else. Nobody was going to lie in and argue with Fogarty. We quickly washed, shaved, dressed, tidied bed, and bed space, assembled for roll call and breakfast. At 0630 with Fogarty in his element we marched onto the parade ground with kit bags over our shoulders, for inspection by the orderly officer of the day.

The parade ground was in complete darkness, it was pitch black, we could hardly see our boots. Military protocol, its habits, and codes of discipline, tend to ignore climatic conditions or any other natural phenomena. This morning the parade ground's geographical position in relation to the winter sun was also ignored. We were inspected by the officer and Piggy Roberts in total darkness. It was cold; I was feeling restless, at the same time my sense of humour was taken over by my perception of the ridiculousness at this military charade of blind's man bluff which was taking place in all seriousness. The inspection ended with the voice of Fogarty shouting orders "Shoulder kit bags, right turn, by the right quick march!"

Our two officers had gone ahead in a small military vehicle together with the kit bags of their own and of the NCO's.

The silent march led by a corpulent Q.S.M. on a lonely country road early on a dark cold winter morning, of a small uniformed band of young first aid men and stretcher bearers in full battle dress and laden with heavy kit bags and bound for the sweltering heat of the Arabian desert and the Suez Canal, would be of a fiction if it wasn't for real.

We halted outside Fleet Railway Station, stood at ease and easy for ten minutes, waiting for our special train.

On arrival at Southampton Docks we were marched to a roped off area where the pleasant site of a N.A.A.F.I. trailer was situated. Permission to fall out was given so that we could partake of a free mug of tea and sandwich. This gesture was much appreciated by a bunch of hungry and thirsty soldiers.

Movement away from the roped area was forbidden, otherwise we were free to walk, talk and relax in this confined space. In the distance further along the dock could be seen a large ocean liner, which was giving rise to some speculation that it was to be our mode of transport. We would not be so lucky, our ship had yet to dock, was the accepted view.

The call of 'Fall in!' from Sgt. Fogarty put an end to our guessing game. We lined up in formation and shouldered kit bags. The rope was removed, 'Right turn, quick march!' and along the dock we marched. 'Halt!, Stand easy!'. We had halted opposite a gangway of the Cunard Liner 'S.S. Lucania'. We were lucky after all. I had never been in a rowing boat, let alone an ocean going liner. Here I was to become a passenger in a 'liner' bound for the East, all expenses paid.

The civilian passengers were safely aboard. Without further ceremony, we were sectioned off in groups of ten, with the longest serving soldier of each group in charge, which in my group was Topper Higgins. We would be allocated cabins where we must remain until instructed otherwise. A ship's steward came on the scene to guide the first group, mine to the cabins which would be our home for the voyage. Other stewards and groups followed in quick succession.

The cabin was small, compact, with two bunks (top and bottom), shower and toilet in a small adjoining annex. I shared the cabin with Topper; he was in charge. The other eight sorted themselves into compatible pairs and did likewise. Topper saw all safely in their cabins, and then came back slumping on one of the two chairs and with a sigh of relief said "We are on our way Taff!" There were two chairs, a small table and a porthole in our cabin, which was on the left hand side of the ship facing the 'sharp end'.

An hour passed. Sgt Fogarty exhausted and looking harassed, came in and enquired of our welfare. He gave Topper a sheet of printed instructions. He also informed us we would be called on deck before the ship sailed and could lean on the ships rail if we so pleased.

On deck looking around seeing all the activity on the ship and on the dockside, people waving from ship to shore and myself in uniform, I wondered what kind of time warp I was in?

Nine days ago, I was sitting, talking, joking with dropouts, pimps and prostitutes and making plans to attend some demonstration or other. I was in a 'topsy-turvy' world and in a whirl.

The S.S. Lucania slipped its moorings and the dockside began to move away.

The vessel was under sail with one very mixed up reservist soldier as part of its cargo. The regimen for the voyage was set out by daily notices posted outside the Q.S.M. cabin (which was spacious), and which we were duty bound to read each day.

We were confined to the lower deck, all other decks were out of bounds. Fraternising with civilian passengers whilst not officially barred, was looked upon with some disfavour, I was in despair with military common-sense.

There were times, however, when we were compelled to move from one deck to another – meal times.

A section of the dining room was roped off, segregating the common soldier during his feeding time from the rest of the 'herd'. The officers and NCO's above the rank of corporal were free to choose where and with whom they dined.

The food was identical in quality and quantity as served to the civilian passenger, as was the waiter service. We were not served with or allowed to purchase any type of alcoholic drinks as were the passengers, officers and NCO's.

We made do with water. Even if we were allowed to purchase drinks our finances would not stretch to the price of the beverages on offer and we fully understood the military does not budget for private soldiers' free booze on Mediterranean cruises. Overall the treatment of the soldiers during mealtimes was exemplary.

A deck patrol of two men at intervals of two hours on and four off was inaugurated, we were not allowed on deck after lights out. The duty of the patrol was to turn back and report any soldier who had the temerity to venture out after lights out at 2200 hours. Why this should have been so, is another one of those military mysteries of an order given to men to obey without some explanation being made. I liked this particular duty, I would have volunteered for it every night. This was not possible as a roster had been set and must be obeyed.

On one of these nightly deck patrols, I was leaning on the ship's rail watching the seas phosphorescent glow in the wake of the ship's propellers. Sgt Fogarty sidled up by my side and asked if I was enjoying the voyage. I politely answered "Yes Sergeant." whereupon he extended the conversation with the question of what was I doing before I was mobilised, because he heard whispers that I was a bit of a 'bolshie'. He wondered if the rumour was correct and if so how come?

I gave him some of my background and especially my eighteen months on the dole.

This intrigued him, but the conversation was terminated by the appearance of the relief patrol. I went below to my bunk.

During these night patrols when I was on duty; I became friendly with Sgt Fogarty, or to put it in the correct context, Sgt Fogarty became friendly with me. It was he who initiated the friendship. After all, a private soldier is rarely if ever, on speaking terms with the disciplinary Sergeant; he normally is enemy number one, and to be avoided at all costs.

He was an Irish Catholic, joined the army in 1915, and stayed on after the Great War. He was active with the British Army in Dublin in 1922. He was also marked by the I.R.A. He had never returned home since. All contact with his family and relatives had been lost. His life and home had become the army. He was single by choice. He had another two years to serve, whereupon he would be discharged with a small pension and nowhere to go.

I was a civilian; he wanted to know about the world of which he had been unaware for too long. He wanted to know about work, what kind of work could he do, he wanted to know about lodgings, how much would they cost. He wanted to know about civilians in total.

Sgt. Fogarty was confiding in me. It was as if I was the corkscrew that had opened the bottle to let his bad genie escape. I respected the trust he endowed in me. His secrets were safe in my keeping.

During our conversations I formed the opinion that his enforcement of strict discipline and his obsessive adherence to the military rulebook was a sub-conscious retaliation for his perceived treatment and isolation of past events that were not of his choosing.

Sgt Fogarty was a sad and bitter man. He was a loner by force of circumstance.

I was a loner by disposition; we had a common impediment. We were two of a kind, perhaps that was why Fogarty talked and I listened. I respected him as a first class soldier, but I did not like him as a man.

Our time on board was taken up with physical exercises before breakfast. Fire and boat drills at odd times, and night deck patrols, and of course meal times, breakfast, lunch and dinner.

A thought often crossed my mind at meal times. If Billy and Joe's café crowd could see me now they wouldn't believe it, and if they did they would be saying 'lucky' bastard. I was saying the same to myself.

I was at sea, a passenger in an ocean liner, with a nice compact cabin in which to sleep, relax and converse with a friend. Enjoying food which I had never tasted before, on route to the land of Cleopatra, the Sphinx, the River Nile and the bullrushes where Moses was abandoned.

The religious, geography, and history lesson given to me by my teachers was coming alive. I was seeing with my own eyes the Rock of Gibraltar, whilst sailing from the Atlantic Ocean through the Straits into the Mediterranean Sea.

My conspiratorial urges and political activities were on hold, and in the bottom of my mental kit bag, where they would remain inarticulate and comatose, until my uniform was discarded and I was again home and in civilian clothes.

I had no intention of 'rocking the boat' or of challenging the military machine, I became a card carrying coward, and a paid up member of the docile silent majority, subdued into this silence by the bellowing authority of Q.S.M. Piggy Roberts and the disciplinary idiosyncrasies of Sgt. Fogarty. This together with the forever oppressive thought of the 'glass house' was enough of a deterrent to keep my head down as low as possible without it disappearing up my own orifice.

I was however, determined to take full advantage of the situation I was in, to enjoy the good food, the relaxation afforded by the gentle rolling action of the ship in the blue warm Mediterranean Sea, and at night with clear sight of the constellations unpolluted by neon signs or street lamp lights. And above all my temporary release and absence from the real world.

My self induced reverie ended outside Alexandria Harbour, where we arrived during a fierce storm, and dropping anchor until the weather abated later in the morning. We disembarked, lined up on the dock side amidst hundreds of men dressed in long 'nightshirts', the majority of whom were barefooted. Humping baskets of coal on their heads and shoulders and running up gangways of steamers tied up alongside. There were also men with handcarts hauling heavy loads of timber up a slight incline and out of the dock.

We marched to a waiting train close to the dock entrance with dozens of young and not so young children holding out their hands with the cry of "Backsheesh!"

Boarding the train was a great surprise after witnessing the primitive working conditions on the dockside. It was modern, and more up to date than the train which had transported us to Southampton. It was electric with overhead wires.

We were on our way to Cairo and passing through the countryside watching scenery change from lush green fields to sandy deserts and back again, with donkeys and camels in charge of peasants in strange dress, and women with their faces covered and hidden. It was all so odd and foreign.

It looked ancient, as if the whole countryside had been embalmed since the days of the Pharaohs and was coming back to life, tangled up with modern gismos. The electric train in competition with the camel train, the biblical donkey with the motor car, the oxen with the tractor. 3000 BC was in retreat with the advance of 2000 AD.

From my uneducated perspective and from what I was seeing from the moving train, the retreat was not a rout. Ancient Egypt would remain ancient Egypt for sometime yet to come.

We may be clever enough to make possible the building of better and bigger pyramids, but they would not be 3000 years old, and of such great wonder

We arrived at Cairo Railway Station to board trucks for the journey to the outskirts of the City, to the little village of Helmea on the edge of the Arabian Desert.

Our accommodation for the unforeseeable future were rows of tents of all shapes and sizes, pitched and erected in the sand by local labour.

There was a large marquee for dining with the field kitchen close to the entrance. There was also a marquee for the NAAFI. The officers' quarters and dining facilities were also in a large tent.

The tents for the private soldiers each holding four men, were equipped with four camp beds and wired for electric light, as was the rest of the tented camp.

The showers and toilets were open to the world with canvas screens which gave just a modicum of privacy.

After dismounting from the trucks and lined up by Fogarty, we were told to sort ourselves out in groups of four to occupy the tents. Thereafter there would be no swapping or changing. Each tent was numbered and that would be our address.

After staking out our place of abode and dumping our kit bags, we made our way to the dining marquee, where a meal had been prepared by soldiers of an artillery regiment permanently stationed in barracks near Heliopolis some distance away. I was hungry and thirsty, my last meal was aboard the SS. Lucania - a long time ago. We were able to purchase mineral water on the train journey but no food.

Back to army cooking and rations. Nevertheless, I enjoyed the meal; I managed to beat the flies to it!

After the meal we were allowed to relax, sort out our kit, ready to dress in khaki drill and toupee for early morning roll-call parade. I tried resting on the camp bed, but it was hopeless, damn flies everywhere, hands, arms flaying and swotting, body permanently on the move. The arrangement necessary to fit the mosquito net over the bed, would not be available until the morrow, we would have to make do the best we could until then.

My first night's sleep on the edge of a desert in a strange country with the distant howling of the pariah dogs, the tent flapping in a slight breeze on which was carried smells and noises of a foreign land, to which my nose and ears was as yet unaccustomed. I was thinking, and I dozed off to be awakened at dawn by the flies as were the other occupants. Topper had been awakened by the night patrol. He was washed, shaved and all dressed up in his new white cook's outfit and away to prepare breakfast assisted by two soldiers and two local natives. The soldier helpers were on a roster basis. My turn would come in due course.

Breakfast was at 0730, and to my astonishment, there was no preliminary parade, we were free, in our own time to eat the meal until 0815. I was always on time and took my place in the queue (I was always hungry!). Plates were communal and stacked on a table next to the dishing out point. We carried our own mug and 'eating irons.' Plate held out, rations slapped on, mug filled with tea from a bucket. No sooner was the food put on the plate than it was covered by flies. At first this was a sickening sight, but I would get used to it and learn to accept the odd fly as part of the diet! Once inside the dining marquee, the flies were swotted and flayed away, they would only return in dozens instead of thousands.

On parade in the sand and to attention, we were told we were in Egypt and on the canal as reinforcement should an emergency arise.

After a 'pep' talk, we were ordered on to personnel carriers, part of a convoy of trucks, ambulances and staff cars stationary outside the camp's perimeter. The trucks were loaded with equipment.

We were on our way into the blue to train and practice the speedy setting up of a front line field hospital. The main effort of this training was given to the erection of two large black canvas marquees and the laying out of equipment, stretchers, tables etc.

Bending down, knocking in tent pegs, wearing a topee and preventing it falling off and sweating like a horse under the thing made life difficult. We were forbidden by Piggy Roberts from taking it off. This piece of equipment was as afar as I and my companions were concerned valueless, cumbersome and a nuisance.

As the weeks went by, even Piggy Roberts could see that the forage cap was the best headgear for the desert work we were doing. It was comfortable and more sensible and it suited him.

It became standard dress when working in the sun. The topee remained an ornament in the tent!

The drivers and mechanics of the vehicle convoy were men of the Royal Army Service Corps. A few of whom like us had also been recalled to the colours. Listening to their conversations, they were not too pleased with this unexpected interruption in their civilian lives.

Whilst working in the field with the R.A.M.C. Sgt. Fogarty was the disciplinary N.C.O. in command. This arrangement was unwelcome by the R.A.S.C. personnel. We knew Sgt Fogarty of old, we knew his strengths and weaknesses, we were used to his ways and not unduly concerned with his strict adherence to the military drill manual. The convoy drivers and mechanics saw him as an interloper and not as one of them. Also Sgt. Fogarty seemed to enjoy harassing them more than he did us. They hated this man and his power of discipline over them. Sgt Fogarty must have been well aware of their dislike, knowing him I doubted if he cared.

The Warrant Officers and NCO's mess tent was a short distance from the main camp and was where Sgt Fogarty spent most of his off-duty hours.

One night around 2300 hours, lying in bed waiting for sleep, a loud shout and cry was heard, then silence, quickly followed by a great hustle and bustle and animated conversations, then silence again.

Myself and the three other occupants of the tent wondered what all the noise and fuss was about. It did not concern us. I pulled the mosquito net over my bed and went to sleep.

Breakfast time the camp was rife with speculation and rumour that Sgt. Fogarty was attacked and severely injured the previous night, and was now in a Cairo military hospital in a bad way. I can state without contradiction that a sense of satisfaction prevailed, especially amongst the R.A.S.C. drivers and mechanics that Sgt Fogarty had at last received his comeuppance.

After breakfast 'roll call' the rumour was confirmed. Sgt Fogarty had been brutally attacked and beaten unconscious by a person or persons unknown. He had since regained consciousness, but was in a very poor condition.

Piggy Roberts then advised anybody who knew anything about this to come forward – long pause –"You will be confined to your tents until further orders and until the military police have completed their enquires. Dismiss!".

A Sergeant and Corporal of the Military Police in their imposing uniform came into our tent, posing the question, "Where were you last night between 2300 and 2315 hours?"

Four corroborative answers were immediately forthcoming. "In bed trying to sleep; we heard a noise but thought nothing of it."

Police enquiries over, parade at 1200 hours, back to normal. Shooing flies, craving for a long cool drink, and glad to see the last of Sgt. Fogarty.

The semi-official explanation given after a week of police enquiries was that Sgt. Fogarty was drunk when he left the Sergeants' mess tent, had fallen over a tent guy rope and had hit his head on a tent peg.

I knew different; we all knew different and could not care less; Fogarty was off our backs.

During my week's turn of duty in the field kitchen, one of the native helpers took a liking to me and we became very friendly. He had a good knowledge of English having worked in army establishments since a boy. He was three years older than me.

At weekends, Saturday from 1200 hours to 2359 hours, we were at liberty to go and do whatever took our fancy; the same for Sunday.

My first free weekend, I went with Topper and a few other men to Cairo. It was chaotic, wherever we went we were followed by a crowd of children with their hands forever held out with the cry of "backsheesh!". We needed "backsheesh" ourselves, as our four bob a day did not go very far in Egypt.

Wandering around the city and especially the red light district, was not my idea of foreign travel. I decided I would explore the city on my own and not be governed by the dictates of a group with different interests. Towards this end, I cultivated the already burgeoning friendship with Mohamed, my kitchen co-worker. My next weekends in Cairo were in his company. His knowledge of the city and the culture of his country he made available to me. He took me to sites and palaces without the cry of "backsheesh!" followers, or the pestering of Dragomen and the never-ending tipping expected from foreigners.

He was my personal Dragoman, teacher and protector. We made arrangements to meet on the road adjacent to the camp's perimeter entrance.

Previously, I made application and received permission to wear civilian clothes when off duty. I along with a few other reservists had stuffed our civilian gear into the bottom of our kit bags. It was now retrieved, smoothed out and put into a condition for wearing. I wondered if Mohamed would recognise me out of uniform?

He was waiting outside as arranged, dressed in a spotless white kaftan, white turban neatly arranged on his head, sandals and blue girdle. He looked very impressive. I was greeted with a smile and a comment on my attire which he had not expected, but was pleased to see me dressed as such. He took hold of my hand. We started to walk hand in hand to the road leading to Heliopolis.

I had often witnessed the custom of holding hands amongst the male members of my Arab neighbours. It seemed odd and out of place to my western eyes and cultural ways. Holding hands in public is a female attribute and not the done thing between macho males!

The holding of my hand by Mohamed, I looked upon as a natural Arabian custom, and subconsciously done. I was not going to offend by withdrawing it; neither was I going to make him aware of my predilection of holding hands only with females.

It was a good half mile walk to the Cairo-Heliopolis road, where it was our intention of boarding a bus. The walk with Mohamed telling me in his faltering English about his family, his wife and daughter, his mother and father, was of a profound encounter with a sensation I had never before experienced.

Two young men of different colour, nationality, and of different cultures, complete strangers holding hands, walking through the sands of the Arabian desert, as close in spirit as one human being can get to another human being without it being articulated, was a heartwarming and emotive moment in my chequered career so far.

This subconscious holding of hands by such a disparate couple was to me, of a transcendental quality, the uniqueness of which was to be repeated only once again in my life.

Most of my weekends when not on camp patrol, fire duty or kitchen helper, was with Mohamed. Holding hands in Cairo's Museums, in the city centre, drinking coffee at a table outside a café on the banks of the Nile and in his humble home with his wife and daughter, eating Egyptian salad, cross-legged on a rug.

"Taffy" Williams and his "Wog friend" became the subject of much barrack room gossip and innuendo by those who did not know me. I chose to ignore it. My friendship with Mohamed was more important to me than the unwarranted speculations of ignorant men.

My stay in Egypt is of a memorable time, and of pleasant moments enhanced by the hospitality and friendship given me by Mohamed. My appreciation of his Pharaoh's legacies, the wonders of his country's ancient heritage, were presented to me, hand in hand on a one to one basis and on site by my dear friend, Mohamed, a direct descendent of the original pyramid builders.

Our training preparations for an emergency were ongoing, and were repetitive and routine by now. We could raise a marquee and dismantle the same in record time, irrespective of sandstorms or the oppressive heat of the desert breeze.

The monotony of this training was however, occasionally broken by the complete outfit including field kitchen, moving into the desert close to the Canal road and pitching camp along its length and moving at intervals of two to three days.

Erecting and dismantling marquees at regular intervals in sweltering heat was hard work, we were fully occupied for most of the day. At night, we slept on the sand on groundsheets with stars as cover and a night patrol of two men, armed with pickaxe handles as protection.

The end of the day and after the evening meal, we could relax. Parades when out in the blue were on hold as were a few other petty military restrictions, water was rationed and the daily shave was voluntary.

I would walk with Topper and a few other men to the banks of the Suez Canal, to watch the different ships as they traversed the 'ditch'.

On one of these occasions, an Italian troopship laden with guns and men, passed by on its way to the Abyssinia war. The Bersagliere on deck having spotted us lounging on the bank, began waving and shouting to us, "The Guardians of the Canal"; we waved back.

R.A.M.C. transport in front of the Pyramids, Egypt, 1936.

Sandstorm! 1936.

Alun (behind man stirring dixie) contributing to the proceedings, Egypt, 1936.

R.A.M.C. transport and tents, Egypt, 1936.
(Note air recognition panel in front of the vehicles.)

R.A.M.C. Dressing Station on excercise, Egypt, 1936.

Would the Anglo-French owners of the Suez Canal Company be pleased at this display of British-Italian solidarity?

My thoughts were with Billy and his friends back home, demonstrating somewhere in London at the obscenity of this unobstructed passage for Mussolini and his fascist army.

At odd times during the day, erecting and dismantling marquees in proximity to the Canal, I was fascinated by the strange juxtaposition of a camel train and an ocean liner moving silently through the desert on a parallel course within spitting distance of each other. It is an 'illusion' of magical proportions that must be seen to be believed.

The perceived danger to the canal had receded; Mussolini's Abyssinia venture was successful. The League of Nations, toothless and helpless went to sleep and died. The National Governments' right wing bias and fears of communism ignored the growing public concerns of the fascist threat.

The appeasers were prominent in the formation of policy. The political establishments of all colours, were so blinded by their hatred for the Soviet Union and its political credentials that the chasm of fascism they were walking into could not be seen. "Ergo", it did not exist.

Roll call parade was normal in the tented camp with the usual crop of rumours.

One morning however, the rumour had a certainty about it; the camp was to be dismantled and all personnel dispersed within Egypt and to the various army garrisons located in the country.

After the midday meal, there was a rush to the company notice board, outside the 'orderly tent'. There, sure enough, was confirmation of the rumour with good news and bad news!

The good news was, the names of all the reservists, together with the information that we were to be on parade at 0800 tomorrow in full kit and ready to move and be transported to Alexandria and home.

The bad news was 'no news' of what was to happen to Topper, Hershal and the rest of the regulars. My ambivalent attitude to this sudden interruption of routine was of a worry. It was as well that I had been given no choice of either staying or leaving, because I would have found great difficulty in arriving at a conclusion. This was one time I welcomed the Army's power of making a decision affecting my life and of which I had no say.

After reading the notice of my impending repatriation, I made my way to the field kitchen. I wanted to tell Mohamed myself before he heard it from someone else, that I was leaving his country the next day.

He appeared distressed when I told him the news, and without a word being said, he grasped my hand, and as was the custom brushed his cheeks against mine, turned around and walked away, across the sand towards his home, in the little village of Helmia.

My friendship with a 'modern/ancient' Egyptian was ended, leaving my memory littered with many incidents and of sight-seeing wonders. But none so potent and evocative as the holding of my hand by a gentle Arab, as he guided me through the archaeological treasurers left by his ancestors.

I walked back to my tent, confused with my emotions all jumbled up, to commence packing for tomorrow's 0800 parade.

I was awakened early by Topper with two hot mugs of tea in his hand, which we quietly sipped outside sitting on the sand, watching the Eastern sunrise over the desert's horizon, upon which I was inclined to meditate if I would ever again be fortunate enough to see this most beautiful of sights.

This very morning at the other end of the Mediterranean, history was being made and where unbeknown to me, I would become a bit player, in a national tragedy with world implications, watched by democratic governments in a hypnotic docility of indifference and political cowardice. With the national government in the role of star hypnotist, lulling the nation into believing in the deception of non-intervention.

We arrived at Alexandria docks. Twenty R.A.M.C. reservists and fifteen RASC reservists under the command of a RASC Sergeant and junior RAMC officer. The Sergeant was being repatriated for medical reasons. An assorted bunch of healthy, weather-beaten sun-bronzed soldiers on the way home to Great Britain and the dole queues.

We got off the train, formed two lines and marched to halt at the foot of a gangway of the S.S. Otranto, a liner slightly bigger than the Lucania.

In single line, we walked up the gangway to reform into two lines on deck, watched by a curious crowd on board. The majority of whom had commenced their journey from Australia.

We were then told by the young officer that we would be taken to our respective cabins, where a printed list of instructions would be found on each bed. He also pointed out that we were soldiers in a civilian environment and would in every respect be treated as civilian passengers, but never to forget that we were still subject to military discipline.

Stewards came and directed us to the cabin we would occupy until we reached Southampton.

The cabin allocated to me and Geordie Lackenby was slightly larger than the one on the outward voyage, otherwise identical. The printed instructions on the bed was from the ships' captain, welcoming us aboard and listing the ship's services and facilities and our table number in the dining room. From the tone of the notice and the sentiments expressed therein it was obvious for all intents and purposes we were ordinary civilian passengers without distinction, our routine would be likewise.

It was 1500 hours and the ship was under way. A knock on the cabin door advised us that a buffet lunch was being served in the main dining hall for all who had joined the ship at Alexandria.

We took off our heavy army boots, put on gym shoes, tidied ourselves up and made straight for the 'eats', where we mingled with the other passengers who had boarded the same time as us.

After the buffet lunch, I made my way to the rear of the ship to watch Egypt gradually recede into the distance.

The fact that I was at the stern end of the ship, looking back at where I had been instead of at the forward end, as to where I was going was a perturbation of some concern.

The security of the army and its freedom from decision making was a seductive thought of some merit. That Topper was contemplating signing on for twenty one years was recognition of the army's seductive embrace.

I thought about it, went back to my cabin, lay on the bunk and concluded that the chaotic liberties, the uncertainties of Joe's café crowd, where every day was different from the one before and where the excitement of insecurity and freedom of movement, the expression of dissent was superior to the dreary repetition of bed and breakfast on time, and the 'clanking silence' of uniformed clones doing whatever they were told.

My experience of both lifestyles was of a preference of giving the thumbs down to the military.

My tenure as a soldier in His Majesty's Army, from a personal point of view was a life with a Jekyll and Hyde mentally in control, with Mr Hyde's stupid humiliations, indignities, and potential horrors being alleviated by the positive actions of the physical and caring attitudes of Dr. Jekyll.

The time for our first dinner as honorary civilian passengers on board the PO Liner SS Otranto had arrived.

Our table was number 4; we had no idea what the seating arrangements would be. We surmised that we would be 'roped in' as was the case on the Lucania. Table no 4 was round, as were many others with places laid for six people. Geordie and I arrived a little early, found table no. 4 and nervously sat down and waited.

The place began to fill, with soldiers and civilians scattered willy nilly amongst the tables. It was evident we were not going to be roped off.

Presently two smart looking ladies came to our table. I stood up and nudged Geordie to do likewise, they sat down and we sat down.

I introduced both Geordie and myself to the ladies, they responded. The conversation was awkward and desultory with periods of silence, which was broken by the appearance of two more ladies.

Geordie and I were introduced to the newcomers as 'Two handsome young men on the way home from the desert.'

It was obvious that the four ladies knew each other having been dining at the same table since embarking in Australia.

This surprising introduction broke the ice, our conversations became animated and very interesting during the meal.

Our personal history in Egypt accounted for, the reason for their visit to England was explained.

The average age of these 'Aussie' ladies, calculated by Geordie, was thirty years.

The remainder of the voyage home was of a holiday cruise quality in the company of these delightful people.

The ship was diverted from its course, to Palma in the Balearic Islands. At the same time, all the soldiers were confined to their cabins, with sanctions if disobeyed. Our confinement lasted some three hours, by this time the ship was back on course and out of sight of land.

According to the Sergeant in charge, our temporary incarceration was a diplomatic necessity.

Apparently a war of some description had broken out in Spain; the ship was diverted to rescue a number of V.I.P's and take them away from the conflict.

We were confined for the sake of diplomacy; it would not be in the interests of safety for uniformed British soldiers to be seen on the ship's rail while the boarding was taking place.

The identity of these VIP's was a mystery; they were secreted away for the remainder of the voyage.

The last evening meal of the voyage with the Aussie ladies was a celebration. They wanted the final dinner together marked as an occasion to be remembered. Geordie and I were their special guests, whose company they had enjoyed and who had made the last nine days of their long voyage a memorable event.

This shared experience of friendliness and kindness would also be a pleasure of memory recall for both Geordie and myself.

The wine and other alcoholic beverages during the meal and afterwards was with the compliments of the ladies as they knew our budget could not afford such luxuries – they told us so!

I was twenty three years old, this was my first acquaintance with the insidious side effects of excessive imbibing of liquor, with the resulting spectacle of a young soldier being escorted on the rolling deck of a liner to his cabin by two lovely ladies, who also had some difficulty in stopping the deck from moving.

Geordie soon followed, escorted by the other two ladies.

I slept with my gym shoes in situ, belt on and trousers off. How came this to be so, I do not know.

Breakfast over, the courtesies of parting were accompanied by smiles, signs of sadness, hugs, kisses, handshakes and final goodbyes. Disembarkation would commence at 1200 hours.

We were the last passengers to go ashore, forming into two squads and escorted off the ship by two R.T.O. sergeants. A squad of fifteen RASC men followed by a squad of twenty RAMC men. Both squads boarded buses and went our respective ways to our depots.

A dream sequence of my life had ended. I woke up outside the Crookham Camp guard room, where it had started some months before. My life as a soldier in the desert and on the Canal, was completely out of context with my life before and after the event. It did not fit in or mesh at either end; it stands alone, the stuff of dreams. An ocean liner sailing through the desert with an escort of camels, a pit boy holding hands on the banks of the river Nile with an ancestor of a Pharaoh's pyramid builder.

To me the whole Egyptian episode, from embarking on the SS Lucania, to disembarking from the SS Otranto, will always seem to be a conjuring trick of such illusory skills that I am still trying to work out how it was done.

I was transferred to the army reserve for the second time with my character enhanced as shown in my discharge book and with my military record unblemished.

I asked the orderly room sergeant to make my railway warrant to Cardiff and the Rhondda. I was keen to see my family and especially my mother, before I once again decided my future.

Whilst abroad I had written home on a regular basis, keeping the family in touch with my whereabouts and wellbeing. I now wrote a card to my mother giving the day and time of my arrival.

My sister Olwen was at the station to greet me. She cried when I left some months ago; she cried again on my return, whilst showering me with kisses and hugs. She was overjoyed to see me.

Arriving at the house, I sensed a major change had taken place during this particular absence of mine. All was quiet, both my mother and father welcomed me with open arms, with my father saying how well and bronzed I looked and telling me to sit, relax and tell him all about my foreign travels.

I was overwhelmed with the unexpected display of paternal concern and curiosity. I liked it and was pleased.

Olwen and my mother after a little while responded to my questioning as to the activities and whereabouts of the rest of my siblings.

Arfon, Betsy and Jean were in primary school, Peggy was in grammar school, Ethel, my elder sister was away nursing and engaged to be married.

Glyn, my brother, two years my junior, was a fully qualified carpenter and was working in London. Olwen was a first year student in college.

I silently included myself in this family roll call as the unpredictable, ne'er-do-well brother on the dole. The change in the family's fortune and outlook imperceptible to them. It was to me, a new family with whom I would have to re-acquaint. A task I would pursue with some diligence as I was fond of my brothers and sisters.

During my first few days with the family it became obvious to me that my father's view of himself and his previous actions, had mellowed. He was more communicative and not so moody to the extent that he enquired if I had been able to play the game of chess whilst in the army. I said I had not played for a long time, the opportunity being rare, the dearth of opponents being the problem.

His face lit up, "When you feel like it, I will help take the rust off your skills", he said. He also commented on the fact that he had not played a decent game of chess since Glyn had left for London.

I have no doubt in my mind that he said this to boost my confidence. I was nowhere near the good player of my brother; he was the player most feared by my father.

The dole queue I rejoined was of the same faces that were there when I left a while ago to do a course of precision fitting. Only this time they were emaciated with their eyes sunk into darkened sockets, staring into the gloom at the back of the head of the man in front who was staring at the back of the head of the man in front.

A bedraggled queue of defeated men, supplicants of a deranged system of phoney economics, subservient to the bankers and city manipulators, whose activities predominated the quintessential struggle of life over death besetting these poor and blighted wretches.

I was out of place in this setting. A well-fed, sun-bronzed healthy young man, with the desert sand still between his toes.

The seventeen-shilling dole money was essential. I kept my place in the queue, staring at the back of the head of the man in front, for five weeks.

My brother Glyn came home from London for a long weekend to be with the family and to see me.

CHAPTER EIGHT

Return to
the City

My brother and I were great friends. We had a lot in common; having spent a lot of our time in each other's company as young boys and adolescents. The trauma of the eviction also drew us closer together. He was as lost as I was away from the old, and confronting the new. There was, however, a great difference in character and personality.

He was my father's son, I was my mother's son. The gene pool was unevenly distributed. I was irresponsible, restless and an unpredictable 'action man'.

Glyn was the exact opposite, solid, dependable and a deep thinker, stuck in a groove without any ambition. The difference in personalities was the reverse. Whereas I had a tendency to be insular and introvert, Glyn was inclined towards the gregarious and extrovert.

His life was a permanent quest for knowledge. He read widely and attended lectures and classes on a variety of subjects. He subscribed to scientific journals and political weeklies. He was also a convinced socialist. All of this seemed purposeless to me. His inherent lack of ambition debarred him from putting his wide knowledge to use or to any advantage.

On the Saturday night, we went together to the local pub, where he enquired of my future plans. He was not surprised when I told him that I had none, and was reasonably content with the present tenure of my position.

He suggested that I return to London, dig in with him and with my permission he would use his influence with his employer to give me a job of some description, and in his words "Afterwards you can take it from there!"

Before his visit I had toyed with the idea of returning to London, his offer clinched it.

Glyn was a foreman carpenter working on a site in Wood Green with his digs not far away. On arrival, his landlady was most helpful in arranging my accommodation. At the moment sleeping space in her boarding house was limited. Her sister who lived a few doors away helped out on the odd occasion by taking in boarders for bed only, meals being taken in her establishment. Thus it came about that I slept in one house and partook of food in another. The total cost was twenty five shillings a week. My 'sleeping house' was in the possession of an 'odd couple.' The wife a passable looking woman of about thirty years, her husband who looked much older was the owner of a fruit stall in the local street market.

My brother was successful in obtaining employment for me on his building site. I was now an electrician's mate at one shilling and sixpence per hour for a forty four hour week, plus overtime with the relevant rates of pay.

It was a very easy job, holding, fetching, and carrying, with the occasional screwing of switches and lamp holders on walls and ceilings that were wired and located.

My mate was a Londoner whose home was in Wood Green, married with three teenaged children; he was also politically conscious.

The first few days in my new surroundings and adjustment to the work ethic, was pleasant and serene in contrast to my previous London life, of which I had a desire to revisit and meet with some old friends, especially Billy and his brother Phillip, and to have their reactions and hear their conspiratorial theories regarding General Franco, the Spanish Insurrection and the Civil War now raging which had broken out on the day I had left Egypt. I remembered the rescue of a number of V.I.P.'s by the ship of which I was a passenger on my return.

This conflict had become the focus of the international and domestic antifascist movements, who saw it with horror and trepidation as a vicious onslaught by the fascist powers on a democratically elected government.

Glyn expressed a wish to accompany me to Praed Street. We arrived at Joe's café on a Saturday afternoon. Joe was absent from his usual place behind the counter. Two cups of tea were served by a stranger. I was nonplussed; the place looked the same, but the atmosphere was somewhat different. I felt out of place in what once was very familiar. There were a few people at the tables, but nobody I knew.

The stories I had told Glyn about the disaffected, the dropouts and political activists that frequented the café, he must by now think was a load of 'hog wash.' Wherein came two girls, one of whom I knew very well. The packet of fags and ten bob girl, and one of many. She spotted me, came over all beaming and pleased to see me. I invited her to sit down, she went back to the counter, returned with a cup of tea and a doughnut. She sat down and became a willing subject of my cross-examination.

She was a mine of information. Joe had not fully recovered from a 'terrible hiding' he took some months ago, as he went to the aid of some of 'your odd friends' when a bunch of fellows stormed into the place, attacked them with sticks and smashed up the café.

She surmised it was also the same crowd of blackshirts who beat "poor Phillip" so badly whilst he was selling the Daily Worker. He was now in a mental asylum. She was visibly upset on recounting the attack on Phillip.

All the girls liked him because of his simple ways and gentle behaviour. I continued my questioning. Billy and John Blackmore had gone to 'some war or other' in Spain. She had heard a few days ago from someone that John Blackmore had been killed. Of Billy she knew nothing.

I finished my examination of this caring girl, by asking her how she was faring, and how was her business. Her reply was, she was fine, but the business wasn't too good. Men were short of money and there were too many girls on the game, but she was managing.

She turned her head and looked around the café, she smiled back to me and said the place had 'gone to bits since you lot left!'

I introduced Glyn at the same time telling her I was working with him on a building site. She looked at me with a feigned look of surprise on her face and with a twinkle in her eyes said, "No more fags for you then! You have all gone bonkers!" She rose up and joined her friend on another table.

I was saddened by the news of John Blackmore's death and apprehensive of Billy's well-being.

We left the cafe, and walked down Edgware Road to Hyde Park; a walk I had done often in the past with Billy.

This time it was with the sole purpose of seeing if a 'Daily Worker' seller was at his old pitch, and to find out what had actually happened to Phillip.

Sure enough the pitch was occupied by Philip Armstrong, chief demonstrator and rabble-rousing organiser in Joe's cafe.

We shook hands heartily, I introduced him to Glyn, after which he gave me a long resume of the events surrounding Phillip as well as the multi-farious happenings pertinent to my old associates of drop outs, pimps and anarchists after the smash up at Joe's café by Mosley's thugs.

He also repeated what the young prostitute had told me about John Blackmore and Billy. He also suggested I go to the Daily Worker's office at King Street, where volunteers to fight in the Spanish Civil War were being signed up, and where it was possible to gather authentic first hand news of Billy and John.

Before I left him at this pitch, he mentioned there was to be a Mosley Fascist march in the East End next Sunday. There was to be a counter demonstration and an attempt would be made to disrupt the march of the fascist thugs.

Most of the old crowd would be in attendance and he would like to see me there.

His particular band of supporters would be assembling outside the Tower between noon and one o'clock. I said I would be there, Glyn chipped in with a "Me too!"

Sunday morning I went alone - Glyn was having a lie in - to the Daily Worker offices and its Spanish volunteer recruiting office. It was confirmed that Billy had been slightly wounded and was now somewhere near Madrid. John Blackmore had been killed as were a number of other volunteers, John Cornford and Ralph Fox amongst them. I was also told that the Republican Forces were in severe trouble and help was required.

My reading of the Sunday press that morning was of a split mentality in the editorial departments with the "Lets keep out of it" brigade in the ascendancy and let the Spaniards fight their own war.

The Conservative majority in the National Government saw it as a struggle against a covert Left Wing and Communist Republican Government.

The Labour party was ambivalent in its attitude as were the rest of the liberal establishment, with the exception of a few brave notable individuals.

The Left, the communists, the dedicated antifascists, saw it for what it really was – a fight for democracy against fascism. A dress rehearsal for the future take-over of Europe by German and Italian despots.

The Heinkels, Junkers and Stukas, were practising their city bombing runs. The Panzers were honing their blitzkrieg tactics. The British looked on, the working classes, the Labour and Trade Union movements were politically impotent. Like the eunuch they knew what to do and how to do it, but couldn't! They organised tins of milk, bandages and sticking plaster, instead of rousing the nation to supply guns, planes and men.

They acquiesced in the gang rape of a country, looking on as voyeurs with sham horror, at the same time advocating and promoting a policy of not intervening and encouraging the rest of the world to do likewise in the hope and expectation that the rapists would desist.

Indecision, vacillation with appeasement as make weight was typical of government responses to foreign crises in the thirties.

The efforts of the working class and the populace as a whole to the plight of the Spanish people was of sympathy, milk and ambulances.

The war went on for over two and half years, and as George Orwell noted, "'The British working class watched as their comrades in Spain were being strangled, and they were never even aided with a single strike.' The British workers disabling malaise of inaction was again evident, a few hundred men had already volunteered to take part with the Spanish people in their struggle. Would I think about it? In the meanwhile a local antifascist protest demonstration would take precedence.

Back at my job of fetching, holding and carrying, I told my mate Tom Adams, that I would not be available for overtime work on Sunday because my brother and I were going to the East End to take part in a protest demonstration against Oswald Mosley and his Blackshirts, who would be marching in the streets of a predominantly Jewish Quarter of the City. He said he had heard and read about the proposed march, and I wasn't to worry about Sunday work. He would like to join Glyn and I on the counter demonstration. House wiring could wait. I was pleased with this most unexpected of antifascist volunteers.

We met Philip Armstrong and his intrepid army of banner-carrying political activists, dropouts, layabouts and concerned antifascist protesters. Together we made our way to the main route of the proposed march.

The road was manned by hundreds of policemen, with a 'squadron of police cavalry' on the periphery, waiting for the call to "charge".

The route was also lined with a seething mass of demonstrators and protesters, incensed by the obscenity of an authorised march of vowed anti-Semites in the vicinity and close proximity to the houses and businesses of a vulnerable section of our society.

The police were out in force to protect Mosley and his organised display of calculated race intimidation and xenophobic paranoia from the hatred of the people and not to protect the people from the malignant objectives and vicious hatred of the Mosley thuggish entourage.

Mobocracy and democracy were coming into confrontation, a stand-off was building up into open hostility. The enforcers of law and order carried out their prime responsibility in a most exemplary manner. They bludgeoned any unlucky protester who had the temerity to approach, or was accidentally pushed to within touching distance of the black-shirted marchers.

This initial over-reaction by the police was to direct the frustrated anger of diverse groups of protesters onto the protectors of the march as well as on the black-shirted marchers themselves.

The protestors surged forward pushed by those behind. The protestors in front being beaten by the police, with the rescuers at the back dragging the beaten ones to safety being bludgeoned in turn.

The 'cavalry' was called, the march continued more or less unimpeded. The entire police force, mounted and on foot, were engaged in a full-frontal attack on the protesting demonstrators. A riot was in progress.

I was knocked down by a charging horse, and saved from being trampled on by the combatants, by the efforts of my brother and Tom Adams dragging me away from further danger at great peril to themselves.

The 'Battle of Cable Street' resulted in many antifascist casualties and arrests, nearly a hundred arrests and an equal number of injured. I am not aware of arrests or injuries suffered by the Blackshirts.

The Battle of Cable Street was an antifascist demonstration, one too many, from which democracy though triumphant had emerged wounded.

It had allowed the indefensible to take place. The outcome of such a crass decision would compel the government to sit up and take notice of the sentiments and antifascist credentials of the majority of individuals who had 'willy nilly' coalesced into a threatening mob.

A Public Order Act was passed which among other things banned the wearing of military style uniforms by political parties.

The sight of Oswald Mosley's black uniformed troops, on the march in arrogant mode down the streets of their capital city, made people more aware of what was happening by default in their name and the realisation of that which was taking place in Germany at this very moment was being duplicated in the streets of London.

The concentration camps would follow if they were allowed to get away with the purveying of their twisted political philosophy of ethnic cleansing and master race dominance.

One of my good acquaintances had been killed and my best friend wounded in an attempt to stop it all happening in a corner of Europe not too far away.

Monday morning and back to house wiring with my mate cock-a-hoop at having been part of the scene portrayed by the lurid headlines in the morning press. Tom Adams was a committed family man who accepted his responsibilities; he was also politically aware but restricted by his domestic life from taking part in overt action. The Cable Street experience had, however, whetted his appetite to pursue more diligently his opposition to fascism.

The next few weeks was of a normal workaday life, with my spare time occupied one way or another with attending local meetings called in aid of the Spanish people. In collecting and helping various organisations towards this end, a pleasant rewarding use of my time.

The tenor of this quiet life was interrupted by an unforeseen and unprovoked event of a most embarrassing kind.

The house of which I was the only lodger and where the husband was a fruit and vegetable stall holder was comfortable and satisfactory.

The wife, however, was becoming somewhat of a problem, which I was having difficulty in handling.

The husband's routine never altered; he would leave the house between 4.30 and 5 o'clock in the morning and journey to Covent Garden in his little van to purchase and transport supplies of fresh fruit and vegetable to his market stall. Within five or ten minutes of his departure, his wife would enter my bedroom, clad only in her nightie, with two cups of tea, squat down on the side of my bed, whilst I lay propped up on the pillow drinking my tea.

At first I took this to be a friendly gesture and which I welcomed. As the days went by into weeks, her conversation, her attitude and gestures took on a sexual orientation.

The timing of her stay became more prolonged; she was touching me and obliquely hinting that her favours were available. She was inviting herself into my bed!

I mentioned my predicament to my brother, at the same time entreating him to cajole his landlady to have me in her house, as a complete boarder, because I knew that one of her lodgers had left a couple of days ago.

Solid Glyn's pragmatic response was, give her what she wants, then perhaps she will leave you alone. I insisted that I could not give what she wanted, as she wasn't my type or my fancy, and I had no intention of getting involved. All I wanted was relief from this compromising dilemma and if Glyn couldn't help me I would look elsewhere for lodgings. Relief was at hand in a most dramatic and violent way.

The usual morning routine took place, husband leaving for the market at 4.30 am, wife entering my room with morning cups of tea, sitting on the bed, clad only in her nightdress, with her usual conversations, spiced with sexual overtones.

Without warning, the bedroom door sprung open with a resounding bang, framing a wild and angry husband accusing me, "You Welsh bolshie bastard! Fucking my wife when you thought my back was turned!" To him it was a straightforward case of "delecto flagrante."

He grabbed hold of me and she started screaming. I said nothing, I felt very guilty, though innocent, and as I have mentioned somewhere before I am a card-carrying coward.

He pulled me out of the bed. I did not resist one tiny little bit, He then got hold of my suitcase and started stuffing my belongings into it. I was standing in my shirt and short pants by the side of the bed. The wife crying, his temper vented on my possessions.

He then caught me by the neck of my shirt, hauled me to the head of the stairs, threw the suitcase down and pushed me after it. I managed to save myself from falling head first. Instead, I bounced on my bottom to the foot of the stairs, with my trousers and shoes thrown on top of me.

The wife was almost in hysterics; I had remained totally silent throughout the whole deplorable fracas.

I grabbed hold of my trousers and shoes, seized my suitcase and rushed into the street, thankful to have escaped with my life and without physical damage.

It was five o'clock in the morning and the street was empty. I put on my trousers and shoes, no socks or belt and moved quickly away from the house, sat on the side of the pavement, and reviewed the situation. I looked at myself and gave a big involuntary chuckle. My predicament at that moment to me, was of a humorous than of a serious nature. I was also by now of the opinion that I was not the first of her lodgers to be caught in "delecto flagrante."

I was very early for breakfast at Glyn's lodgings. I went to his room; he was in bed, but awake. He looked at me with the remark of 'What the hell has happened to you?' I told him. The bed shook with his laughter; I laughed with him.

I informed the landlady that I had been thrown out of her sister's house by a suspicious husband and could she find her way to give me full board?

Her answer was prompt and positive which reinforced my view that her sister's "tricks" with lodgers were a fact of which she was well aware.

It was a change to eat and sleep in the same house and away from a temptress.

We went home for Christmas. My mother and father were pleased to have all their family around them. We were getting older; Ethel, Glyn and I had left home for good. Olwen was in a student residence, "four down, four to go". It was inevitable, my mother knew it but she didn't like it.

Boxing Day. I walked the mountain with Glyn and Tim our dog to the old home valley. It was dying – its life crushed out by pit closures and migration of youth. The weeds of despair had taken over that which was once a proud and vibrant society, that made a virtue of survival under the most difficult and horrific circumstances. Time moves on without heed of life's resistance to its passing. All my friends had moved out, a few like Glyn and I were at home for Christmas but we too had changed. The original "eccentric" thirteen no longer lived in the valley. Their adolescent hopes and ambitions were now being played out as adults in an uncertain and uncaring world.

The work schedule of house wiring, the repetition, the routine, had become boring. I had worked conscientiously for three months and I was becoming restless. There was more to life than fitting switches and fuses. I did not want to make the job of electrical mate a career. My life of rejected jobs and potential careers was growing and I was about to add another. I was beginning to suspect my capabilities and willingness to hold and keep a job for any length of time.

Why couldn't I be like my brother and other people I knew, who once they had a job were terrified of losing it and would subject themselves to all kinds of pressures and indignities to keep it.

I knew I was introverted and a loner; at the same time I had confidence in myself and was a great optimist.

What was unseen and around the corner was always a challenge. I had yet to learn that life is a series of seeing around one corner after another and the older one gets, the corners straighten out and the way at last becomes clear.

I was six feet two inches tall of good physique, black hair, grey eyes, fairly intelligent, healthy and an ex-serviceman. Good Metropolitan Police material.

I would join – a hare-brained scheme if ever there was one, that my friend Billy would be proud of.

In my activities of street collecting for Spanish Aid, I approached a constable on his beat, had a long chat with him, obtaining the necessary information of what was required, and how to apply.

In due course I received an application form which I completed by answering a multitude of questions. I waited some two weeks before I received a reply. My application was favourably received and I was asked to attend an interview at an address in St John's Wood. I had not spoken or hinted to my brother or anyone else about my intentions.

The evening prior to the interview I went to Hyde Park to listen to the speakers and hecklers air their contrary views about the Civil War in Spain. I met Phil Armstrong at his 'Daily Worker' pitch and had a talk with him. I nonchalantly mentioned that I was going for an interview with the hope of joining the Metropolitan Police.

A look of incredulity registered on his face, followed by a tirade during which he cast aspersions on my sanity.

'After what happened to you at Cable Street, I would think you would be the last person who would want to do the same to others!' he said.

He hit home, right on target. I then told a lie; I said I was only joking, and changed the conversation.

I returned to my lodgings, went straight to bed, but could not sleep pondering the morrow,

I have been asked a hundred times or more over the years, 'What decided you to fight in Spain?'

I have no facile or ready answer available, and the truth on offer is only partial. The emotions and motives for my decision were complex.

I was bored with my work, unsettled, independent, irresponsible, wanting a change, to test, challenge and satisfy my curiosity of what was around the corner; but this time with the knowledge that my antifascist credentials and first aid expertise would be of use around the corner, where my friend Billy was already.

The look on Phil Armstrong's face when I said I was thinking of joining the

Metropolitan police and his following remarks wherein he questioned my sanity was a deciding moment that re-railed my thoughts and attitude that had temporarily jumped track.

I jettisoned a possible police career, in favour of an impulsive act which this time coincided with a reason I had expressed many times in the past; the fight against fascism.

The bridge between the impulse and the act is a highly personal process. One that men rarely divulge to each other, even when they themselves are conscious enough to trace its intricate path.

There is a no-mans-land between conviction and action into which the majority of humankind never ventures. Today the final determining factor which set each single one of over 2,000 British in motion on their democratic crusade died with 530 of them. Those of us who returned will probably guard some small part of the secret to the end of our lives.

My interview was at King Street to volunteer into the 'International Brigades'. The interview at St John's Wood was a non-starter.

Alun (left) at Victoria Station in December 1938 with the returning
members of the British International Brigaders. His clothes were provided
by the French Communist Party. His companions are unknown.

Alun at left behind and between hatted men and women.
(stills from British Television and Film Archives)

CHAPTER NINE

Trying to get into a War

That evening I told my brother I was leaving for Spain in the morning. He expressed the view I was bereft of my senses, and it was typical of my irresponsible attitude in relation to the family and to myself.

He was my father's son and like him when confronted with the awkward and the illogical, would retire in their blossoming solitude, the spectators of life, into their own little observation towers, roaming the timeless universe in strange quests and severe detachment from the human ant heap.

The stay-put and take no risk of the poets, philosophers and thinkers whilst sitting on their behinds with their hands to their foreheads, doing nothing other than looking down on the likes of me, looking up at them, was to me, at that time, a dead end occupation. I would do what I had to do and think about it later.

Early on the Friday morning in the middle of January 1937, I presented myself at the King Street office, at the rear of Covent Garden. Here volunteers were being briefed for the journey to Spain.

The non-intervention policy was in full operation and 'neutral' against the democratically elected Spanish Government. The Foreign Enlistment Act of 1870 was made applicable in regards to the conflict, with a penalty upon conviction of two years jail. I was about to break the law, be a criminal on the run for having the temerity to join in the struggle in defence of freedom from the depravation of fascist dictators.

I was teamed up with four other volunteers, two from Glasgow and two from Yorkshire. For some reason, I will never to know why, I was made leader and given a sum of money to pay for continental cross ferry tickets, valid only for three days. Failure to return home after expiry, would classify us as illegal entrants. We would be fugitives.

From now on, until we reached the Spanish Frontier, because of the murderous lie of non-intervention and the Foreign Enlistment Act, our journey would be of a clandestine nature with all the risks disclosure would involve.

My instructions for the journey to Paris were simple. I was to carry underneath my right arm, a copy of the London Times, with the title plainly showing. On arrival at the "Gare de Nord" we would walk nonchalantly towards the main exit, where I would be 'accosted' by a young lady who would point to the Times, remove it from under my arm and we would follow her. The train arrived on time and I was approached by a young pretty female. She relieved me of the London Times, and with a gorgeous smile linked my arm and escorted me out of the station. My four companions following close behind. Outside the station, we entered two cars waiting nearby and were transported to a seedy looking part of Paris, to be deposited outside a café, which we entered, were served with a meal and told to wait. Eventually our pretty escort returned, and took us to a house in a most insalubrious suburb of Paris, where we were interviewed by a tall elegant lady, none other than Charlotte Haldane, the wife of Professor J.B.S. Haldane, who at the time was the Daily Worker's Science Correspondent. Charlotte was the British representative and one of the organisers working at the Paris Office of the 'International Brigades.'

After receiving a new set of clandestine travelling instructions from this fascinating lady, I was handed a sum of francs for train fares and incidentals. We were then taken to a room in a large block of flats; our lodgings for the night.

After a most uncomfortable night in this noisy tenement, we boarded a train at the Gare d'Austeriliz for Perpignan and the Spanish Frontier, where a contact would be waiting to receive us. On arrival at our destination, we waited on the platform as instructed for the approach of our contact. There was no sign of such a person.

We moved to the station entrance and waited again without success. We were becoming concerned with this unexpected hitch in the clandestine operation. Feeling very conspicuous 'hanging' around the station, we moved away to a small tree-lined square a little distance from the station. There were benches on the square, one of which we occupied to relax, discuss our predicament, and form a plan of action.

One of us would not be conspicuous standing alone at the station entrance. I would go there, wait fifteen minutes; and return to the square if contact was not made, with a view to working out the best method of contacting the local communist party, who we knew were in on the clandestine operation.

I waited the fifteen minutes, help was nowhere in sight. I made my way back to the square and my companions. They had vanished and the bench was empty with two gendarmes waiting near there to arrest me. The other four had already been arrested and taken to the Commissariat Central Police, to where I was promptly escorted.

At the Commissariat, I was stripped-searched, questioned by an authoritative civilian, who spoke fair English and was very courteous in his attempts to gain information of what was the purpose of my visit to Perpignan. Where was my passport? Who else was involved with me? etc.

All my answers were a spontaneous pack of lies. The interview ended with the statement; I was trying to cross over into Spain, which was illegal and in contravention of the non-intervention pact. I was put into a cell on my own. The other four were in another part of the building and treated as a case separate from mine.

The following morning, I was interviewed by an English-speaking lady lawyer, who informed me because I was in possession of a sum of money I would not be charged. The others were penniless and deemed 'vagabonds.' She also told me I was to remain in custody, while the others were arraigned, and further enquiries made about me. After which I would be released and escorted to the British Consulate at Marseilles. The fare was to be paid with the money found in my possession on arrest.

I was released after seven days of almost solitary confinement. My companions were sentenced to fourteen days imprisonment as 'English vagabonds.' At the same time as I was let out, I was joined by a fellow Welshman whose predicament was almost identical to mine. His party had been apprehended a day or two after the arrest of our group. Before we finally left the commissariat, we were photographed from all angles, finger-printed and plaster-casts made of our hands. The Secret Service were taking no chances.

Jack Roberts, a fellow Welshman was my new travelling companion. A revolutionary "Red" in mind and deed. A born fighter against injustice. He reminded me so much of my friend John Blackmore who had already died fighting for the same cause that Jack Roberts was volunteering for and trying to emulate. Jack's story is graphically told in a book entitled 'No Other Way - Jack Russia and the Spanish Civil War' - a biography by his grandson, Richard Felstead (Alun Books, Port Talbot, 1981).

From the moment of our meeting outside the Commissariat, it was obvious to me that Jack would be the dominant partner to a willing follower. He was fourteen years my senior. We were put on the train for Marseilles for the explicit purpose of reporting our plight to the British Consulate, as stranded citizens in need of assistance to get back to Great Britain.

What money we had between us was confiscated with the exception of a few francs, and given to our secret service escort for train fare. After boarding the train this gentleman melted into the background and out of sight, until he surfaced some days later at Toulouse Station.

Outside Marseilles Railway Station, Jack and I stood, looked around and saw humour in our situation. We were criminals, fugitives from justice, 'stony-broke', not knowing a word of French and hoping somehow to get to the British Consulate for help. With lots of gestures, little maps drawn on odd scraps of paper, and the words 'Britanico Consulato' shouted by Jack at people for whom we asked the way, eventually got us there.

We were shown into a room and told to wait. After what seemed an inordinately long time, we were ushered into a small ante room, to be confronted by a greying Consulate General with a look of contempt on his face and a nasty smell under his nose, at the audacity of these two odd characters asking for help.

How dare they? And we hadn't yet uttered a word.

My initial urge at first sight of this official 'donkey' was to walk out. I knew we weren't going to get help. My respect for authority however, came to the rescue. I stayed as Jack put our case of how we had been on the 'booze' in Paris, and the train we had caught for Calais, had somehow and mistakenly landed up in Perpingnan. We were penniless, and at his mercy and goodwill to assist us in getting back home.

He didn't believe our story (we didn't expect him to). The nasty smell under his nose got stronger. He attempted by questioning us to glean information of our contacts and route of the clandestine operation that brought us to Perpignon. We repeated our protestation of innocence of getting on the wrong train. He rose from his chair, scowled at us, and with a look of disdain and supercilious tone of voice, he addressed us from on high, accusing us of being common criminals of contravening and ignoring the non-intervention pact, and the foreign enlistment acts of two countries. He was not going to assist us in any "way shape or form" to get back home to England. An official representative of the Great British Empire had verbally mugged and refused help to two of its unfortunate citizens when in need. We were then thrown out of the Marseilles office of the British Consular Service, officially, if not physically.

On emerging from the stuffy room with its pompous ass into the Mediterranean air, Jack's anti-establishment and revolutionary fervour would have razed the Palace of Westminster to the ground and turned Buckingham Palace into a public lavatory.

The prejudice and arrogance of the occupants of the Consular building behind us was symptomatic of a very sick and unequal society, where its citizens when in need of help are treated by well-paid civil servants as non-persons, and a local nuisance, not-worth-the-bother, in any "way, shape or form." Like the man said! The door closed on this ugly face of officialdom. We walked away with a much more pressing problem of bladder expansion. Our body requirements of replenishments and relief had been on hold since vacating the jail house at Perpignon.

A distance from the Consulate, we spotted an underground toilet. We descended the long stone steps and when near the bottom a loud French scream was hurled at us by the matron in charge of the female facilities, which we had mistakenly entered. We turned about and quickly rushed back up the steps. Her screaming French abuse got louder as she chased us up the steps on to the street. We ran for our lives until we were lost in the ethnic mix of people that inhabited the dockside area of the city.

We were in possession of empty stomachs and full bladders, we had little money, unable to speak one word of French and were fugitives in a foreign land. Our circumstances were so bizarre that Jack and I laughed and relaxed. Nature's antidote to panic was in control.

We wandered the streets of this cosmopolitan city seeking out something familiar, which we eventually found in the window of a small café. A sign which read

'English tea served here'. We entered, sat down and were immediately attended by a young waiter. Jack held up the index fingers of his hands and said 'tea'. The waiter then said in faltering 'student English.' "Two cups or one tea pot?" Surprise, surprise! Jack answered "Two cups please and two pieces of cake."

I then whispered to the young lad a request to use the toilet and would he show me where it was. He smiled, took me by the arm and led me to a door next to the counter marked 'Hommes'. I was learning French. I returned, relieved, with the contented grin of a Cheshire cat. Jack upped and followed my example.

Two cups of hot water arrived with tea bags tied to the handles, two slices of cake, a small bowl with lump sugar and two spoons, but no milk! We dunked the tea bags, sugared the tea and ate the cake, with Jack all the while letting of steam by giving vent to his feelings in his best Welsh valley accent, with the perfidious behaviour of the British Diplomatic Service in general, and with particular reference to the local representative.

At the end of his tirade, which I am sure could be heard back at the Consulate. A lady sitting at an adjacent table who had been watching us since we entered and who no doubt by now was intrigued by the two strange English speaking people drinking tea and, one with a large chip on his shoulder, who was not inhibited in advertising the fact. She came over to our table and said in perfect English "I gather from the conversation which I could not help but overhear, that you are in some difficulty." She then took out of her handbag a piece of paper on which she wrote the name and address of the chaplain of a seaman's mission in the port of Marseilles, together with street names and directions of how to get there.

She returned to her table, called the waiter, paid her bill and on her way out of the café, she leaned over and wished us good luck, and in passing, said that our bill has been paid! She was through the door before it dawned on us what she had done.

A complete stranger had taken the trouble to assist in solving our present quandary by giving name, address and location of a place that may be in a position to help us, plus paying our café bill.

This was a voluntary, unsolicited, act of kindness and generosity, an altruistic moment of such a rarity in my life, that it has reserved a place on my shelf of memories all for itself.

With the lady's notes of directions, we had no difficulty in finding the seaman's mission. Jack explained our difficulties to a very receptive chaplain; a most patient and understanding man. He could see we were different from the normal characters he dealt with on a daily basis, especially when Jack asked him if he would be kind enough to send a cablegram to the clerk of the Caerphilly District Council, requesting money for our fare home.

The chaplain agreed to Jack's request. He also gave permission and made arrangements for us to have full board and lodging until such time as a reply was received from Wales.

On the morning of our third day at the Mission, we were invited to the Chaplain's office where he presented Jack with a money warrant from his friend the clerk of the Council. We both thanked him for his help and kindness. After which he put forward the suggestion, the warrant would be of more value when changed into real money, which he would arrange within the next half-hour.

With a pocket full of francs, we made our way to the railway station, purchased tickets for a through journey to London via Toulouse, Paris and Calais. This reduced our pocket full of francs to zero. We couldn't care less; we were on our way home and freeing ourselves from the mess of a clandestine 'cock-up.'

Getting off the train at Toulouse, Jack was intrigued and drawn to a rowdy drunk shouting the praises of the Spanish Republican Army, while at the same time my attention was being solicited by our Secret Service shadow who we had lost after our departure from Perpignon.

He invited us into the bar of the station café, and in perfect English with a French accent, he enquired of our choice in drinks. Jack desired a cognac, I wanted a long cool drink; he also had a cognac. With the drinks in our hands, we retired to a table to savour them. He then with a pleasant smile recounted our movements of the last four days, including the incident at the ladies toilet, which he thought was hilarious.

During the rest of the conversation, it was plain where his sympathies lay. He was sorry that the gendarmes of the day at Perpignan had been so awkward, they all knew what was going on and most closed their eyes; it was the same all along the frontier. His job ended at Toulouse, as soon as we got on the train for Paris, we were no longer his concern. Ten minutes later, we shook hands and he saw us on the train, wished us "Bon voyage" and "Bonne chance".

Jack and I parted at Victoria Station, devoid of all possessions except one franc and two shillings between us. We did however, have decent beards and a good odour! We hadn't shaved, bathed or had a change of underwear for nigh on fourteen days. We shook hands, unaware that we would again be shaking hands and in the near future under a set of circumstances totally different from the present. With Jack holding a rifle, with a bandolier slung across his shoulder, and I, with a bag full of field dressings and with a Red Cross band on my arm, as we met on our separate paths on the way to the front line and the Battle of Brunete. Jack made tracks for Paddington, Abertridwr, and home. I went to King Street in the hope of obtaining a little money to maintain myself in London for a few days while I reviewed my position and decide my next move.

I was questioned about the problem at Perpignan which they knew about, but not who was involved. After the questioning and answer session was over, a lady in the office wanted to know where I was going and what were my intentions. I told her that all I wanted at that moment was a change of underwear and a bath. They all smiled at this. My dishevelled appearance said it all. The lady who posed the question invited me to her home, if I could wait a half-hour or so. I accepted her offer and thanked her.

I was given five pounds by a person of some authority who at the same time hinted that I have 'another go' at getting to Spain because men of my military first aid experience were badly needed out there.

The lady took me to her home, where she lived with her widowed mother, and brother of nineteen years, who worked in a local garage. With his permission I was given a clean set of underwear, socks, underpants, and shirt; he also let me use his razor. I emerged from the bathroom completed refreshed and at ease, to be told that I could stay with them for a few days whilst looking for lodgings, or whatever else my intentions were.

The mother was an active member of the Communist Party, her daughter likewise a Party member and an employee at King Street. I stayed with this kind family for three weeks. My army quarterly reserve pay which was due the following week, plus the seventeen shillings I received from the dole after much haggling over red tape, contributed to the cost of my bed and board.

I have often been asked many questions about Spain. One of the most difficult to be confronted with, is why didn't I let my mother and family know I was back in England and not in Spain, where my brother had told them I had gone? My explanation is straight-forward and simple.

As far as my mother was concerned I was already in Spain, and even though I was back in London, I was undecided whether or not I would have 'another go'. If I did, it seemed pointless to me in causing her a repeat trauma when as much as she knew I was already there. Irresponsible, thoughtless maybe, but it was without malice.

Towards the middle of March, I once again presented myself as a candidate for the International Brigade. This time I was a member of a group of eight volunteers. The procedure to get to Paris was almost identical to my previous attempt.

At Paris we were again interviewed by "Charlotte the Harlot", as she was affectionately known! But this time there was a difference in procedure and outcome to my previous attempt at entering Spain. Myself and three other volunteers, Robbie from London, Geordie from Sunderland and Jim Jones of no fixed abode, were to remain in Paris. The other four members of the original party of eight were to proceed on their way to the Spanish Frontier.

We were held back because of our expertise in certain aspects of military techniques. Robbie was a signaller, Geordie a tank driver, Jim Jones a guardsman and me a first aid man. To what use and where our expertise was to be tested was at the moment unknown.

Jim Jones became my new and close companion for the next eight weeks. He latched on to me for reasons peculiar only to himself. He was a strange person, very reticent with the look of a haunted man. Tall and well built, I guessed his age to be middle thirties. He spoke with a cultured accent. That he was an ex-guardsman was visible by his demeanour and bearing. He never divulged which Guards regiment he was in or his rank. The name Jim Jones was an alias that much I found out during our weeks of relationship. That he had been a commissioned officer of some rank, he never confirmed. I am however, of the opinion that he was so.

The four of us, as temporary residents of Paris, lived in a comfortable room in a small tenement block near a restaurant where food was provided. The Bistro alternating with the tenement was where we spent most of our daytime. During the evenings at this bistro we were entertained by sympathisers and people from the Paris recruiting office.

Ten days elapsed. One morning very early, we were called to see Charlotte, who gave us the reason for the delay in our movements and our stay in Paris. We were part of a special group of well trained ex-soldiers of various nationalities, German, Italian, Polish, but mostly French.

We were being transferred to Bordeaux, from where we would be carried by fishing boats to Santander on the northern coast of Spain, with the view of helping the Asturian and Basque people in their defence of this northern enclave of Republican Spain, where a major Nationalist offensive was in the offing.

Later in the morning a bus pulled up outside the bistro where we were waiting. We entered to join twenty five to thirty volunteers of all nationalities bound for the same destination. There was also a Communist Party member as our courier aboard.

Our arrival at Bordeaux was expected. We were taken to a building, given a selection of sandwiches and a glass of wine and introduced to the people with whom we would be billeted until we left for Santander. The date of this assignment was uncertain.

We were paired off by the courier with Jim Jones as my partner; Robbie and Geordie, the other two Britons in the group were also paired. Jim and I were then handed over to a pleasant looking couple in their late thirties. The courier who spoke a little English introduced us as 'Deux voluntaire Anglais'; our hosts nodded and shook hands.

The courier then told us we were to remain with the couple and be available and on call at any time. Maybe in a day, a week or longer, he did not know when. The couple indicated the way and shepherded us out of the building into their car.

As we drove off, the couple started talking to each other only to have their conversation suddenly interrupted by Jim Jones speaking to them in their language. I was flabbergasted, at the moment I did not know what Jim was saying. The wife turned around and with a big smile, said "Bien, merci beaucoup." That was the end of all conversation until we got out of the car some time later.

During the evening, when we were alone, I asked Jim what had he said to the couple in the car to stop them talking. They were talking about us said Jim, and not to have them embarrassed later on by finding out he could speak their language, he thought it best to let them know that he could understand and speak French.

With tongue in cheek I said, "Quite right, Jim." I had been with this man for nine days in Paris and this was the first time I knew he was conversant with the language.

Our host owned a slice of land consisting of a small vineyard, a vegetable plot, chickens and two goats which they maintained with the help of two labourers.

They were proud parents of daughters, aged fourteen and seventeen, communist party members and of Basque origin. Hence their sympathies for the Spanish people in the present conflict and their generosity and overwhelming kindness in having us as guests.

The first few days at the little chateau was of a slight strain, my shyness and introvert physche was a great hindrance. Jim's reticence and surly behaviour of 'oui's' and 'nons' when being questioned about something or another, was most disconcerting. Our hosts I am sure could sense and see the difference in their guests' personalities. In the beginning they tolerated Jim and went overboard in making us at home, welcomed and comfortable.

A week went by without a word as to our movement. José, the husband's name, insisted that formalities were out of place; first names were of a more friendly way of address. His wife's name was Consuela, his eldest daughter Ampara and the young one Marie; their names all indicating their Spanish lineage.

Jose was in daily contact with the local organisers responsible for our wellbeing and would report to us all that was happening in efforts to fulfil the task that we were here for. The main problem apparently was, because the Nationalists had declared a total sea blockade of all Spanish ports, the fishermen who would ferry us across the bay wanted to be absolutely certain of the blockading movements of the Nationalist and Italian warships. Their boats and lives were at stake.

The second week of our stay was more relaxed, Jim was integrating in his own way, he expressed a wish to help out on the plantation, which Jose acceded to; Jim became a third labourer.

I also expressed a desire to do something useful. I was shown by Consuela how to mix the chicken feed, replace the old litter with new, how to collect the eggs and grade them to size. By the end of my stay in this little chateau near the Petit Gironde, I was a first class 'chicken attendant.'

In the evenings, I would sit in the lounge with the family being taught French by the seventeen year old Ampara, in exchange for me teaching her English. With the occasional game of chess with Jose, whom I can only remember beating once during the whole time. After the evening meal, Jim would either walk around the estate or retire to his bedroom; he never mixed with the family.

At the side of the house was a large grassed open space where the girls would have me play ball games of various kinds, some new to me. A most enjoyable pastime. At weekends and when not in school, the girls wanted to be in my company most of the time.. I was a great novelty; they would shout at me and tease me in their French language and Gallic ways and have great fun at my expense.

The Civil War in Spain, the sole purpose of my being with this family, was relegated to the background. The tranquillity of my immediate surroundings, the extended welcome by Jose and his wife, the friendships of his daughters, all assisted in an amnesiac hiatus. Also the natural phenomena of the brain's inability of thinking or concentrating on more than one thing at a time was compensation. Antifascism and the Civil War were temporarily forgotten.

By the middle of the third week, the spell was broken. As dusk was falling a car arrived to take us away. We wished our hosts goodbye, they seemed sorry to see us go. Young Ampara didn't want to know, she vanished.

At the dockside rendezvous, we met Geordie and Robbie and twenty five to thirty other men. We were given a small haversack containing bread, cheese and a bottle of water. This was intended to sustain us on the voyage and on landing.

Around midnight, we were escorted to the fishing vessels lying alongside. Split into two groups, we then boarded. We were on our way, in a hold, stinking of fish!

The boats chugged their way out of the harbour into the Bay of Biscay with Santander and a war the next stop. The sea was calm, but the roll of the little ship made me feel very sick. I found my way to a secluded corner of the hold and saw my food for the second time that day! I thought I was dying, and I couldn't have cared less at that moment. Jim came over to comfort me, he put his arms around me and drew me to himself, I got better quickly, I didn't like his embrace and broke away saying I was much better!

Daylight crept into the hold and we scrambled on deck. The world was all blue and empty with the exception of our two little boats rolling in the swell.

The execution of the plan was, that, with luck, it would be dark before we were in sight of land, thus avoiding the blockading patrol. We would disembark, with the boats going back and well out to sea before daybreak.

As the sun was setting we were within thirty miles of landfall. An Italian warship was in sight, we had been spotted. In international waters, as such we were safe for the moment. The boat's skipper decided to turn back, the chance of a safe landing was nil. If he approached the coastal limits we would be blown out of the water.

The Nationalist army with the assistance of the Italians and the German Condor Legion with the immense destructive power of its latest artillery pieces and bomber aircraft was sweeping across the Basque country, with defensive positions crumbling before the onslaught.

We arrived back at Bordeaux late in the afternoon of the next day, tired, disappointed and very 'fishy' to be collected by our erstwhile hosts later that evening.

Consuela by the look on her face was pleased to see us back safe. Jose was also pleased to see us but voiced his opinion at being stopped in our efforts by an Italian Fascist warship, which had no business being there anyway.

Ten days later, a second attempt was made at running the blockade with almost disastrous results.

It was midnight; we were almost within the coastal limits, when a gunboat came from nowhere sweeping the sea with its searchlights, with the sounds of heavy machine gunfire pointing in our direction. The fishing boats were not prepared to risk a landing, instead they turned back for home. The searchlights picked us up, but took no action, no doubt because we were heading out to sea. This was the second and last abortive attempt at landing token help, to the hard pressed Basque and Asturian people.

In between my blockading exploits and attempts at a landing, my life at the little chateau was a pleasurable and at time of hectic proportions. My duties as 'chicken-keeper' combined with the boisterous attention given me by the two girls and the occasional games of chess with Jose kept me fully occupied.

There was, however, a slight blur on this mirror of country life. Young Ampara was showing signs of puppy love, she was developing a crush on me, which I found very difficult to avoid or contain. I did not want to be rude or hurt the young adolescent by word or deed, furthermore I too had become enamoured of this young girl. She was nearly eighteen, I had just turned twenty four. Her actions, her looks, her touches, her attention to every whim of mine was an indication to me of her willingness to bite the apple and forfeit her cherry!

Without being arrogant or presumptive on my part, I know I could have. I wanted to, but I didn't. I left the little chateau near the banks of the Petit Gironde as celibate and the young girl as intact as when I arrived.

This was the first time, since I last flattened the grass on 'Joby Meadow' that my libido had awakened and demanded attention!

Her parents did not seem to notice their daughter's overt attentions to my needs and movements. If they did, they made the choice of ignoring it, as a temporary adolescent blip in her young life, which would end at any moment on my departure. I have the feeling they took that course and they ignored it.

Another of my problems was Jim Jones, I respected his privacy and the secrets of his haunting, but when this six foot four giant of a man and an ex-guardsman to boot, with covert homosexual tendencies who by now also had a crush on me, attempted to paw me and by innuendos propositioned me in the seclusion of the bedroom. I became very angry and told him in as few words as possible, what he could do to himself, but not to me! I was fuming, yet somehow understanding with a sense of pity for this sad man.

I had already formed the opinion that my companion Jim Jones was thrown out of a Guards regiment because of his sexual orientation. His haunting look was the sign of a deathwish which he intended fulfilling, but did not know how. Jim's wish was granted at the Battle of the Ebro. He is now at peace, buried with his secret where he fell, along with many of his comrades in the olive groves that flourish in this most beautiful part of the Ebro Valley.

Later in the evening, following the second abortive attempts at landing, a car arrived at the chateau, its occupant informing all within range that we would be going to Bordeaux railway station that night for transportation to Marseilles, where we would board a ship for Barcelona.

The military situation in the Basque region had deteriorated and was in Franco's favour. The uneven struggle was nearing a conclusion. The day after our departure to Marseilles, the town of Guernica was destroyed by German bombers.

I gathered my few possessions, razor, comb, soap, towel and a change of underwear. Jim did likewise. We said our goodbyes to our carers and thanked them for their hospitality during the past six weeks.

Our previous departures were more or less preludes for a possible return. This time it was final; we all knew it, especially young Ampara. On hearing the news at first, she did her usual vanishing trick, but this time as I was getting into the car, she appeared from nowhere, rushed over, kissed me full on the lips and with tears running down her cheeks, said "Bonne Chance, Alun."

The sound of my name uttered in a beautiful French accent by this young pubescent girl with a sob in her voice, forever lingers on, with its echo resounding in the valleys of the long ago.

CHAPTER TEN

The 15th International Brigade

At the port of Marseilles we were moved around for a few days, hiding in different houses, halls, outhouses, until finally one day as night was closing in, we were smuggled aboard a cargo ship bound for Barcelona.

We were a motley band of volunteers of all nationalities with a large contingent of Americans, and about a half dozen British, plus Geordie, Robbie, Jim and myself.

We were all dumped into a hold and forbidden to go on deck before the ship left harbour. Whilst waiting to leave, this assortment of men somehow managed to gravitate into their respective language groups. The English and Americans saw themselves, as the saying goes, separated by a common language. I joined myself to the group wherein were a number of my fellow Welsh countrymen among whom was Harry Dobson, a product of the Rhondda Valleys, like myself. I knew Harry on two counts, his reputation as a firebrand, he having served a jail sentence for incitement to riot. The other because he had been very friendly with my sister, Ethel. We had a lot in common and plenty to talk about.

Around midnight, the ship cleared Marseilles harbour into the Mediterranean and the Gulf of Lyons. We were now allowed on deck. It was a relief to be out of the claustrophobic atmosphere of the dark and crowded hold. I along with Jim, languished on a secluded part of the ship's deck in order to grab some sleep, which seemed to be the ambition of all the hold's late occupants.

It was late afternoon. I was leaning on the ship's rail taking in my first view of Spain and its shoreline, some one and half miles in the distance, when there came one hell of an almighty bang. The ship shook, tried to get airborne, before settling down at a crazy angle.

Shouts of 'Torpedo! The ship's sinking!' came from every direction and in every language. Jim grabbed me and made for a lifeboat that was being lowered; it was full. We looked around for another as well as for life preservers of any kind.

I have vivid recollections of those last few minutes; of the coolness of most of the men in this most perilous of circumstances. There was no jostling, pushing or shoving and no hysteria.

The ship was sinking fast. The last lifeboat had been lowered and because of the ship's angle and its death lurches, the boat tipped over emptying its human cargo into the sea. Jim and I jumped into the water and quickly made for the upturned boat and like many others clung to its side as the ship went down. In less than ten minutes from the time of the torpedo hitting the "City of Barcelona", it had disappeared.

There were many men in the water, some with life preservers, others hanging on as best they could to bits of wreckage. Jim and I grabbed hold of one man who was in serious trouble and managed to haul him to the side of the lifeboat of which he took hold. There were many such acts of like kind being played out that May morning in the sun in the Mediterranean Sea off the coast of Malgrat, north of Barcelona. The lifeboats that were afloat made for land, a mile and a half away.

I was a good swimmer. I knew I could make it to the shore if help was not soon forthcoming. I mentioned this fact to Jim. He smiled, it was the first time I had seen him smile in the seven weeks of our relationship. In spite of all the stress and trauma of the situation at that moment, the sight of Jim Jones' smiling with the lifting of his haunted look, relaxed the tension I was undergoing, as did the swearing and shouting of words of encouragement to one another, as we swam around, those of us who knew how, keeping the ones who couldn't swim, afloat.

Fishing boats quickly put out from shore, picking up all the survivors that were in the water and delivered us on to land, to the shocked population of the small town of Malgrat.

Harry Dobson, my two blockade comrades, Robbie and Geordie along with lots of others were enjoying hot coffee dispensed by the local citizens. They had landed safely in one of the few lifeboats. Many volunteers went down with the "City of Barcelona".

Within a couple of days of the sinking and subsequent rescue, we were on a slow and painful stop, start, crawling train journey to Albacete, a small capital in the region of La Mancha and the windmills of Don Quixote, the subjects of Cervante's imagination. Here was the headquarters of the International Brigades and where on arrival we were taken to an army barracks and segregated; those with previous military service and those without.

I was interviewed by Peter Kerrigan, British Commissar of the International Brigades, who then handed me over to an American who questioned me about my army service. After which I was given a uniform of sorts and later a haversack with a Red Cross emblazoned on it, filled with bandages, field dressings, tourniquets, syringes and ampules of morphine. I was told I would be sent to the front line at Jarama, with half a dozen or so German volunteers as a first aid man for the Thaelman Battalion until a replacement of a German nationality was found. After which I would be transferred to the new American Washington Battalion that was being formed. My Bordeaux comrades together with Harry Dobson and his group were being processed elsewhere and lost to me. It would be many months with much happening in the meanwhile before I saw any of them again.

A truck came, I clambered aboard with a crowd of Germans and Spaniards as company. One of the Spaniards was to be our guide. A solitary Welshman bemused by the hectic pace of events since vacating the little chateau on the banks of the Petit Girond with its fun of ball games with two young girls and the tranquility of quiet chess games in the homely company of Jose and his wife the lovely Conseula. To be suddenly pitchforked into a jabbering crowd of Germans and Spaniards and being transported to the front line of a bloody war. That I was going to have a problem with communications did not seem to matter. My main and only concern at this most difficult juncture of my exciting chequered career was to retain ownership of my life and survive whatever I was now committed to, which attempts at burial and drowning had so far had failed to get me to relinquish.

The truck stopped a little distance away from the trenches. We jumped down to be escorted to a dug out in the side of a small hill, which by all the activity surrounding the place, I assumed was Battalion H.Q. My assumption was correct. The party was greeted by a person of some rank who came to me after talking to his countryman. One of whom must have told him I was English, because he greeted me in broken English and said he was very pleased to have a first-aid man back in the Battalion.

As dawn was breaking, I was given a tin mug of hot coffee, after which, with the rest of the new reinforcements I was taken into the front line trench and guided by one of the soldiers on duty, to a part of the trench where a space had been made for the storage of stretchers. The Red Cross on my haversack had already indicated my status. All was quiet, or in the words of the official communiqués, "Sin Novedad"; my entry into a war was peaceful and undramatic.

My first three days as a front line first aid man was uneventful. The only sign or noise of war was the occasional crack of bullets as they went harmlessly overhead. My fourth day was of terror and a touch of panic. For a reason unknown this sector of the front line was the target of mortar bombs and artillery shellfire, which lasted for ten minutes, then ceased.

I was told by the battle-hardened soldiers of the Thaelman Battalion, that this was to be expected. It happened occasionally. I did not like it one bit; I certainly was not going to make a career of dodging shells and bullets.

Within a few seconds of the end of the bombardment, there were shouts of "Sanitario!" - that was me - Spanish for medical aid.

A young German volunteer was sitting on the floor of the trench with a few of his comrades around him. They moved aside as I approached to reveal the hand of this young man, hanging by the wrist, almost totally severed by a piece of shrapnel and with blood pouring out. This was the first time I had seen blood caused by war.

Momentarily I was shaken but training came to my assistance. I promptly applied a tourniquet, to stop the flow of blood, then proceeded to apply a field dressing to the wound and bind the almost severed hand with bandages to his forearm. He was quiet and weak with the loss of blood and in shock. He was put on a stretcher and carried by the bearers to an assembly point near the Battalion Headquarters from where he would be ferried by ambulance to the dressing station, some three to four miles to the rear. This was the first of a great many wounds I was to dress and tourniquet during the ferocious battles and periods of "all quiet" in the near future.

The front line first aid medical services of the International Brigades were inadequate and in some cases practically non-existent. The number of stretcher bearers was limited. I cannot recall seeing more than six to a battalion. Front line doctors were a rarity and of those in the front line their casualty rate was very high. I worked with Dr. Randall Sollenberger of Baltimore and Dr. Robbins of New York; both were killed at Brunete.

The doctors at the field dressing station were remarkable men. Under the most difficult and heartbreaking conditions, they performed wonderful feats of surgery. A severely wounded soldier's potential for survival was increased by 100% on arrival at the Field Dressing Station. The dedication and work of these doctors was bordering on the miraculous.

One of the many problems experienced by me was the delay and difficulty in getting the wounded from the assembly point at the front line to the dressing stations at the rear. The ambulances that carried the severe casualties were subject as of routine to aerial bombardment. The Red Cross was of no protection, it being ignored. The shortage of ambulances also exacerbated the difficulties.

The delay in collecting the wounded from the immediate vicinity of the front line was of practical concern. Deaths at these assembly points while waiting was inevitable, either by enemy fire or the severity of their wounds. The lack of stretcher bearers, the distance separating the front line from the dressing stations was of crucial importance. To require the walking wounded to travel this distance under battle conditions was asking a lot of these already traumatised soldiers.

A wounded man in the movement and chaos of battle is immediately dependent upon his comrades to drag him to safety if at all possible. Otherwise he is left where he lay, until a first aid man or stretcher bearers can help him, which is a very dangerous, foolhardy undertaking and a act of amazing contradictions.

The appalling appetite for slaughter in man is demonstrated with great clarity at a front line clearing station, where soldiers lay in mortal agony and where the screaming of falling bombs blend with the groaning agony of these damaged men, as they were being pulverised yet again in a deliberate act by their fellow man.

The pronouncements by the Generals that 'War is Hell' are mere words. Hell is a product of the imagination and without substance. War is real and unimaginable, Hiroshima, and the Holocaust for instance.

My experience and participation in two wars of my century will testify to the undeniable fact that man's will to destroy each other has no boundaries. Nature has made no provision to check this insatiable destructiveness in man. In war, all things perish at his hands; neither speed, wariness, cunning nor camouflage are of avail against intelligent means. Man adapts to a destructive end. He beats nature, he wounds her to her death in her great purpose of life - more life.

The days passed. The sector was quiet with the exception of short burst of machine gunfire and the odd mortar bomb being lobbed over. There were no serious casualties. I was learning Spanish. I could communicate a little more with my German comrades. Spanish eventually became the lingua franca of all the Brigades.

Ten days away after my 'baptism of fire' I was instructed to report to Battalion H.Q. where I was told I was being transferred to the new Washington Battalion at Tarazona, within the hour, the time of my replacement's arrival.

At Tarazona de la Mancha where the battalion was billeted, I was taken by Steve Nelson, the battalion Commissar, to a small barn, which was the 'surgery' of Dr. Randall Sollenberger and the headquarters of his small team of first aid men and bearers. I was the only one of his team to have experience of battle conditions. I was peppered with questions, which I took pride in answering. It was a change to converse in my language after ten days of hand signs, gestures, and feeble attempts at Spanish.

Dr. Sollenberger, a native of Baltimore U.S.A. was a few years older than me. During the weeks I was with his team, we became very friendly. He was curious about my background and about Wales in particular. Because of my Welsh accent he could not associate me with the English, to him I sounded different and foreign.

From this moment on and until the Battle of the Ebro, I was a first-aid man with the American Lincoln Washington Battalion in all the great battles of the Civil War. These are well documented, with the International Brigades having pride of place as the shock troops in all major engagements. With the exception of Teruel, which was captured by purely Spanish units of the Republican Army in a swift offensive during a snow storm of blizzard intensity on Christmas Day, the International Brigades were at the forefront of the fighting.

I am always amazed and envious of some of the memoirs I have read and of the various battles in which the writers participated; of their blow-by-blow accounts of events, skirmishes, ambushes, near-misses, place names, times, dates, map references, tactical errors, hysteria of retreats, the defence or loss of strategic points.

It is only by my reading of some of these accounts, do I realise that I too was there, but with an entirely different perspective, unrelated to the finer points of military planning, geographical locations, or the ebb and flow of killing engagements.

During my times in battle, I was always 'bomb happy' and unaware of a map reference as to exactly where I was, or what was happening where I wasn't. The names never registered with me. Of the rivers we crossed, the Pueblos, valleys and Sierras we advanced to, occupied and then forced to retreat from.

I witnessed most of the carnage from a height of six to twelve inches from ground level. A kind of worm's eye view of the bloody proceedings. I became an expert in the taste and texture of the Spanish earth. My body, for days and nights on end had the unnatural propensity of hugging the ground as I went about my business of applying tourniquets and field dressings, in between crawling to the aid of wounded soldiers and scratching around in the dark, locating the mournful cries of volunteers in awful trouble.

My accounts and recollections of these battles are mundane, and unexciting in comparison to the events and incidents meticulously noted by the memoir writers. The big picture as recorded by these authors in their detailed blow-by-blow accounts passed me by. I and my fellow first-aiders were more concerned with the distance to the field dressing station and the availability of stretcher-bearers.

In spite of this and irrespective of battle fatigue, there were moments when the big picture permeated my consciousness where sites and map references struck a chord of a personal nature to become vivid on recall, as well as the names of the battlefields where the bloody evidence of "man's inhumanity to man" was demonstrated and strewn around. I remember soldiers in great agony. I remember seeing soldiers mutilated beyond recognition. My mind sees as of yesterday, soldiers with smashed legs, soldiers with arms almost severed and hanging from their shoulders, and men dead without visible marks on their bodies.

The unforgettable battles at Brunete where soldiers died from loss of blood with swollen tongues filling their parched mouths for want of water. And Pardillo where the brave Dr. Sollenberger and the wounded he was attending were blown to bits by aerial bombardment, and where later I received a bullet in the leg.

I remember Teruel in a blizzard where a bitter wind was blowing through a railway tunnel used as a clearing station and shelter from the shells and bullets, causing havoc on the men of the Lincoln Battalion as they fought with the rest of the Fifteenth Brigade in the attempt of thwarting a major fascist offensive.

My memories of the Ebro River crossing have never gone away. Where Harry Dobson was killed and Morris Davies was badly wounded by a burst of machine gun fire, as we were standing together talking on the side of a hill close to the front line. I must have been standing at the correct angle for survival otherwise, I too, would have gone down. My second lucky miss of the war so far!

Harry dropped with a slight moan and died almost immediately★. Morris was hit in the stomach; he fell to his knees. I padded his wound, tied his legs to his stomach and urged the bearers to get him back to the dressing station as quickly as possible. Morris survived, but the war for him was over. With the stretcher bearers now in charge, I made my way to where further urgent calls were being made for my services.

An incident during the storming of Belchite, I shall never forget. Machine guns in a church tower were holding up the advance. It was shelled and caught fire. A great many enemy soldiers sheltering inside were burnt to death. An exception was a young Spanish soldier who was brought to the casualty assembly point with his clothes still smouldering and his body one massive blister from head to toe.

Editor's Note:

★ Harry Dobson was evacuated from the battlefield and died of wounds at Falset Cave Hospital behind the Ebro. Leah Manning MP stayed by Harry's bedside through the night that he died on 29th August 1938.
He was subsequently buried in a communal cemetery nearby. According to the written records his name was recorded as "Harry Dolsom". For further information see the 1st Len Crome Memorial Lecture "Beyond the Battlefield: A Cave Hospital in the Spanish Civil War" by Dr Angela Jackson, 2002.

I did not know what to do; he was beyond help and he was in great pain and conscious. One of the Spanish bearer's bent down, said something to him, stood up, took out his revolver and put the young man out of his agony. The horrors of the Sierra Pandols is another vivid recall. On a ridge of solid rock, we were bombarded for days and nights without shelter from the hot shrapnel and thousands of chunks of flying rocks, and where trying to pull Brazell Thomas of Llanelli to safety he was hit a second time and died. I left him where he lay, to aid his friend Evan Roberts, also from Llanelli, who was badly wounded with a smashed arm. I managed to drag him to some sort of safety. Evan survived; his injured arm was amputated. I remember Frank Proctor of Liverpool, (a friend of mine), collapsing into unconsciousness without apparent cause or reason. Until a further inspection revealed a sliver of steel, the thickness of a darning needle peeping out of his temple, with small spots of blood showing at its entrance and exit. Frank died within minutes.

I remember gentle Tom Howell Jones of Aberdare, lying on his belly with his rifle still in his hand and a gaping wound in the back of his neck. His dentures lay on the earth by the side of his mouth and me wondering what to do with them.

I remember how helpless I felt on occasions and how my terror with the Thaelman Battalion at Jarama, had become benumbed and hidden away with my emotions, together with my doubts, would they ever surface again with the intensity and sensitivity of yesteryear.

My saddest memory of all was two days before the big Republican offensive to relieve the pressure on Madrid. I made the journey to Mondejar, where the British Battalion was at rest with the intention of locating my friend Billy. I assumed that is where he would be.

He was there and when he saw me, he did not believe his eyes. His greeting was typical of him, in the same vein as was his greeting of a year or two ago, when he greeted me then with "Where the hell have you been these last four years?"

The variation this time, "Good God, Alun, what the hell are you doing here?" My reply was, "The same as you Billy", which brought a smile to his face.

He took off his glasses, wiped them and then introduced me to others of his acquaintance.

Later on, we went to the little village where he knew of a photographer and where he would like a photo of us taken together as a momento for the future. Billy's future lasted another three days; he was killed during the storming of the town of Villanueva de la Canada. He, like hundreds of his comrades has no known grave and like his friend, John Blackmore before him, no marker or sign of who he was, why he died or for what? The photo, still in my possession is, as he intended, a momento of a loyal and trusted friend, at a very unusual moment in our lives.

There was a period during the war when I was fully aware of the 'big picture', and as anxious as anybody to know where I was and where I was going.

A massive offensive by the fascists on the Aragon Front broke through the Republican lines in a dozen or more places. Their preponderance of men and

Alun (seated) and Billy, Spain, June 1937.
Billy was killed three days later on June 19th 1937.

material, Italian Battalions, German tanks and guns manned by their own nationals. The German Condor Legion with their superior and abundant aircraft made the contest a foregone conclusion.

A retreat became a rout, with all that it entailed. For me and hundreds like me, it was a time of near panic. Running, hiding for three days and nights. Not knowing where we were or in which direction to run.

I was with a large group of stragglers of the Lincoln Battalion which had reached the outskirts of the town of Corbera and where a stand was made. The skirmish resulted in a number of killed and wounded.

The wounded were placed in a partly demolished house and tended by myself and 'Tiny' Holland, a six foot something, a native of Chicago, who was also a first aid man.

The tanks, which had caused such havoc and casualties of the small defending group, were coming nearer. One of which sprayed the building which housed the wounded with machine gunfire. Tiny and I dashed for cover at the rear of the building, leaving the wounded. We looked around for a sight of the defending stragglers. They had disappeared. Tiny and I and the wounded were on our own. In the distance we could see the enemy infantry in the open, heading in our direction. The cracking of the bullets overhead also denoted their intentions.

Tiny Holland's immortal words, 'Those sons of bitches will kill us if we don't get the hell away from here quickly!' dashed any hesitations we may have had of honour and glory by staying with the wounded.

We got up from our prone position and got the hell away from capture or the fulfilment of Tiny's prediction. We ran until we were exhausted and breathless in the direction we thought the others had gone. That was away from the shooting behind, to what we hoped was some sort of refuge in front.

Towards dusk the shooting behind had eased, and seemed to have moved in another direction. We decided we would continue our escape during the hours of darkness in the direction we were now going, in the hope of finding help, or the river Ebro, which we knew could not be many miles away.

For three days, Tiny Holland and I skirted enemy outposts, dodging patrols and sentries, hiding by day and moving by night. On the fourth morning of our flight, hungry and bedraggled, we were hiding at the rear of a small hut in the middle of an olive grove. We saw some men in the near distance, making their way through the grove. We had a problem; should we make a break and run or stay put in the hope they would not see us?

They came closer, and closer, as decision time came, Tiny whispered to me, 'I am certain I heard them talking quietly in English.' As they came nearer, his suspicions were confirmed. We revealed ourselves, with Tiny shouting, ' We are Americans!'

There were five in the group, all stragglers of the British Battalion, who like us had been on he run for four days. We exchanged experiences. They had not seen any sign of the enemy that morning, hence their reason for breaking cover and moving like us towards the Ebro, which one of the group had the notion was not far away.

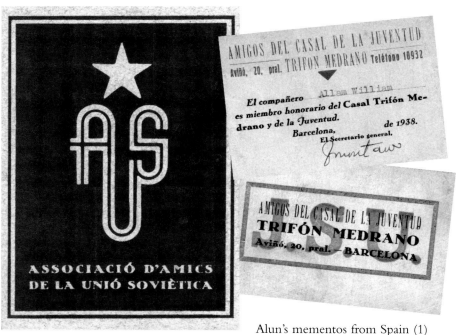

Alun's mementos from Spain (1)

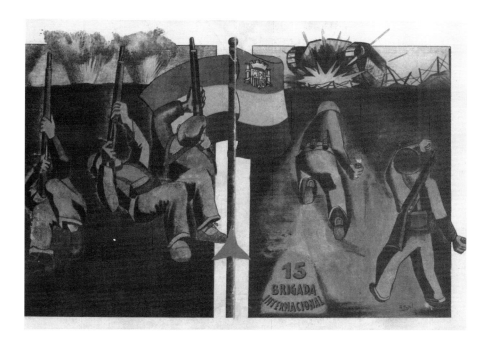

CADA ACTIVISTA UN SOLDADO MODELO

Testimonio de honor y agradecimiento al Activista

Nombre *Soldado Alun Williams* Batallón *57* Compañía *E.M.*

Ejemplo para todos sus camaradas de disciplina, de trabajo, en la defensa de la Causa del Pueblo contra la reacción y la invasión extranjera.

El credo de los Activistas:

I. Asimilar con rapidez la ciencia militar.
II. Ayudar a los demás combatientes a mejorar su técnica de lucha.
III. Cuidar las armas como mi propia vida.
IV. Conocer todas las armas de combate.
V. Ser un campeón de Unidad, digno representante del Gobierno de UNIÓN NACIONAL.
VI. Trabajar sin descanso para aumentar la capacidad política de los combatientes teniendo como base los 13 puntos del Gobierno de UNIÓN NACIONAL.

VII. Luchar sin descanso contra los derrotistas i provocadores.
VIII. No estar satisfecho en tanto haya un luchador analfabeto.
IX. Tener como consigna, ser el más fuerte en el ataque y el más firme en la resistencia.
X. No descansar en tanto quede un soldado que no sea ACTIVISTA.

El Comisario,

John Gates

El Comandante,

Sam Wild

CADA ACTIVISTA UN CAMPEÓN DE UNIDAD

Alun's mementos from Spain (2)

Alun's mementos from Spain (3)

CARNET DE HONOR

SE le nombra Combatiente de Honor de la 35 División del Ejército Popular Regular, como Voluntario de la Libertad. Por sus acciones fué en nuestra nación expresión firme de la avanzada del Frente Popular y de la Democracia del Mundo, en lucha contra el fascismo invasor.

Los soldados de la División, todos los españoles, no olvidarán jamás a los que con ellos defendieron la independencia del suelo nacional, cubriéndose de gloria en las batallas en que intervinieron.

Al lanzar nuestro ¡Vivan los Voluntarios Internacionales! afirmamos que la República Española conseguirá su independencia total.

España, octubre de 1938.

El Jefe de la División   El Comisario Delegado de Guerra

COMBATIENTE A. Williams.

Alun's mementos from Spain (4)

They were as hungry and exhausted as we were, but the fear of capture drove us forward. More so when gunfire was heard in the distance and the rumble of tanks at the back of the olive grove.

We ran, fell, scrambled, crawled and ran again. We reached the river, the tanks and gunfire getting closer. We could see soldiers on the opposite bank in hastily prepared positions, waving and beckoning us across. How to get across was the problem. There were no bridges, boats, or any means available to make the crossing. There was no alternative, but to wade in and swim across. I had confidence in my ability as a swimmer to reach the other side. It was painful to see the agony of doubt in some of the others.

It was 'make your mind up time'; bullets were cracking all around, thumping into the olive trees and plopping into the ground. It was sink, swim, be killed or captured. All seven took the swim option. Four of us managed to reach the other side. Two were drowned and washed downstream. One hesitated and waded back, I presume he was killed. I did not know any of their names.

We scrambled onto the bank, half naked and shivering, and made as much distance away from the river as possible, before collapsing from sheer exhaustion.

We were no longer alone, hundreds of stragglers had managed the crossing, some by boat, some by swimming, but most by means of a bridge crossing which was later blown up by the Republican troops.

Every man who reached the safe bank of the river had similar stories to tell of their flight. Of dodging the enemy, of hiding fear, hunger and exhaustion, and of the wounded left behind. A few like Tiny and myself had eluded capture by the merest of margins.

Stragglers were finding units, and a semblance of order and discipline was becoming established. Tiny and I found the remnants of the Lincoln Battalion that were enjoying a stew of some concoction. It was the first solid food we had eaten for five days. Whatever it was it tasted wonderful.

I was parched with thirst, with a swollen tongue for twenty-four hours at the Battle of Brunete. I was hungry with stomach-ache on the Aragon and Ebro for five days. Twin body requirements that are only appreciated when absent or unavailable, a most unpleasant experience. Bobby Beynon's mug of water and slice of bread would have been both welcome on these occasions. Such were the thoughts in my head at that time.

The return of stragglers became less frequent as the days went by. It became evident that no more of our lost comrades would be returning. The four Battalions of the 15th International Brigade rested in the dust and sand, a little distance from the river with an occasional scouting and observation party along the river front.

The losses during the retreat had been enormous. The Brigade had to remain in the line for some time yet. The enemy occupied the left bank, the Republican Army the right bank of the river Ebro. Both sides had taken a mauling and were licking their wounds.

A period of quiet prevailed. The International Brigades were moved to reserve positions a few miles back and to a well deserved rest. During which time, the strength of the Battalion was augmented with young Spanish soldiers, fresh from their training, and with new volunteers from the U.S.A. The preponderance of the Battalion would henceforth be Spanish.

I had been a first-aid man with the American Battalions in every major battle from Jarama to the Big Retreat. My only absence being the three weeks in hospital and convalescence after being wounded at Brunete, which was the one and only time I slept between sheets and in a bed during the whole of the Spanish Campaign.

I wanted to join my fellow countrymen in the British Battalion. There was no particular reason for this desire, other than a change to the familiar, after the oddities of the American ways and languages. I went to the H.Q. of the British Battalion resting a half mile away. I saw Alan Gilchrist, the Battalion Commissar and to whom I put my request. He was very surprised when I told him I had been with the Americans for over a year, which he thought was odd, because the British Battalion were always short of qualified first aid men. He took me to see Sam Wilde, the Battalion Commander, who agreed with my request. He also couldn't understand why I had remained so long with the Americans. I went back to the Lincoln Battalion accompanied by Alan Gilchrist who had a word with George Watt the Lincoln's Commissar to regularise the ad hoc transfer. Tiny Holland was sorry to see me go, as were a few other yanks who had been bandaged and tourniqued by the 'Limey doc.'

The next six weeks was of training for what was to be the most ferocious battle of the Civil War. The Battle of Ebro. Twelve weeks of organised, unyielding mass slaughter.

The Republican Army crossed the River Ebro at midnight in a manoeuvre that caught the enemy completely off guard.

The last time I crossed the Ebro was by swimming, this time it was in a rowing boat with six other soldiers and manned by a Spanish fisherman, as part of the 15th Brigade, the second wave of troops to cross.

As the sun was rising artillery fire was targeting the river approaches as the Battalion emerged on a sandy strip of shore. The next three months was a nightmare of advancing, retreating, and defending with only short periods of relief and rest.

There were times when the Battalion was cut off and fought their way out with many casualties. The horrors of the Ebro Battles are epitomised in the struggle for the ownership of the strategic heights in the Sierra Pandols. These heights were of rock and the battleground where the bursting of shells and mortar sent showers of flying rocks and shrapnel in all directions. The only protection from such missiles was flat on the belly on the rock surface and blind hope

My clothes were stiff and caked with blood and very lousy by the time we were relieved and away from this rock-strewn abattoir. There was no earth to cover the dead. When we left the Pandols, the ridges were marked with cairns of stones where the bodies of our comrades were placed. I have often wondered if they are still there on that god forsaken place; or has Franco's vandals desecrated them as happened to all the graves and markers of the dead of the International Brigades?

These battles in the Sierras of Spain were my worst experience of the war. Not of terror, I had lost that long ago, but of sheer frustration with the conditions and logistics of getting the severely wounded down to safety from a mountainside, continually raked by shell and machine gunfire, as well as air bombardment.

The stretcher-bearers were faced with an almost impossible task. It was a mile from the ridge to an ambulance or any wheeled transport that could get near enough in that inhospitable terrain.

Darkness was the best time for the bearers to do their work. The snag with this was that the most severely wounded could not wait until sunset. Their chances of survival depended on speed to get them to the Field Dressing station, some four miles back. The bravery of the ration party in their nightly runs to the base of the mountain for ammunition, food, water, and field dressings was an achievement, made more remarkable by the successes. They always escorted the walking wounded on this hazardous journey.

The International Brigades' part in the Civil War was coming to a conclusion. The Prime Minister of the Spanish Republic, Negrin, signed an agreement with the non-Intervention Pact to the effect that all foreign persons involved in the conflict were to be repatriated immediately. It was vainly hoped that the Nationalists would reciprocate with their Italian and German troops.

The Battle taking place along the Ebro front at the time was as fierce as any of the previous six months. The rumour that the Brigades were to be withdrawn had no effect on the fighting in which they were now involved.

The last day of action before the battalion was withdrawn from the line was as bloody as any engagement they had suffered in the past. The action started with three hundred and seventy seven soldiers of whom one hundred and six were British, the rest Spaniards.

The following night when the battalion left the line, two hundred and seven had been killed or missing. Of the one hundred and seventy survivors, fifty-eight were British. The line had been held until relieved.

My willingness to continue the fight against fascism was being modified. The inevitable defeat was now obvious. My instinct for survival was in conflict with the principal of martyrdom for a cause. I worked hard at it, and came to the conclusion that I was no longer ready for martyrdom.

The fight for the cause of anti-fascism was over in this neck of the woods, and in this part of Europe. Self-sacrifice was no longer an option. Perhaps another time, another place, but not right now. It was over! I am a survivor, my father said so; my instincts tended to agree. I was not going to make him a liar. Those 'sons of bitches' were not going to kill me.

The fascist army with superiority in numbers together with the Italian Divisions and the German Condor Legion with their modern tactics and weaponry used and tested in actual combat was too much and overwhelming. We were out-manned, out-gunned without adequate air cover, short of ammunition, in rags and hungry. Messrs Chamberlain, and Daladier, authors of the hideous non-intervention pact had loaded the dice against us.

The repatriation agreement was signed. The 15th Brigade together with all fifty eight men of the British Battalion crossed a rickety footbridge over the river Ebro for the last time near the town of Asco.

For me the war was over. I was home with my family the first week of December. I had survived, physically unscarred with the exception of a slight leg wound. Mentally I was also relatively undamaged. The horrors I had witnessed together with my own personal experiences was in denial and the subjects of long spells of amnesia.

One of nature's ruses in her extensive repertoire for survival is her disappearing trick of mental nasties.

The obscuration by the brain of unpleasantness and impalpable facts of life and its preference of highlighting and selecting the pleasant and enjoyable moments is a healing process of quiet efficiency - it was for me. When required the horrors and nasties locked in my memory have to be dragged out screaming at being disturbed. Whereas the memories of the good and the nice, slide out of their own accord with pleasure of their revelation.

Within days of my home-coming, I became very quiet and introspective. Balancing the weight of my past irresponsible and hectic behaviour with the weight of a burgeoning future. At the same time recognising a fundamental change in myself. I was no longer the impulsive optimist loner of yesterday. Instead I was seeing in myself a careful, thoughtful, non-risk-taking loner. Living one day at a time with every tomorrow a bonus.

The following four weeks was a difficult period. I had become a local hero and was in demand by different groups and organisations to address them on aspects and subjects relevant to my experiences in the Spanish Civil War and to my part in that conflict. My introvert self was in the ascendancy. I was shy in front of people. It was only on the insistence of my siblings and parents I acceded to some of these requests.

Public speaking was at first an uncomfortable chore, akin to the nervous tensions I experienced during the war. It was, however, a challenge to shyness, which I was determined to overcome. Most of the meetings and speaking sessions were pleasant and encouraging. One such meeting nevertheless was most hurtful and affected my attitude towards people in a way that was foreign to me.

I was addressing a packed public hall of diverse people where I was continually being interrupted by hecklers, especially so when I mentioned the bombing of Barcelona and Guernica.

Loud calls of 'Liar!' and 'Communist propaganda!' were hurled at me from various parts of the hall.

I finished my address in spite of these interruptions and personal invective doubting the veracity of my statements. I was congratulated by the meeting's organisers for my stand against the hecklers. These hecklers were the least of my problems. During the course of the meeting, I sensed a feeling that I was speaking in a vacuum. The audience was hearing, but not listening to what I was saying or telling them. I concluded they were curious about me and not what I was telling them. A piece of paper waved to an ecstatic crowd some time ago had confirmed their complacency and mitigated their complicity, conscious or otherwise in the greatest con trick of all time. Appeasement had reached its logical conclusion. "If you can't stop him, join him." Hitler's signature was alongside Chamberlain's in the declaration of 'Peace in our time.'

This was the last meeting or gathering I addressed. Forbearance and tolerance of people and my willingness to understand their concerns and prejudices went overboard. I went home, crawled into my shell and opted out of all '-isms' political and otherwise, active or benign.

I would find my own kind of peace, living with the shades of my friend Billy and his comrades in their unmarked graves, with truth at the bottom of her well by their side, looking up at the heavens hoping to see the Holy Ghost descending gently upon us in the likeness of the Dove of Peace. Instead, it is bawled out of heaven by the appeasers and comes tumbling down dead with the shock.

The world will little note, nor long remember what we
say here, but it can never forget what they did here.
                        Abraham Lincoln

I end this part of my life story in the first half of the twentieth century by paying homage to a body of men, the like I doubt the world will never see again.

We were there in a foreign land, men of all nationalities, of colour, creed, race, religion and cultures. From all parts of the world; Iceland to Australia, from the tortured lands of Central Europe to the affluent democracies of the West.

A truly international force of volunteers, spurred to action by the heartfelt cries of "No Pasaran!" of a beleaguered nation and its people. The coming together for a common and single purpose of this pot pourri of nationals was in itself a unique event.

In the peaceful surroundings and conditions of their homes, they would have individual classifications attached to their characters and personas. Students, ideologues, cranks, rogues, eccentrics, political refugees, poets, intellectuals, dreamers, politicians, adventurers, vagabonds, and quite ordinary men who defy classification like myself, and who were of the majority. We all had the positive idea in pursuant of a negative one. An idea 'against' and not an idea 'for'.

The last war for a genuine idea was the Crusades. The crusading soldiers were against Islam and not for Christianity 'per se'.

The International Brigades were against fascism and not for the Spanish Republic 'per se'. No more and no less. The main venue for the test at the time happened to be in Spain. They died there, not for glory or gain, but to halt the march of fascism there and then.

We failed. The fascist triumphal cry of "Adelante!", "Forward!" prevailed on to World War Two, the Holocaust "et al."

The Spanish battlefields were where men last fought for an ideal. Modern war is so inherently demoralising and destructive, that a war for a genuine ideal becomes impossible.

The volunteers of the International Brigades will be remembered in history as the last of the great warriors who fought and died for a genuine ideal.

Alun Menai Williams, 1940.

Epilogue

The second part of my life in the latter half of the century, begins with my wedding and marriage to a lovely girl. The embodiment of my idealised woman; who, like myself, was a loner and of introvert disposition. We were a matched pair with almost identical personalities. Resulting in fifty seven years of companionship, great happiness, mutual respect, and above all, a love that transcended petty differences and which remained constant in its intensity, throughout our togetherness, until the day she died.

My life with "Goldie" was a survivor's reward for the series of traumatic events that had befallen me long before our chance meeting and the cementing of our bond of togetherness, only once thereafter was this bond ever broken.

An involuntary separation of concern and foreboding took place during the period. When man's long creep from slime to glory was for the second time in my century put in peril. Its forward progress suspended and its outcome disputed over six long horrific bloody years. When once again, I put on a uniform to become an active participant as a member of the Royal Air Force. In a programme of competing nations in organised continental vandalism on a grand scale.

A whole continent was torn apart and laid to waste. Its treasures of antiquity and modernity reduced to smoking rubble, and where tens of millions of beings were killed, tortured, and made to suffer unimaginable horrors and indignities, and the land mass between the Urals and the Atlantic became a "monumental" war grave, filled with the dead victims of man's insatiable desire for slaughter.

Written history does not record a natural disaster that stands comparison with the scale of devastation, annihilation and the horrors of the man-made catastrophies of my century.

Will "Homo sapiens" ever admit to its apparent inherent genocidal tendency and curb its will, and appetite for senseless slaughter?

It is my hope the lessons so painfully learned in my time are taken on board, and the national bellicose parroting of the totem call of "blood, sweat and tears", banished from the lexicon of the 21st Century and replaced by "hope, peace and tranquility."

These sentiments, I am sure, are laying dormant somewhere amongst the detritus of a flawed human spirit, waiting to emerge.

My time on this beautiful planet is now limited. It is time to get off.

Six of my closest and life-long friends have already preceded me, and moved off. The stay of four of them was of a comparatively short duration, but of a varied and exciting kind.

Billy — the dedicated anti-fascist and International Brigadier - killed in Spain.

Ifor — the pimp, friendly philanthropist, and air gunner, missing on an air raid over Berlin - presumed dead.

Brinley — the young Salvation Army Cadet, and trumpeting sheep rustler, a stretcher bearer in the 8th Army - killed in action.

Bobbie — the most"eccentric" of the lot and naval telegrapist - went down with the Repulse off Singapore- presumed drowned.

Dai — a gentle pragmatic being, died in a wheelchair. Immobilised after a pit accident some years previously, aged 64.

Our Priscilla, who with a wink, a smile and a haughty look, "touched" us all. After a successful career in the Probate Service, died of cancer - aged 70.

They've left me to tell their stories...